"A very important contribution. The contestation over value and essence of democracy is here to stay for the foreseeable future, both domestically, notably in the West, and internationally in terms of what makes world order. The book's theme speaks to most fundamental themes in the study of politics, government, and international affairs: What is democracy? How do we defend democracy? What's the relation between law and democracy? What does rule of law really mean? Thus, it deals with topics and questions that are central to any political science curriculum."
—**Robert Schuett**, *University of Durham, UK*

"Turner and Mazur's approach to the topic of democracy is original and, to my mind, persuasive; it departs insistently from theories that rest on idealized and normative notions of democracy. Instead of proceeding in this philosophical vein, the authors ground their alternative approach in political contingencies. The argument is conducted at a very high intellectual level. Connecting the authors' arguments to those of Max Weber and Hans Kelsen adds a history of ideas dimension to the book's theoretical heft."
—**Peter Baehr**, *author of* The Unmasking Style in Social Theory

Making Democratic Theory Democratic

This book addresses a timely and fundamental problematic: the gap between the aims that people attempt to realize democratically and the law and administrative practices that actually result.

The chapters explain the realities that administration poses for democratic theory. Topics include the political value of accountability, the antinomic character of political values, the relation between ultimate ends and the intermediate ends that are sought by constitutions, and a reconsideration of the meaning of the rule of law itself. The essays are inspired by the demystifying realism of Max Weber and Hans Kelsen, including explications of their views on law, constitutions, and the rule of law.

The book will be of interest to social and political theorists, philosophers of law, and legal theorists, and for discussions of democratic theory, the administrative state, constitutionalism, and justice, as well as to readers of Weber and Kelsen.

Stephen Turner is Distinguished University Professor at the Department of Philosophy, University of South Florida, where he is also Director of the Center for Social and Political Thought. He has written extensively on issues in social and political theory, especially related to Max Weber and his critics and successors, on liberal democracy and expertise, on Durkheim, on the history of social science, and on cognitive science and tacit knowledge, complex organizations, the history and philosophy of quantification, international relations, legal theory, and normativity.

George Mazur is a scholar in international law, trained in Russia, who is presently an independent research scholar at the Newberry Library, Chicago. He has edited two memorial volumes on Morgenthau: *One Hundred Year Commemoration to the Life of Hans Morgenthau (1904–2004)*, 2004, and *Twenty-Five Year Memorial Commemoration to the Life of Hans Morgenthau (1904–2005)*, 2006, among other works, including (with Stephen Turner) "Morgenthau as a Weberian Methodologist," *European Journal of International Relations*, 2009.

Making Democratic Theory Democratic

Democracy, Law, and Administration after Weber and Kelsen

Stephen Turner and
George Mazur

NEW YORK AND LONDON

Cover image: NaturaLight/Alamy Stock Photo

First published 2023
by Routledge
605 Third Avenue, New York, NY 10158

and by Routledge
4 Park Square, Milton Park, Abingdon, Oxon OX14 4RN

Routledge is an imprint of the Taylor & Francis Group, an informa business

© 2023 Stephen Turner and George Mazur

The right of Stephen Turner and George Mazur to be identified as authors of this work has been asserted in accordance with sections 77 and 78 of the Copyright, Designs and Patents Act 1988.

All rights reserved. No part of this book may be reprinted or reproduced or utilised in any form or by any electronic, mechanical, or other means, now known or hereafter invented, including photocopying and recording, or in any information storage or retrieval system, without permission in writing from the publishers.

Trademark notice: Product or corporate names may be trademarks or registered trademarks, and are used only for identification and explanation without intent to infringe.

Library of Congress Cataloging-in-Publication Data
Names: Turner, Stephen P., 1951– author. | Mazur, George, author.
Title: Making democratic theory democratic : democracy, law, and administration after Weber and Kelsen / Stephen Turner and George Mazur.
Description: First Edition. | New York : Routledge, 2023. | Includes bibliographical references and index.
Identifiers: LCCN 2022046276 (print) | LCCN 2022046277 (ebook) | ISBN 9781032420158 (Hardback) | ISBN 9781032420110 (Paperback) | ISBN 9781003360810 (eBook)
Subjects: LCSH: Democracy.
Classification: LCC JC423 .T776 2022 (print) | LCC JC423 (ebook) | DDC 321.8—dc23/eng/20221108
LC record available at https://lccn.loc.gov/2022046276
LC ebook record available at https://lccn.loc.gov/2022046277

ISBN: 978-1-032-42015-8 (hbk)
ISBN: 978-1-032-42011-0 (pbk)
ISBN: 978-1-003-36081-0 (ebk)

DOI: 10.4324/9781003360810

Typeset in Times New Roman
by Apex CoVantage, LLC

Contents

Theoretical Preface: Democratic Theory, Law, and
Administration, in a World of Divergent Values   ix

Introduction: Nine Chapters on Democracy, Law,
and Administration   1
STEPHEN TURNER AND GEORGE MAZUR

1   **Democracy, Liberalism, and Discretion: The Political**
    Puzzle of the Administrative State   26
    STEPHEN TURNER

2   **Improving on Democracy**   43
    STEPHEN TURNER

3   **What Are Democratic Values? A Twenty-First-Century**
    Kelsenian Approach   54
    STEPHEN TURNER AND GEORGE MAZUR

4   **The Ideology of Anti-Populism and the Administrative State**   66
    STEPHEN TURNER

PART I
Free Speech, Pluralism, and Toleration   85

5   **Religious Pluralism, Toleration, and Liberal Democracy:**
    Past, Present, and Future   87
    STEPHEN TURNER

viii Contents

6 **The End of Clear Lines: Academic Freedom
and Administrative Law**   100
STEPHEN TURNER

PART II
Fundamental Political Theory   **123**

7 **The Method of Antinomies: Oakeshott and Others**   125
STEPHEN TURNER

8 **Decisionism and Politics: Weber as Constitutional Theorist**   141
STEPHEN TURNER AND REGIS FACTOR

9 **The Rule of Law Deflated: Weber and Kelsen**   162
STEPHEN TURNER

Acknowledgments   177
Index   178

Theoretical Preface

Democratic Theory, Law, and Administration, in a World of Divergent Values

The essays presented in this book are in the category of fundamental political theory. They deal with a small set of basic political concepts, particularly democracy, law, and administration, and an equally small set of meta-political concepts, particularly ideology and various related concepts, such as the fact–value distinction, legal science, pure theories, and expertise. There are many ways of writing about such topics, but given the shibboleths of the present day, it is often useful to deal with them through commentary on other thinkers, which is what we have done in most of these chapters. This is a strategy with advantages and disadvantages. The disadvantages stem from indirectness: the ideas are presented in the voice of past thinkers, rather than in *propria persona*, and not always in terms that are precise enough or directly applicable to present concerns. Moreover, they are prey to the conflicts of interpretation that inevitably arise when larger issues in the history of ideas are extracted from their local contexts. The advantages are closely related: allowing the dead to speak avoids the reductivism to present political passions that characterizes much of present academic discourse, by showing that the topics are not simply the projection of current prejudices, but rooted in fundamental conflicts in the intellectual domain of the political that transcend the immediate and the local.

Attending to historical sources is also a form of discipline. Philosophy is fundamentally a kind of dialogue, and it is valuable to the reader to know who the dialogue partner is. It is also useful to help distinguish what are original claims and what is part of the normal context. But the greatest value of doing commentary is discipline: to comment on, interpret, or elaborate the arguments of an actual thinker forces one to address the structure of their reasoning, rather than slogans their thought has been abridged into. It also allows the writer to identify the specific differences between what they are saying and what someone else is saying. But it must also be said that this kind of dialogical writing, almost inevitably, obscures the systematic thinking of the interpreter. The compromise we have made here is to present chapters representing many years of reflection on key thinkers, particularly Max Weber and Hans Kelsen, but to add this extensive theoretical preface in order to fill gaps and to provide orientation to the reader, as well as to update the theoretical content of both thinkers by introducing an element of agency theory. The chapters presented here thus represent something approximating systematic thinking, but without a systematic presentation. This preface is designed to provide the outline of a more systematic account. The chapters will themselves be described in the introduction, which follows.

The core idea of the book is simple: democracy is a largely majoritarian procedure of law making and leader selection for a state with a significant administrative and judicial apparatus. Moreover, law and democracy are linked: democracies produce decisions through legal procedures, and law is the means by which the decisions are put into effect. Kelsen has a term for this: metamorphosis. It is exemplified for him by the transformation of the idea of justice into law and freedom into a form of government. He gives the example of "The metamorphosis of individual happiness into satisfaction of socially recognized needs," those "recognized by the social authority, the law-giver, as needs worthy of being satisfied, such as the need to be fed, clothed, housed, and the like," such that "the idea of justice is transformed from a principle guaranteeing the individual happiness of all the subjects into a social order protecting certain interests socially recognized as worthy of being protected." He adds that "[T]here can be little doubt that satisfaction of socially recognized needs is very different from the original meaning the idea of happiness implies, which, by its very nature, has a highly subjective character" (Kelsen, 1947: 391–92). This metamorphosis

> is similar to that which the idea of freedom must undergo in order to become a political principle. Since genuine freedom, that is, freedom from any kind of social authority or government, is incompatible with any kind of political organization, the idea of freedom must cease to mean absence of, it must mean a special form government: government exercised by the majority, if necessary against the minority of the governed. The freedom of anarchy turns into the self-determination of democracy.
>
> (Kelsen, 1947: 391–92)

The notion of metamorphoses will loom very large in our explication of basic issues in this chapter. Democracy is a prime example of a concept that is metamorphosed by turning it into specific procedures within a democratic legal order. These procedures are democratic in the sense that they result from choices made according to pre-existing procedures and validated in some fashion by "the people," meaning political equals.

Notions like "justice" and "freedom" and "the people" are transformed when they are turned into procedural facts and transformed again when actions are taken by the agents of the state to implement these procedural facts. These are the basic metamorphoses central to democracy as the term is usually understood. There is no way for the "people" to act collectively without their "wills" being turned into something very different from what they individually will, and what they can be said to will collectively through law be transformed as well. Max Weber put the point more brutally when he said that the will of the people was for him a fiction. Fictions can be politically and even theoretically useful, but they are still fictions. This is what differentiates what will follow here from much of what passes as political philosophy, and makes it political theory. Political philosophy can traffic in abstractions; political theory needs to deal with the transformed versions of these abstractions into administrative fact, the transformed versions of policy ideas, and with the means of their transformation. The means are the political order itself, which is made up of procedures, sanctions, and delegated and discretionary powers. But political theory has its own problematic abstractions or fictions.

The idea that "democracy" in practice means no more than "that which is produced and enacted involving the participation of citizens through legal procedures" seems simple, and it is. But it is a radical departure from what passes as "democratic theory" and "rule of law" thinking today. What is the issue? From the time of François-Noël Babeuf (1760–1797), there have been attempts to go beyond a spare definition of democracy in terms of democratic procedures to identify "real" democracy as something bigger or more fundamental and to claim that the concept of democracy itself implies various policies that would make democracy "effective." Often this point is made more strongly: that a given political practice or policy is a necessary condition for "genuine" democracy or law.

Much of what passes for "democratic theory" today consists of attempts to tease out these supposed implications. Some of this discussion is concerned with serious questions that go to the heart of the problems of liberal democracy, such as the question of how much freedom of speech is necessary for a voter to be meaningfully informed and thus meaningfully able to participate. Some of it is ideological sleight of hand, by which the particular policy preferences of the author are said to be implied by the concept of democracy. Some of it depends on the idea that democracy requires a powerful state with few restraints if it is to be a real instrument of "the people." From this point of view, libertarianism is the antithesis of "democratic."

Contemporary political theory, as well as writing about democracy generally, is constrained by an academic consensus on the political good and a self-imposed task to justify certain tendencies in political life itself. Much of this thinking has addressed the problem of justifying the interventionist welfare state. This is perhaps no surprise. Liberalism was in crisis at the end of the 1930s as a result of the depression, the acceptance of the necessity to overcome the narrowness of written constitutions and the paralysis of divided parliaments, and the apparent success of "planning" and totalitarian, or proto-totalitarian, regimes whose animus was anti-liberal and collectivist. The solution to the crisis of the 1930s was the welfare state—a compromise forced by the fact that, as R. T. Tawney explained to the victorious Labour Party, there was simply not enough money to redistribute in order to make a difference in people's lives, but what could be done was for the government to provide extensive services. This was not a new model: it was Bismarck's. But Bismarck had based his policy on anti-socialist *Realpolitik*.

For true socialists, and for theorists on the Left, the still capitalistic welfare state was a disappointment. It lacked a justification that matched the high aspirations for a solidaristic socialist society with planning, collective ownership of the means of production, and equality that had powered what the Spanish socialist Julio Alvarez del Vayo called the *March of Socialism* (1974): the inevitable triumph of these ideals. There was, nevertheless, a pragmatic, political justification. It satisfied, or spoke to, the interests of many segments of the electorate. But it left intact basic "liberal" political and legal forms, liberal rights, and stretched some of them, for example, in relation to immigration. The social and racial divisions of the Bourgeois order evolved without disappearing, and new divisions, and social movements around them, emerged. The quest for a unity that would overcome these conflicts, and for an ideology that produced unity through a particular concept of "justice," remained the Holy Grail of this line of thinking, and dominates normative academic political thinking today (Forrester, 2019). This literature is also marked by its hostility to Kelsen and Weber for their realism and legal positivism.

A parallel literature exists in connection with law and the idea of the rule of law. Indices of the rule of law include long lists of *desiderata* that states might live up to. The question of whether some regime is acting in accordance with the rule of law could be a legal question, if there is a legal definition or authorized enforcer of the concept. But if it is merely a contested idea, a matter of opinion, it needs to be decided in accordance with the legal procedures of the political body, such as votes by representatives. From the point of view of much present legal philosophy, this is a radical thought. The National Socialist experience seems to justify the idea that a legal system can be said not to be genuine law and to expand the notion of genuine law to include the policy preferences of the particular theorist of law. This is a temptation to ideologize the concept—a temptation that both Kelsen and Weber vehemently resisted.

Despite the importance of these issues, they are not the concern of the chapters in this volume. The chapters here are based on the radical idea that choices about law and the means of making political decisions are themselves choices to be made democratically. To be genuinely democratic and genuinely in conformity with the rule of law, from this point of view, one must follow the law, allow the definition of "democratic" to be a matter of democratic decision, and decline the temptation to claim that a legal order is not really legal or that a democratic electoral procedure itself produced through legal democratic processes is not democratic. These kinds of assertions have their place and deserve to be taken seriously as ideological statements, rather than as academic theories. But they are matters that should be decided democratically. They belong to the people and to the decision-making processes they agree to through legal procedures, not to expert opinion, though experts are free to promote their ideologies and concerns in the public square, along with everyone else. Needless to add, the kind of argument presented here depends on a distinction between fact and value and—because of the central role of ideology and ideological conflict in democratic politics—between fact and ideology. Its aim is to exclude ideology and doctrinal considerations from the basic framework of discussion of the key concepts. But this requires some explanation, particularly with respect to the concept of values.

Facts and Values

The basic distinction observed by both Weber and Kelsen between matters which are valuative and matters which are not in itself controversial. It will not be our concern to unravel the issues with these concepts in any detail. The idea of "normativity" as a supra-empirical force has been addressed elsewhere (Turner, 2010), and the complex history of the fact–value distinction in the twentieth century has as well (Turner and Factor, 1984). Kelsen rooted his version of the distinction on facts of cognition. He distinguished facts as the subject of what is sometimes now called "cold cognition" from the results of emotion-influenced cognition or "hot cognition." Cold cognition involves ordinary empirical claims, or claims about something object-like, such as a law. Hot cognition is relative to the cognizer.[1] The defenders of rationalistic ethics wish to turn issues of justice, which appear initially as relative to the cognizers, into matters of cold cognition. But they do so on grounds different from the grounds that are normally given for factual claims about the objects of cold cognition. The fact that there is a difference will suffice for our purposes. But there is an observable consequence of this: what people value varies considerably from person to person. Moreover, the grounds for claiming values are fact-like themselves also vary considerably. And these variations are politically relevant for democratic theory. They imply that the metamorphoses involved in collective action traditionally represented by the notion of the will of the people, which presents this will as a unity, is a political fiction.

Discussing what varies from person to person with respect to aims, desires, and what people regard as valuable is fraught with problems. The term that bedevils this discussion and needs to be clarified is "values." The term acquired its present meaning in nineteenth-century neo-Kantianism and purported to name a metaphysical reality in the realm of spirit existing distinct from one's "valuations," which were one's personal preferences for the realization of a value, meaning "what you wanted." The term has survived as a stand-in for many very diverse items: culture, dispositions, revealed and unrevealed preferences, articulated dogmas, ideologies, moral truths, anything involving "normativity," and so forth.[2]

The point we can take from this is the following: the background to a political act, such as voting, is complex and involves an amalgam of experience, belief, emotion, sense of the transcendent, and so forth that is individually variable and largely tacit. The act of voting, for example, to select a leader, is in any case not an expression of anything a simple as a value. We can represent political choice in these terms only as a convenience. But there is nevertheless an important point to be extracted from this: the metamorphoses from this complex background to the simplicity of the political act of voting in the case of such a thing as a selection of a democratic leader involve a great deal of complexity and a substantial transformation. And the law governed-collective processes of election and representation are also a metamorphoses.

For the purposes of this volume, we nevertheless will mostly stick to the notion of values, though in several places, different and better language will be used, and the better language of others will be explained. The advantage of the term is convenience. It provides a simple way to discuss the non-factual aspects of political conflict and political agreement. It has been used in this way for so long that it has shed its metaphysical baggage and become an umbrella term for these non-factual elements of discourse. When used in this way, it does have some important advantages. The central facts of politics are facts about agreement and disagreement, and the process of collective decision-making by procedures that permit decisions in spite of value disagreement, and sometimes allow for the resolution of value conflicts through discourse. To the extent that liberal democracy is government by discussion, and to the extent that there is a non-factual element to discussion, values in this sense are important to liberal democracy. And the common ground for discussion also contains these non-factual elements.

The picture of values and value conflict and agreement that underlies the chapters in the volume is complex, and because it is only indirectly stated in the chapters, an introductory explication will be useful. Weber has the phrase, "ultimate values." This is a place to start, but not to end. If we are to use the notion of values in its non-metaphysical common sense, each of us has things we value: some of these are intermediate or instrumental values or things which are means to further ends, while others are the ends toward which our actions are ultimately directed. The value of "salvation" is the value that figures in much of the discussion of political values in the era of Weber, so it is a convenient place to start. It is an end in itself and is ultimate in the sense that there is nothing to achieve through salvation other than the properties that come with salvation, such as eternal life. Salvation serves as an organizing principle for moral life: one can always ask whether a given act leads to salvation or prevents it. The acts, however, are themselves values or have value: an act of kindness, or fulfilling an obligation, or piety, may help in attaining salvation. They are thus valuable, but for the person seeking salvation, they are also instrumental or intermediate ends, to be motivated by the "ultimate" values they help to realize.

Weber gives the example of the subject of *Pilgrim's Progress* (Bunyan, [1678/1684]1975), who forsakes his family for salvation: that is a case in which an ultimate value overrides and conflicts with other proximate values, such as loyalty to one's kin and acceptance of one's responsibility to them. This sounds irrelevant to politics, but for Weber, it is the essence of political value choice. He notes that Machiavelli praised the Florentines who placed the defense of their city ahead of their souls. And this is his point about politics in general. One cannot consistently be a Christian and submit to the law of love and engage with the means and risks of violence necessary for the political leader or indeed the citizen.

But this way of thinking leads to a puzzle. It serves to make sense of the moral rejection of politics as such: the cases of this that fascinate Weber are the Tolstoyan whose rejection is based on pure Christianity or the hypothetical anarchist who destroys without any hope of either early victory against the state or a heavenly reward. For Weber, these were real types—or approximations of real types—which an understanding of the politics of his own time required. His legal philosopher ally Gustav Radbruch made the same point about principled rejections of the law ([1932]1950: 118–9). They could not be refuted, because they appealed to something higher than the law.

The law, in this way of framing matters, is a value. But it is also a fact. This takes some explaining. Procedures are legal facts; once a value is made into a law, it becomes a legal fact. As a consequence, the relation of the distinction between procedures and content and the fact–value distinction is complicated by the fact (or at least tempts confusion as a result of the fact) that the procedures are themselves produced according to procedures and that the choices of procedures themselves reflect "values" or political preferences. It is tempting to say that all of these things are shot through with values. Both procedural or "constitutional" questions and policy questions, questions about what laws to enact, are debated in terms of notions like justice, freedom, and the question of who "the people" are. But once a decision has been made to adopt a procedure, such as a constitution, it becomes, through metamorphosis, a fact; or as the Scandinavian legal realist Karl Olivecrona put it, law as fact (1971). Its valuative character belongs to its history. Kelsen, it may be noted, routinely distinguished the "historical" aspects of law from their "scientific" ones. By doing so, he meant to separate the operative legal realities from their decorative valuative and ideological associations (Kelsen, [1949]2006: 282).

What does this have to do with democracy? In some rough but meaningful sense, there is a difference between values (and the normative realm) and the natural or social realm. This difference is paralleled by the difference between the procedures of a democratic legal order and its content. The concept of metamorphosis is key to this difference. It makes perfect sense to say that a constitution or law expresses an ideology or is "ideological." But at the point it becomes law, it is a fact and a fact of a particular kind. Georg Jellinek, who was a friend and ally of Weber and a teacher of Kelsen, used the odd expression "the normative power of the real" or of "the factual" (see Bezemek, 2019: 73). Procedures and practices, which are facts, become "normative" or felt as normal and correct simply as a result of being followed routinely.

To confuse matters more, values themselves have a factual side: they are Janus-faced in the sense that they are both internal to people or subjective and have the appearance at least of being external and "real" in the sense of an ideational reality. This relation is usually marked by a distinction between the ideal values and subjective "valuations": the "natural" aspect of the fact in the case of valuation is its subjective character. It is a psychological and individual fact. Law, in contrast, is neither. But it has its own Janus faces: it becomes an objective natural fact as well as a normative systemic fact. The confusion arises from the idea that the law is intrinsically valuative. It is better to say that it is both normative and natural but from different points of view. But the kind of "normativity" is different.

Kelsen and Weber both treat legal science as a normative science and observe a distinction between the law as it is actually carried out and acted on by judges and others and the "normative" object of the law itself as a logically organized and intelligible system. But for them, this system is simply a different kind of fact, a normative fact, not a non-fact. It is a fact in the neo-Kantian sense of a *faktum der Wissenschaft*, a fact as an object of inquiry that is intelligible or understandable, but not one containing a supra-empirical "normative" force. Kelsen puts it this way:

> at least part of the essence of the law . . . appears to occupy the realm of nature, to have a thoroughly natural existence. If one analyses a parliamentary enactment, say, or an administrative act . . . one can distinguish two elements. There is an act perceptible to the senses, taking place in time and space, an external event . . . And there is a specific meaning, a sense that is, so to speak, immanent in or attached to the act or event.
>
> (Kelsen, [1934]1992: 8)

Weber makes the same distinction when he speaks of *Verstehen*, which means both the understanding of an action or utterance and the understanding of a system of ideal objects, such as mathematics. The legal procedures of a democratic legal order belong to the realm of fact in the sense of the "realm of nature." The existence of "values" in the minds of people and of value conflicts in these minds and between people also belongs to this realm of fact in this "natural" sense. The values themselves do not. They belong to the ideal or normative realm.

There is nevertheless a connection between the two orders. For Kelsen, to be law, according to international law, it must be "effective," meaning that people generally obey, for whatever reason. Weber has a parallel formulation. So the normative and the "sociological" realities of law must to some extent correspond. People of course do not always obey the law, so the correspondence is imperfect. The law is interpreted differently by different people. It is perhaps not surprising that these distinctions are not observed in common discussions of democratic theory and public discourse, and there are indeed principled objections to them. But most of what passes for democratic theory simply ignores these distinctions and treats such things as "democratic norms," as normative facts with a real existence that is simultaneously a subjective reality, in the sense that they are thought to be actual forces in people's lives. One might cite Talcott Parsons' idea of a central value system as a sociological force or Philip Pettit's idea of common knowledge as a theoretically developed version of this conventional way of thinking. But to do so exposes its implausibility. These are both theoretical constructs that characterize in a short-cut approach a huge diversity of personal opinions, interpretations, dispositions, and so forth. The "will of the people" is thus a political fiction, while the valuations that cause people to act in a particular way are facts.

Democratic Theory, and Democrats, Against Democracy

When a political theorist like Robert Dahl says that the US constitution should be, or could be "more democratic" on the basis of "democratic theory," he is not saying that the laws approved through democratic procedures could be enforced more rigorously or that the procedures could be followed more exactly (1989: 231). He is making a valuative claim, depending on a preference for a particular valuative definition of democracy that is different from the one arrived at through the means of the law. He is entitled to his opinion, but it is a category mistake to treat this notion of democracy as belonging to the same category as fact. It might be thought of as a preference in constitutional policy or as an ideological statement. It may even be "empirical" in the sense that one may associate it with empirical facts and put it into a model of types of regimes. The comparison produces a fact. But it is a fact only in the special sense that it differs or corresponds to a non-factual standard, even if the non-factual standard is itself made up of facts. In such cases, it is the selection of the facts, or the criteria for selection, that is valuative.

This may seem counterintuitive. Isn't "democracy" itself a value? Isn't law a value? The constitution? Isn't it a value? Yes. But only in the Janus-faced sense, we have noted. Neglecting this distinction is where confusions set in. Some of this is innocent confusion from a misapplication of common sense. Some of it is doctrinal, resulting from a denial of the fact–value distinction, the law and politics distinction, or from an insistence on the law as a moral reality beyond the mere facts of its institutional structure and the fact of sanctions, or on the claim that law is merely an ideological superstructure. Both Weber and Kelsen fought against these confusions. But their opponents, such as Natural Law thinkers and Carl Schmitt, as well as other anti-liberals of various kinds, along with defenders of an egalitarian view of the essence of democracy, have traded on them. Their views dominated much of the post-twentieth-century discussion, and today, their influence is such among students of political and legal philosophy educated in the era after Rawls' *A Theory of Justice* (1971) xviii Theoretical Preface

that merely to be broadly aligned with Kelsen, as H.L.A. Hart was, is grounds for anathematization (cf. Forrester, 2019: 44–45)

It would be an interesting but not terribly constructive polemical project to sort through all of these confusions and identify the precise points at which they vitiate the claims in question. They can perhaps be understood more constructively with the help of Kelsen and Weber themselves. But a few problems need to be addressed first. The first is an important but somewhat hidden and confusing distinction between *kinds* of values, or kinds of roles of values in valuative reasoning, in which each kind has its own Janus-faced character. Weber repeatedly discusses ultimate values, of the sort that motivated Pilgrim when he abandons his family. But as we have noted, if there are ultimate values, there are non-ultimate ones. The non-ultimate ends are still ends. But they are, rather, intermediate ones, ends that are conditions for the achievement of other ends. This is a role in reasoning, however, not a categorical distinction between categories of ends. This requires some explanation. An intermediate end for one person can be an ultimate one for another or in another case of means-ends reasoning. Thus, democracy or the rule of law can each be both a means to higher ultimate ends or ends themselves: ends sufficient to die for.

Once we get used to the distinction between intermediate and ultimate ends, and the result that an intermediate fact can be a value, or valued, we can clarify a whole series of issues. Weber at one point says that one could take free trade as an ultimate value, but that it would be ridiculous to do so. So, the distinction between an intermediate and an ultimate value is not to be found in the "value" itself, but in what we make of it and where it fits into our own scheme of values, and in the practical relations between values, especially the fact that achieving a value depends on the prior achievement of other values. Weber thought that one thing that a professor could teach, without affirming values, was whether a person's values were consistent and whether they were achievable. Some of these would be intermediate values, which would be instrumental in the achievement of other values.

For most thinkers about law, whether they articulate the thought or not, the law is an instrumental value. It brings about something people want, such as civil peace. Civil peace is a condition for the achievement of their ultimate values, but not normally taken as an end in itself. But it also has the Janus-like character of being simultaneously value and fact. Most of the time, for most people in the West, "democracy" is a value, but an intermediate value, and also a fact on the other Janus face, which is a condition for action. It can be taken as an ultimate value and indeed might be as part of a justification for war and, therefore, of sacrificing lives in support of this value. But in practice, democracy is something that happens between people with many different ultimate values and possibly many different valuative conceptions of democracy. And it is a factual condition at the same time.

From the point of view of many thinkers, values can be reduced to something simpler, and collective, such as Talcott Parsons' central value system, or a hegemonic ideology, or to principles that can be ascribed to some collective object, such as a national state or society. This is convenient, in a sense, because it allows us to talk about "democratic values" as a package to which one may or may not subscribe. Subscription is an all or nothing thing: one either accepts them or rejects them, like a theology. But "values" is already a shortcut term, a portmanteau covering everything from emotional dispositions to theologies, and these are even more drastic shortcuts. So, it is important to see what is being cut out by these terms—what the long way is. One thing is immediately apparent: people do not have, as individuals, a coherent non-conflictual value system, unless they have gotten one from a doctrine, and even then there is a tension between the doctrine and reality, as is well known to students of totalitarianism. Nor can individuals articulate their "values," which is to say that the term "values" is ordinarily being used to cover many things that are neither articulated nor articulable.

It would thus be a rank simplification to say that a given polity is underwritten by a set of shared values and that politics within the polity is a matter of coming to shared values through, for example, discussion, in the liberal case, or coming to compromise through procedures. But it would be closer to an adequate account to say that given the diversity of values, politics is a means of reconciling them. It becomes a means because, despite the differences in outlooks and values, there are intermediate "values"—meaning values in the Janus-faced sense of also being facts, for example, institutional facts about law or procedure—that are common to people who do not share ultimate values. "Common," however, need not mean something like a genuinely shared mental state: people will interpret a value, such as civil peace, in different ways. They need only be close enough to the aspect of "fact" to gain acceptance or endorsement.

To put this even more simply, politics is the business of securing intermediate ends. The task of the politician or political leader is to invent or define such ends and persuade people to value them. There is a certain fluidity to these ends, and this makes for the ebbs and flows of politics. The methods of achieving them are constantly under revision, their successes and failures lead to the opportunity for political revision, and so forth. Reductions to abstractions, such as the claim that the goal of politics is civil peace, justice, or freedom, do not explain the level of detail that would illuminate these ebbs and flows. But they nevertheless are useful ways of talking about the problems of politics, for they are terms that characterize intermediate ends. One wants freedom, security, or justice, for something else—salvation, happiness, and well-being. The rule of law and "democracy" are ordinarily intermediate ends. But they do not, under the right circumstances, conflict. Other intermediate values do conflict.

The Kelsenian view of democracy involves a close link between the rule of law and democracy, understood in the metamorphosized sense. The rule of law is a matter of procedures determined by procedures to establish or change law. What makes something "law" is its creation according to law—legal procedures. Customary law is different, but it is inherently "democratic" in the sense that it is broadly accepted by the people as law. Law, understood as a coercive order, meaning one which involves sanctions, is the instrument of democratic rule. Without law, there is no "rule" and therefore no rule by the people, even in the metamorphic sense of rule according to democratic procedures such as voting and representation, which are "democratic" in the sense that the people participate in their creation through procedures established through laws made according to legal procedures. There is a regress here: the justification of law is always and only more law. One which never goes beyond law—beyond the metamorphoses, for example, to "justice" or natural law— but only to prior law, which for Kelsen included what he called primitive law, law without a state.

Value conflict at the level of intermediate ends requires some special explanation. But it is at the core of what follows in this volume. We can make a very crude distinction between two kinds of value conflict: those which involve an intrinsic connection between the conflicting values, such that they are always found both together and in conflict, and those which arise because of special circumstances but which normally do not involve conflict. One might desire an athletic populace and one that appreciated fine art. It might be difficult to devise a policy to achieve both simultaneously, but not an insurmountable one. Others are intrinsic to particular domains. Weber's ally Gustav Radbruch gave the example of the following antinomies between legal values: certainty, justice, and expedience ([1932]1950: 107–12). Occasionally, these values might coincide in a law or legal judgment, but normally, they pull against each other, and sometimes come into stark conflict, as when an appeals court decides that the endless pursuit of justice in a case is overridden by the need for legal closure in order for the law to function as law, or an expedient legal gimmick is used to avoid a tough case, or justice requires action in the face of uncertainty and inexpedience.[3]

Understanding these intrinsic conflicts is something that in what follows we take to be at the core of political understanding as such, which is to say a part of meta-political thinking. Weber has a term, "ideal interests," which he pairs with material interests to capture the notion of valuation. He analogizes ideas about the world to train switches that direct interests. With this, we get a familiar picture of politics as the pursuit of interests, mediated by ideology. There is no need to elaborate on this picture. It becomes more interesting when it is linked with the problem of intrinsic conflicts. This is sometimes treated as the "problems of liberalism," and there is indeed a close connection. A typical example is Voltaire's "no freedom for the enemies of freedom," which captures the intrinsic problem—and conflict—between freedom and security, when security is required for the practical exercise of freedom. It is these kinds of conflicts that define politics. But understanding them and distinguishing them as a fundamental type requires a good deal of unpacking. In this case, for example, it is not clear that one could not simply abandon freedom and choose security, though this might prove to be an unpleasant and unacceptable outcome. But it is clear that one cannot have freedom in the desired sense without security of some kind from the enemies of freedom.

This kind of reasoning can be applied to an enormous number of concepts and conceptual dyads. The variations on the Hegelian master-bondsman (or slave) relationship are perhaps the one that has been the subject of the most ingenuity: the master is not really the master, because there is a sense that he is enslaved by the limitations inherent in the relationship, and the slave, similarly, is nor fully a slave because he possesses something the master cannot. These formulations are clever, and perhaps worth thinking about, but depend to a great extent on the way they are formulated. The same can be said for reasoning about limit situations, a favorite strategy of Weimar thinkers, and especially Schmitt, which yields such notions as Marcuse's "repressive tolerance," in which tolerance appears as repression at its own limit: a variation on the "no freedom for the enemies of freedom" problem, in which there is no tolerance for the enemies of tolerance. Similar kinds of arguments, some quite plausible, can be made in relation to such dyads as freedom and equality: the totalitarian dictator or party elite who ruthlessly enforces equality becomes, by doing so, unequal. The protector of the equal human dignity of all becomes, by doing so, the greatest in dignity, and thus eliminates the possibility of equal dignity for those who are protected. One can go on ad infinitum in this vein, but we will not. In what follows, we will be more concerned with pragmatically real political facts and actual personal choices. The slaves will be slaves, and the masters will be masters. But one should remain mindful that the hysterical inflation of such concepts as dignity played a role in National Socialism and that similarly inflated concepts have played roles in other ideologically driven movements.

To forestall a misunderstanding of this volume, particularly its discussion of antinomies, an additional word about value conflicts is necessary. The traditional political value conflict in liberalism is between freedom and equality. What kind of conflict is this? It is evident that there are practical problems in achieving both, given present institutional realities, such as private property. Policies may need to face conflicts between prioritization of some ends that more closely fit the idea of freedom and some other ends that leads to some kind of equality. But these abstract notions need to be applied in order to conflict, and even to formulate a conflict, one must specify the terms in a particular way or in a particular application. And this dependence on formulation allows for arguments that reformulate the terms in such a way that the conflict can disappear. Philip Pettit provides a reformulation of freedom as non-interference in terms of what he calls non-domination, and this allows him to treat many of the kinds of interventional practices that promote equality or well-being as consistent with this new form (Pettit, 1997: 51–79). The conflict between "pro-life" and "pro-choice" accounts of abortion has been absolutized in the United States in terms of the incompatible principles of the sanctity of the lives of the unborn and the sanctified principle of women's control over their bodies. But most countries have managed to define these things in less absolute terms and produce laws that restrict abortions to particular stages of gestation.

Limit arguments have their uses in relation to such conflicts: they can show how values pursued without respect for other values and for on-the-ground realities ultimately defeat themselves. But they represent situations unlike those that typically occur, and thus distract us from the situational character of all political action: the fact that value conflicts arise only in specific situations governed by particular facts and involving particular conflicting values. The trolley problem is a famous artificial example that would never arise in practice. The antinomies of concern to political theory do arise in practice. It is not always that a legal verdict is torn between justice, expedience, and certainty, for example, or even between equality and freedom. But situations where they do conflict nevertheless do arise routinely, and the conflicts arise at the practical level of implementing the values. Sometimes, they arise systematically, and these cases are of special interest.

Agency Theory and Protections Against Misrule

Judge Jed Rakoff quotes Jefferson as writing that "I consider [trial by jury] as the only anchor yet imagined by man, by which a government can be held to the principles of its constitution"[4] and laments the fact that the *de facto* replacement of jury trials by plea-bargaining has eliminated this anchor. The role of the jury was to control the judges. police, and prosecutors, to prevent them from abusing the discretionary power they possess. The systematic use of "prosecutorial discretion" and the deference of the courts to agreements between prosecutors and defendants, which the courts nevertheless must formally approve, are an example of a systematic conflict between expedience and justice. As Rakoff points out in his book, the effect of this is that the innocent plead guilty and the guilty go free. It is such systematic conflicts and conflicts between the emergent system and commonly held values that drive constitutional revision and improvisation. But the quotation points to something more basic: all of these "powers" are carried out by people, people engaged in human relations, with all the uncertainty, scope for error, interpretation, malfeasance, cheating, and ideological distortion this implies. And this familiar Kelsenian point also connects the metamorphoses discussed earlier to agency relations: they are actions of humans.

Most of these issues arise in connection with problems of discretionary power, which are themselves problems of principal–agent relations. This also requires some explanation. There is a famous article on the 12-inch fish, which deals with the following routine scenario: a fish and wildlife agent inspects the catch of a family fisherman and finds, among the caught fish, one which is just short of the 12-inch limit. Should they use their discretion and ignore it, or arrest the fisherman? The regulation is directed at the long-term consequences of fish stock depletion; the error is small and innocent, but the legal remedy is draconian (Jaccard, 1999). The dilemmas faced by ordinary administrators, however, between personal feelings and long-term consequences, are ubiquitous and not necessarily shared with voters in particular groups. This is the stuff of politics when there is a legislative remedy. But it is also the stuff of administration and administrative discretion. This is a part of politics that is often ignored in political philosophy, and even in political theory, though it has been forcefully revived in connection with the recent interest in Kelsen's arch-opponent, Carl Schmitt.

Although it is not the sole theme of any of the chapters, the topic of discretionary power is taken up in various places, and a long digression about them is necessary. It is in connection with this kind of power that most of the practical issues of democratic constitutions and law relating to legal and quasi-legal processes arise. Weber was concerned with a particular feature of the modern state: bureaucracy or the administrative state. His great fear was that mammoth bureaucracies would be beyond political control. This is a simple case of a principal–agent problem: the bureaucracies are, in constitutional theory, servants. In principal–agent problems generally, the issue is one of representation: of the exercise of the authority involved in the relation of speaking for or acting on behalf, or for, another, whether a person or group of persons. The problem is one of trust: is the agent acting as the principal would, or in their interest, or in their own or the interest of others? The "solutions" to this problem are devices that monitor or control the agent on behalf of the principal. The "on behalf" element is crucial: it requires a new agent, and another principal–agent relation, which is also subject to abuse, as a consequence of the discretion understood as part of the relation, which in turn can be violated and require another monitor or controller, or at least a check, such as a check on the judge that the jury provides on behalf of "the people."

The idea of a jury of peers is an example of representation in which an abstract idea of the people is turned into a procedure. So are elections, governed by law, and by various traditions of civil discourse, rights of free speech and petition, and so forth. The agency relation between "the people" and their government is through these procedures, a point Kelsen made repeatedly (Kelsen, 1955). Needless to add, these are fraught processes encrusted with ideology—a crust Kelsen sought to remove. There is no collective agent called "the people." There are people with divergent values acting collectively through procedures. The procedures provide a means of replacing conflict with an artificial agreement, which individuals may come to accept or reject. But for our purposes, the issue is this: the inherent slippage between the individuals and their "will" and the actions of the authorized agents of the state in carrying it out: their "representatives" and the bureaucrats who administer the law. This is the core agency problem of democracy. It is also the reason for the legal remedies that are improvised to control the agents, such as frequent elections or rules governing appointments. The slippage is inherent: there is a gap between "justice" and the policy that is produced by metamorphoses into law and policy. But the gap is filled by discretionary power.

xxiv Theoretical Preface

What does this have to do with fundamental political theory? Kelsen's notion of metamorphoses cuts two ways. On the one hand, it is a reminder that the participation of the people in legislating for themselves through the legal means of legal democratic procedures is a transformation from their desires into the form of a system that ultimately relies on legal coercion. It should also be said that the transformation almost always involves not only the additional problem of administration, including administration by the courts, and the agency relation created by that relationship, but also the likelihood of unanticipated consequences. There is thus a need to control the agency relationship and correct for unanticipated consequences. Much constitutional and legal revision takes the form of this kind of course correction or monitoring: having juries or corporate bodies to approve decisions or take over aspects of them in a division of powers is a way of controlling discretion and monitoring an agency relationship. There is no formula for producing these devices, and there is a kind of path dependence to change: past choices of devices often constrain future ones. One can think of constitutional traditions as themselves doctrines or solutions that become fixed in place and constantly added to by improvised revisions and reinterpretations rather than simply being replaced in total when something goes wrong. In this way, past solutions become kludges—structural elements that are too embedded to easily alter because doing so would require altering all the improvisations that corrected them. History, a history of these improvisational and path-dependent creations of legal and political devices thus becomes tangled up in the popular understanding of a political and constitutional tradition.

The number of these controls and the doctrines justifying them is very large, but a few examples should suffice to explain the thought. A constitution may recognize "rights" and even call them natural or pre-political, but by metamorphosis, they become legal facts that constrain rulers and therefore provide a check on the agency relation that gives them the power to act on the behalf of others. Electorates may choose to constrain themselves through constitutional devices on revision, such as the requirement of supermajorities, because their long-term self does not trust their short-term self to perform the right metamorphoses into law. Kelsen was especially concerned about the problem of minorities, which is intrinsic to democratic majoritarian procedures, and suggested means of protecting minorities (and therefore protecting the legal order from minority defection), such as granting forms of self-rule or subsidiarity to smaller regional units. All of these can also be seen as protective measures against the kind of resistance and conflict that would threaten the legal order itself—measures taken by sober majorities who foresee that they may one day be in a minority and also that protecting minorities protects the legal order from problems of majoritarian or administrative overreach.

Political life is inherently composed of people acting under legal authority on behalf of other people. These are all principal–agent relations. So, it should be no surprise that law and political action in support of policies should also be composed of improvisations in controlling them. The flexibility implied in principle agent relations, one of which is "representation," nevertheless allows for the possibility of agents acting against or to change the principal, and therefore for the state to change the people they are accountable to and claim to act for. The possible variations of the phenomenon of agents acting in ways they consider to be justified but are at odds with the wishes of the principal, in which judges and politicians are tempted to evade democratic control, are numerous, and the responses to them through political action or law are often plagued with difficulties. There is no denying that "representation" is intrinsically and continuously problematic, and the temptation to use the flexibility granted to agents or representatives to intervene by influencing them or using their powers is always present. Dealing with this would require a different book or library of books. We can point to *Liberal Democracy 3.0* (Turner, 2003) as part of such a library: it is concerned with the problematic role of experts, a paradigmatic case of a relation of trust that easily goes wrong by violating its own difficult-to-enforce implicit terms. Legal structures designed to protect the autonomy of judges, which itself is a protection against the misuse of law by others, also protect abuses by judges. There is no escape from such issues, or from their provisional character, and therefore from their character as "political," in the sense of being subject to policy determined through political means.

It should also be stressed that solutions to the problem of trust inherent in principle–agent relations are not always benign or "democratic" in the sense familiar from traditionally democratic political traditions. A strong leader who is authoritarian but relatively uncorrupt, in the sense of adhering to the law and to a personal "mission" beyond self-aggrandizement, may "solve" the problem of trust in a particular situation. Similarly, the party discipline of an ideological party or the analogous discipline of a religious movement in politics, visibly enforced, may have the same effect. These solutions conflict with the solutions characteristic of liberal democracies or "open societies" in which open discussion serves as a check on representation. But even government by discussion is transformed by metamorphoses into a legal order with limits. There is a further transformation into administrative rules and yet another into administrative practice and decision-making. And there are different checks in these cases, and different possibilities of abusing these checks, such as bureaucratic secrecy—an issue for Weber.

Legal checks, however, are never sufficient. Kelsen's arch opponent, the Harvard political theorist Carl J. Friedrich, added something important to this discussion. There is a *de facto* as well as a legal form of discretionary power. Friedrich, who considered bureaucracy to be the heart of government, and the emergence of bureaucracy the start of the modern state, had one great political idea: the rule of anticipated reactions ([1937]1950: 49). He considered this rule to be a description of the way in which bureaucracies exercised power. They acted as they pleased, regardless of formal legal constraints, but did so in such a way as to avoid the reaction that would produce new legislation to control them or judicial intervention. Thus, the *de facto* power of bureaucrats was limited, but only by the prospect of political or juridical opposition. But the existence of this zone of *de facto* power is partly a consequence of the law itself: of the ambiguities that bureaucrats exploit, and the limitations of the legal means of controlling them. But legal means depend on the will of people to use them. The power of bureaucrats depends in part on the unwillingness or inability of courts and legislatures, and even their superiors in the executive, to discipline them. And there are many other elements that support these powers: the willingness to accept claims of expertise, the ability of bureaucrats to ally with supporters and coerce opponents, the ability to exploit bureaucratic secrecy, and so on.

Policy and constitutional improvisations designed to control the agents of the state can fail. They can produce bad policies as well as good. At the extremes and in the long run, they can fail to produce what we think of as a stable democratic polity. A "constitutionalism" that ignores the possibility of constitutional failure is misleading, and a theory of democracy that ignores this will also be misleading. There is no guarantee that democratic procedures will generate the kind of policies and practices that are intermediate values for a sufficiently large and diverse middle of the population to avoid polarization into mutually hostile sectarian groups with different intermediate values which struggle for power. Preventing polarization and other deep conflicts requires not only political creativity, but conditions that lie beyond politics, in the realm of culture and the conditions of geopolitics and economics.

"Democratic" legal procedures do not magically produce what we conventionally think of as democratic regimes, with leadership competition, a flexible policy arena, pluralistic discussion beyond sectarian divisions, a public arena of discourse that translates into administrative action, and a political community of people (and parties) with an open society "democratic character" that accepts political responsibility in a sober and tolerant way. The experience of such a regime can have educational effects producing civic habits that facilitate these "democratic" features. But they do not automatically produce them. Indeed, well-intentioned policies may do the opposite: generate novel divisions that appear to the people involved as existential threats. That these kinds of divisions become stable, and the governments that attempt to manage them become unstable, is a potential consequence of democratic procedures. Policy improvisions may fail; the political creativity to produce them may be so constrained by the ideological commitments that a party adheres to in order to produce the trust and solidarity it needs to survive may prevent it. The temptation to think of a constitutional or legal order as self-guaranteeing, "A Machine that Would Go of Itself," as Michael Kammen titled his history of the US constitution (2006), is great. The possibility of constitutional failure or inadequacy is always present and indeed is much of the reason for improvisation. But there are no guarantees that the improvisations will work.

Stephen Turner and George Mazur

Notes

1 As Kelsen and in his own way Weber both pointed out, this separation of fact and value was a late intellectual achievement. Kelsen discusses this in *Society and Nature* (1946), where he gives a historical account of the emergence of law from vengeance (Turner forthcoming); Weber, in a parallel way, as part of the disenchantment of the world (Turner, 2015).
2 Carl Schmitt wrote an essay on "The Tyranny of Values" ([1960]2018) denouncing this terminology. Heidegger did as well ([1935, published 1953]2000: 199–200).
3 The sources given here are from "Continental" legal thinkers, but the same issues arise in the common law tradition, and are commonplace among serious contemporary legal thinkers. An excellent example is James Boyd White's recent discussion of the tensions and conflicts between legal goals in relation to the model penal code. He makes, in different language, the same argument that underlies this volume and is detailed in Chapter 7: that different values are intrinsically in tension in the law, or as he puts it that the code is "riven with unavoidable tensions and contradictions" (White, 2019: 18), and that the pursuit of one of them to the exclusion of the others leads, as he puts it, to "incoherence" (White, 2019: 16).
4 Letter from Thomas Jefferson to Thomas Paine, July 11, 1789. https://founders. archives.gov/documents/Jefferson/01-15-02-0259

References

Bezemek, Chrisoph. "The Normative Force of the Factual: A Positivist's Panegyric," In *The Normative Force of the Factual: Legal Philosophy Between is and Ought*, Edited by Nicoletta Ladavec, Christoph Bezemek, and Frederick Schauer. Cham: Springer, 2019, 65–77.

Bunyan, John. *The Pilgrim's Progress from This World, to That Which Is to Come*, Edited by Roger Sharrock and J. B. Wharey. Oxford: Oxford University Press, [1678/1684]1975. www.gutenberg.org/ebooks/131

Dahl, Robert A. *Democracy and Its Critics*. New York: W.W. Norton, 1989.

del Vayo, Julio Alvarez. *March of Socialism*, translated by Joseph M. Bernstein. New York: Ferrar, Strauss, and Giroux: Hill and Wang, 1974.

Forrester, Katrina. *In the Shadow of Justice: Postwar Liberalism and the Remaking of Political Philosophy*. Princeton: Princeton University Press, 2019.

Heidegger, Martin. *An Introduction to Metaphysics*, translated by Gregory Fried and Richard Polt. New Haven: Yale University Press, [1953]2000 (Publication of Lecture Given in 1935).

Jaccard, Don. "The Case of the Eleven-Inch Fish: A Study in Administrative Discretion," *Policy Perspectives* 7: 51–58, 1999.

Kammen, Michael. *A Machine that Would Go of Itself: The Constitution in American Culture*. New York: Routledge, 2006.

Kelsen, Hans. "Foundations of Democracy," *Ethics* 66(1): 1–101, 1955.

Kelsen, Hans. *General Theory of Law & the State*. New Brunswick: Transaction Publishers, [1949]2006.

Kelsen, Hans. *Introduction to the Problems of Legal Theory*, translated by Bonnie Lischewski Paulson and Stanley L. Paulson. Oxford: Oxford University Press, [1934]1992 (Originally Published under the Title *Reine Rechtslehre. Einleitung in die Rechtswissenschaftliche Problematik*. Leipzig: Franz Deuticke).

Kelsen, Hans. *Society and Nature: A Sociological Inquiry*. London: Kegan Paul, Trench, Trubner & Co., 1946.

Kelsen, Hans. "The Metamorphoses of the Idea of Justice," In *Interpretations of Modern Legal Philosophies : Essays in Honor of Roscoe Pound*, Edited by Roscoe Pound and Paul Lombard Sayre. New York: Oxford University Press, 1947.

Olivecrona, Karl. *Law as Fact*, 2nd edn. London: Stevens & Sons, 1971.

Pettit, Philip. "Liberty as Non-Denomination," In *Republicanism: A Theory of Freedom*. Oxford: Oxford University Press, 1997, 51–79.

Radbruch, Gustav. "Legal Philosophy," (translated by Kurt Wilk) In *The Legal Philosophies of Lask, Radbruch, and Dabin*, with an Introduced by Edwin W. Patterson. Cambridge: Harvard University Press, [1932]1950, 43–224.

Rawls, J. *A Theory of Justice*. Cambridge: Harvard University Press, 1971.

Schmitt, Carl. "The Tyranny of Values: Reflections of a Jurist on Value Philosophy," In *The Tyranny of Values and Other Texts*, Edited by Russell A. Berman and Samuel Garrett Zeitlin (translated by Samuel Garrett Zeitlin). Candor: Telos Press, [1960]2018, 26–41.

Turner, Stephen. "Entzauberung and Rationalization in Weber: A Comment on Iván Szelényi, and Incidentally on Habermas," *International Political Anthropology* 8(1): 37–52, 2015.

Turner, Stephen. *Explaining the Normative*. Oxford: Polity Press, 2010.

Turner, Stephen. "Kelsen: Methodological Individualism in the Social Theory of Law," In *The Palgrave Handbook of Methodological Individualism*, Edited by Francesco Di Iorio and Nathalie Bulle. London: Palgrave, forthcoming.

Turner, Stephen. *Liberal Democracy 3.0: Civil Society in an Age of Experts*. London: Sage Publications, 2003.

Turner, Stephen and Regis Factor. *Max Weber and the Dispute over Reason and Value: A Study in Philosophy, Ethics, and Politics*. London: Routledge & Kegan Paul, Ltd., 1984.

White, James Boyd. *Keep Law Alive*. Durham: Carolina Academic Press, 2019.

Introduction

Nine Chapters on Democracy, Law, and Administration

Stephen Turner and George Mazur

The relation of democracy to law and administration is a perennially fraught theoretical problem, but aspects of the problem become visible and the subject of theoretical reflection when they become political issues. The administrative state, and the question of how "deep" it is, has become an issue in American politics, just as the parallel question of the "democratic deficit" of the European Community became an issue two decades ago, and has continued to evolve and add issues about the relation of democracy to the rule of law. Each has generated its own literature. There are several basic bodies of thinking on these problems, which do not closely relate to one another: political philosophy, political theory, legal philosophy, public administration, history of ideas, administrative history, sociology, and perhaps others. We will draw on each of these in various ways. But theoretical problems become especially salient as a result of immediate problems in the public and political sphere itself. And the administrative state has become a political flashpoint. The reasons for this require a brief discussion. The distinction between the essays in this volume and "democratic theory," which explains the title of the book, requires a somewhat more extended one.

Why It Is Salient Now

What the problem of democracy, law, and administration is, who is the problem, and how it is understood vary radically between political standpoints. Although this book is not concerned with deciding the issues between them, it is concerned with explicating the issue itself. The "left" version of this problem, in its American form, is this: in principle, the goal of reform politics is to bring economic life under the control of a participatory, deliberative, public process which, through its egalitarian character, would bring about a consensual democratic socialism that provides flourishing for all people, largely through emancipation from the bad consequences of capitalism. The "right" engages in deceptive tactics to prevent the realization of such policies, especially (but not only) by inventing pro-capitalist legal constraints on government action, often in collusion with conservative academics, resulting in what

DOI: 10.4324/9781003360810-1

a recent critique of James Buchanan calls *Democracy in Chains* (MacLean, 2017). These are the kinds of constraints that make it difficult to address the great questions of the day, such as climate change, pandemics, and gun control. From a certain policy perspective, these require restrictions that are unwelcome to resistant and backward parts of the electorate, whose members are in denial and subjected to the misinformation provided by corporate-sponsored "merchants of doubt" (Oreskes and Conway, 2010), who abuse the freedom of speech. In practice, the kind of extensive and intrusive policies that would produce the desired results requires an extensive expert-controlled administrative apparatus. But this apparatus can operate only with rules, authority, and discretionary power. It therefore requires hierarchy and a concentration of power, centralized for efficiency and independent of the specific demands of politicians and insulated against political pressure. But there is a deeper conflict as well: the idea of participatory democracy, which is inevitably in conflict with expert-driven bureaucratic rule. And there is a left critique of democracy in favor of "epistocracy," which would amount to the rule—which one commentator refers to as an oligarchy—of the academically credentialled. But there is also an alternative "left" view, which is frustrated with the ordinary processes of legal electoral politics and envisions a reform alliance between the enlightened or progressive elite and "the people" or social movements that captures the political energy of these movements (Turner, 1996; Calhoun et al., 2022).

The "right" version of the problem, in its American form, is this: the political system is faced with constant demands for state services—payments, subsidies, regulations, and other things construed as human rights to well-being, such as health care—each of which requires administration, none of which solve the problems they are intended to solve. These demands are episodic, popular, and emotionally or justice driven but with complications and implications that are not understood or are oppressive or burdensome. To protect against policies of this kind—which is to say almost any policy—that serve to increase the power and cost of administration, it is necessary to constrain state power through legal means, ultimately based on constitutional or legal principles that are taken to be more deeply rooted than the emotions of the moment driving the policy demands (Marini, 2019). This backstop is under constant threat from the administrative state itself, and from the judiciary, which avoids conflicts with the bureaucracy and by the legislature, which avoids the task of directing the administration. There is a more purely legal form of this problem, dependent on the question of whether the US constitution allows the delegation of law-making authority to administrators, and the larger question of the extent to which the courts should "defer" to the decisions of administrators (Hamburger, 2014, 2017).

The "right" response to these policies has been to point to the larger cultural transformation that has resulted from administrative action and policies of reform (cf. Shils, [1978]1997). The administrative pursuit of what came to be called "equity," based on legislation formally devoted to "equality," produced

Introduction 3

a category of preferred groups, which in turn incentivized claims of victimization. This led to, as Christopher Caldwell calls it, *The Age of Entitlement* (2020), or as Charles Sykes names it, *A Nation of Victims* (1992). Much of the American welfare effort has been devoted to issues of race, and figures such as Thomas Sowell have argued that the effect of these policies was to harm the communities:

> The disasters in the social reforms of recent years alone are all too apparent and painful. One need only mention urban renewal, public housing projects, welfare, and the inner city schools to realize that the "experts" have produced more than their share of disasters.
>
> (Sowell, 1975: 204)

Because the actual policies are often expert-driven, the populist right also focuses on expert failure, a ubiquitous feature of expert-governed administration and policy-making (Koppl, 2018).

The elites in the United States, who dominate the administrative state and compare to the Eurocrats of the European Community and the Enarchs of France and their counterparts throughout Europe, are well aware of these conflicts, and have developed their own view of "democracy." The progressive movement in the United States in the early twentieth century sought explicitly to harness the energies of populism to the leadership of experts, who would lead them in the right direction. By the 1930s and 1940s, in support of the Roosevelt administration, elite opinion reinterpreted democratic politics, rejecting the idea of the ordinary citizen being rational and competent, taking the "realist" view that democracy was a matter of consent rather than participation and that the task of politics was to offer a choice that was instructed by the well-informed. As Carl Friedrich put it, "Enough common men, when confronted with a problem, can be made to see the facts in a given situation to provide a working majority for a reasonable solution" (1944: 423). This "made to see" working majority was democracy enough. His ally Talcott Parsons dismissed the liberal democratic idea that "the public must be taken fully into government's confidence and treated as responsible adults" as a "compound of rationalistic and utopian bias" and compared it to the idea that "medical practice should be abolished since it is incompatible with the human dignity of a sick person to submit to being helped by someone more competent than himself" ([1942]1954: 172n). As one critic put it, "the notion that the common people's words are, like grunts, mere signs of pain, pleasure, and frustration, is now axiomatic among our Ruling Class" (Codevilla, 2010: 20).

The European Community version of this problematic is that its legitimacy depends on outputs rather than inputs, that is to say on results rather than acceptance through the transparency of democratic representative processes that produce decisions and policies (Scharpf, 1999). The European Parliament, which has legitimacy because it is the product of voting, lacks the essential

4 Stephen Turner and George Mazur

element of inputting, the right of initiative, which is reserved to the European Commission itself. It can do little more than complaint and assent. The actual power in the EC is in the hands of the people who define the choices—bureaucrats who are experts—which is to say the administration (Tsebelis and Kreppel, 1998). The term "democratic deficit" was coined to describe the governing style of the European Community, but it applies more broadly: to all systems which are de facto controlled by administrators, however superficially democratic its processes appear to be. Yet such systems are deeply rooted in a variety of polities and defended precisely for their efficacy. And in the face of domestic partisan conflict, yielding power to such bodies is a kind of solution.

What This Book Does

The essays that follow are not an attempt to take sides on substantive issues, including the issues that have been outlined here, but an attempt to provide a framework that enables understanding them. Max Weber and Hans Kelsen were on different sides themselves: Weber as a kind of aristocratic liberal, Kelsen as a social democrat in Austria, or left liberal in the United States. But in the case of both Weber and Kelsen, and this book, "meta" arguments do have the effect of taking sides, in the sense that they can serve to exclude positions as inadequate or problematic or place them in a light that differs from the one their adherents want to place them in. That is intended here as well. As a general matter, political philosophy and political theory both suffer from the neglect of the fact of administration itself and its political significance.

The book is thus primarily concerned with the relation between three concepts, democracy, law, and administration, as they apply in a real, diverse, and changing world. This text does not include an elaborate meta-philosophical explanation of what kind of text it is, though a core contrast between theoretical styles is taken up in Chapter 5, the method of antinomies. But in order to forestall any confusion, to distinguish it from other kinds of texts in the area of political theory and political philosophy, and to leave open questions for future discussions, it is appropriate to provide a few limiting comments to explain what it is not. Each of the three concepts is "normative" or valuative in some respect, which would tempt a normative thinker into transforming it into a standard of "the best," or "most fully realized" version of the concept—in Weberian terms, into an ideal type, but with "ideal" taken in a normative sense. In the case of democracy and law, this would amount to abstracting some concept that might be presumed to underly these, such as "justice," and purifying it in such a way that it can be taken as an external rational standard by which to judge actual democratic institutions or ascribe a *telos* to them.

Why not go the familiar route of abstracting concepts such as justice to purify them in a way that allows us to draw normative conclusions? We can distinguish a genuine human conversation, of the kind that actually occurs among citizens of a democracy, from the virtual citizens that populate democratic theory and theories of justice. The actual citizens would be individuals. There is a natural fact of value relativism here: different people value different things, believe different things connected to these values, and have grounded their preferences in different experiences. They would also be attuned to the fact of metamorphoses: the changes that would result from enacting them as law, through legal processes of elections, referenda, and representation, and the metamorphoses that would follow as they were carried out in courts and by administrative agencies. All of these things would be part of their conversation.

The alternative is to instruct the citizen in the true essence of these things, or the principle that underlies them and can be validated by reasoning that goes beyond this kind of conversation—transcends it and secures results on a higher level. The strategy is found on both the Rawlsian left and the Straussian right, as represented by John Marini (2019). This is what an ideal model purports to do as well: provide an ideal standard outside of prosaic reality with which to judge it. And it purports to do it on the basis of the reasoning of an ideal reasoner, a virtual rather than an actual citizen, or a political being. Rawls' "veil of ignorance" is a model virtual being. Strauss's equally virtual philosopher has knowledge of natural rights and can derive normative results from nature.

There are many variants of this kind of virtualization. What they do is eliminate the elements that make "conversational" political reasoning possible: knowledge of others, knowledge of probable outcomes, and knowledge of the particulars of the actual situations faced by those making political and constitutional choices. The promise of virtualization is to provide some sort of moral certainty as a foundation for politics; its effect is to ideologize the concepts. The promise of conversation is to provide an understanding of actual others and, in this way, perhaps to persuade the other conversationalists to change their views, or even to arrive at a novel compromise, based not purely on transcendental considerations, on which they may or may not agree, but on factual, prudential, pragmatic, and empathic ones, on which they might. For the conversationalist, the metapolitical problem is to understand how this is possible and what the ever-changing conversation is about; for the absolutist, the metapolitical problem is how to criticize the conversation on the basis of higher knowledge.[1] The goal of the essays in this book is the opposite of the goal of the absolutist: to understand differences and agreements rather than to judge. The means of doing so is to clarify the relations between contested concepts by de-ideologizing them, in the manner of Kelsen and Weber, a manner which will be explained in several chapters.

It is certainly true that democratic conversation contains theoretical terms such as representation and legal terms such as sovereignty, and that these are contested terms not only in the public sphere but also in the professional communities of political theorists and lawyers. But it should be clear why primary democratic conversation is resistant to the kind of reduction and idealizations characteristic of "democratic theory." The public conversation not only includes and extends this contestation but also includes many more "political" concepts and rhetorical strategies, such as a tendency to mythologize, absolutize, affirm transcendental grounds, theologize, personalize, appeal to emotion, anthropomorphize, defer to experts and argue about deference to experts, appeal to solidarities such as citizenship, race, ethnicity, religious identity, and exclusions based on various forms of "othering," to name only a few. These all provide considerations that bear on the problem of political form, in the extended sense found in the "Theoretical Preface."

The agency relations described in the "Theoretical Preface," and the political and legal inventions that are devised to correct for the intrinsic problems of trust and moral hazard in relations of delegation, are inherently improvisational. There are always new challenges to the means of protecting against abuse and misrule, and the primary conversation, where it turns to questions of political form, law, and administration, is concerned with the workings of these protections, with inventing more of them, and with their unintended consequences. It is a necessary consequence of the approach that the task of defining the good, or the right, is left to the primary conversations themselves. The "Theoretical Preface" and the chapters that follow are concerned with providing a way of understanding the agency problems and value conflicts that motivate many of these primary conversations.

The language for discussing meta-ethical and meta-political issues, especially the concept of values, is highly problematic and inadequate. We have chosen the shortcut of taking over the terminology of values and value conflict from Weber and Kelsen, a terminology that at least has the virtues of both clarity and complexity. It is nevertheless cursed with the legacy of neo-Kantianism, as are, in different ways, all thinkers on these topics. The nature of this curse and the prospect of emancipation from it are issues that are not taken up here, except in a cursory way in the "Theoretical Preface": explaining the Janus-faced character of valuations and their role as both facts and values. We have been concerned in this book with only one of these faces: the factual one.

All of the substantive considerations discussed in the "Theoretical Preface" are consistent with the view of values that will be the main subject of this volume: that there are irreducible tensions between the values at stake in the improvisational solutions to political conflicts—that is to say, within the instrumental, non-ultimate values that people must mutually acquiesce to in order to cooperate. Some of these value conflicts are intrinsic to the traditions in question: antinomies. In this respect, the volume is in direct conflict with the tradition of democratic theory that has grown up in the post-war period. A serious consideration of the improvisational nature of policy in the face of value conflicts and especially the antinomic conflicts to be discussed here is consistent with neither a "scalar" view of democracy nor with the practice of constructing "ideal theories" and using them as a standard to judge existing solutions. But the more basic issue is this: these theories are not themselves democratic or the product of democratic processes. The factual situation with which the primary conversation deals is one in which there is a huge diversity of opinion. To make democratic theory democratic would be to engage in this conversation on equal terms. The kind of "validity" with which we are concerned is "democratic validity," which in turn is the metamorphosized fact of the validity conferred by the legal procedures of democratic rule. To return decisions about what democracy is to the people themselves requires abandoning the idea that "democratic theory" in the usual sense can be anything other than special pleading for an ideological persuasion: something that is a legitimate part of a democratic conversation, but not one that overrides it.

Absolutes and reductive claims are, in a sense, anti-political. They abstract from the political world in ways that distort what is humanly desirable and practically possible. This is one implication of Kelsen's idea of metamorphoses: a noble ideal looks different when it is converted into a coercive system of law, where unanticipated consequences and moral complexity rule. Even Rawls grasped this when he translated his abstract principles of justice into lessons about liberal politics (Rawls, 1993) and international affairs (Rawls, 1997, 2001). We will return to this topic in the chapter on antinomies. But this book is not about ethical theory, and we will avoid the byway of metaphilosophical analysis here, for the most part, except in the occasional aside. It will be useful, however, to briefly contrast the approach here with the tradition of "democratic theory" represented by such figures as Robert Dahl, who can stand for our purposes as a representative of this tradition.

Dahl mixes empirical and valuative considerations in his construction of the notion of democracy, which is itself a variant of Babeufism. For him, democracy is explicitly "a scalar concept" (Baldwin and Haugaard, 2016: 4). There is always the possibility of more democracy, which for him does not mean a state that more perfectly reflects the desires of its citizens or one which arises from the procedures of collective decision-making they have adopted, but a state that reflects egalitarian *desiderata*. At the end of his life, he was even more vociferous about this (Dahl, 2003), attacking the American constitution for denying "equal participation and contestation to all citizens" and calling on Americans to "rethink the conditions necessary for a genuine democracy" and comparing it unfavorably to other polyarchies (Hochschild, [2015]2016: 13). This view of democracy as scalar is even clearer in the empirical and also scalar approach to democracy found in Stein Ringen, the subject of the chapter, "Improving on Democracy." To be sure, there is an empirical aspect to these approaches to democracy. Dahl thought that young people in the 1960s were demanding the "democratization of a variety of social institutions" (1971: 11) and implies that this is a part of a larger "historical process" (1971: 10). But he also spoke of highly contested and problematic policies as "democratic ends," implying that the ends people actually choose democratically are not democratic ends (2001: 61). Ringen similarly more or less assumes that everyone would prefer living in a Nordic welfare state if they were sufficiently aware, informed, and empowered and constructs his empirical indicators of "democracy" accordingly.

What is "wrong" with this? In one sense, these exercises are innocuous: they are someone's opinion, perhaps shared with others, perhaps not, about policies that they take to be desirable, and that have some support with the public, and which the public might itself regard as inseparable from their conception of "democracy" or their idea of "what is really democratic," or characteristic of states whose policies they approve of. They are not so innocuous if they are taken literally as assertions about what "genuine" democracy is. Weber and Kelsen were careful to separate the two issues: defining democracy in a way that is useful for legal or sociological analysis and characterizing it in a way that reflects their preferences. They also distinguished their definitions (which differed) from the policy content of democracy, the culture of democratic citizens, and other things that might or might not be empirically associated with democracy, but which were neither legal nor procedural facts.

They also recognized that politics was not "scalar": that what motivated politics was the existence of conflicting values, imperatives, differing cultural backgrounds, and differing practical situations which required tailored responses, and which had effects on what kind of politics was possible. Weber puts it succinctly:

> I hold the view that what dominates the sphere of values is the irresolvable conflict, and consequently the necessity of constant compromises; no one, except a religion based on "revelation," can claim to decide in a binding form how those compromises should be made.
>
> (Weber letter to Robert Wilbrandt, 2 April 1913; collected in Weber, 2012: 406)

Weber's discussion of the legal tradition emphasized one of these conflicts: between procedural justice of the kind dear to *Rechtsstaat* liberalism and the substantive justice sought by socialists. Constitutional orders reflect solutions to these inherent conflicts, as well as adapting to the specific demands of the situations faced by the order in question. They all involve metamorphoses in their transformation into law, and equally importantly, in the metamorphoses of law into administration.

As noted in the "Theoretical Preface," a large element in metamorphoses from ideals to state practices is the reality that government involves agency relations: relations in which one person acts on behalf or in the name of another person. Agency is, so to speak, the human side of the legal facts of metamorphoses. Representation is one example of this, among many. When a bureaucrat acts in the name of the executive, or on the basis of expertise, these too are agency relations. This was a major underlying concern of Weber's discussion of democracy: for him, pure democracy was purely consensual. As soon as authority, specifically the authority of party leaders, entered into it, it was no longer democracy.[2] We need not go so far. But Weber recognized that office holding, and the exercise of official authority, was a deviation from pure consent. We accept such deviations by our agents as a practical matter. But we also invent ways to constrain them to act in our interest and prevent them from acting against us, and this is at the core of much of the restrictive constitutional practice that Dahl objects to. For many of these thinkers, constraints on governments and their powers to arrange and rearrange society are the problematic obstacles to genuine democracy. But the problem of agency and the need for restrictions extends to participation and equality: "participation" takes forms that are open to corruption and unequal influence. Placing restrictions on forms of participation through democratic procedures is simply democracy in action, rather than democracy according to opinions about what procedures should exist or what ends they should serve.

Needless to add, the inherent conflicts can be formulated in a variety of ways. They have the character of abstractions and are most easily represented as ideals. The "method" of formulating these conflicts is discussed in the chapter on antinomies, "The Method of Antinomies: Oakeshott and Others," where various examples are given. But the focus of this book will be on one particular set of conflicts, which arise in the triad of law, democracy, and administration—an analog to Gustav Radbruch's triad of justice, certainty, and expedience. Democratic practice requires all three. Each is a "value" or means, and each is associated with its own internal cluster of values, which themselves conflict, just as Radbruch's group of three conflicts. One can bond democracy and the rule of law together in theory as Kelsen did, such that law is the instrument of democracy: violations of the rule of law are thus violations of democracy. But the addition of the reality of administration complicates this picture. In theory, administration is a silent partner to politics and law: merely an obedient instrument. Kelsen thought that ambiguities in the law were merely a form of permission given by lawmakers for judges to act freely within the ambiguities. The same interpretation could be given to administration. But this means that discretionary power can dwarf that which is democratically agreed to.

The topic of concern to Dahl and his followers might be summarized by the phrase they are prone to employ: "the conditions of genuine democracy." The problem with this phrase, from a Kelsenian and Weberian perspective, is that there is a difference between "genuine democracy," meaning the kind of democracy with the kind of policies that the theorist in question prefers on their own ideological or normative grounds, and the democracy, with all its checks on agency and all the cumbersome features this involves, that "the people," through these procedures, have actually voted for. This is more than an obscure theoretical issue. Catharine MacKinnon, a one-time teaching assistant and protégé of Dahl, openly advocates the use of law, Kelsen's "coercive system," to bring about social change. She quotes Patrick Lawlor's comment that "unconscious, partly non-intentional and impersonal prejudices are built into many of our modes of behavior and our institution," the thought which is at the core of her critique of male-centric law. She goes on to quote his comment that "A change in structure (law) would help bring about, re-enforce, or co-operate with a change in heart" and endorses his conclusion that "we cannot wait for changes in heart—usually they take time and much pain, and generally the law has a wonderful effect on the head" (MacKinnon, 1989: 235). The changes in people's attitudes and beliefs she seeks are those which she believes to be harmful to women. Initially, they are legal changes women are expected to adapt to; presumably, they become normalized eventually and thus democratic. But at the time they are introduced and theorized, they are presented as conditions for genuine democracy.

If these are not changes anyone has consented to or been asked to consent to at the time they are made into law, this kind of coercion is by definition anti-democratic. If they are arrived at through ordinary democratic procedures, they are part of the ongoing process of legal revision designed to assure the conditions that people believe to be conditions of democracy. She correctly describes what she is doing as "feminist jurisprudence," which is to say that she is seeking to transform the ideology of judges with discretionary power as a way to change the law as practiced in advance of, and in order to produce a "change of heart." Changes she has advocated for, for example, in the definition of sexual consent, have been implemented through administrative discretion under Title IX. It is here that the problem of democracy becomes apparent: the supposed conditions of genuine equality she takes to be "democratic" conflict with what people elect their representatives for or take to be reasonable or fair at the time they are imposed. The imposition is reminiscent of the attempt to create the new socialist man, which was a failure to achieve its professed aims, but one which nevertheless was consequential for the formation of a certain type of person and also a certain type of resistance.

We may expect people to disagree about questions about preserving or extending democracy through legal, constitutional, and administrative improvisations, and we may expect people to provide doctrinal as well as pragmatic arguments for their answers to these questions. Things become sticky when, as part of this, "the people" are told what they can think, or arguments and doctrines, or discussion of them, are banned, or whose *Umwelt* [environment] is manipulated. People who are unfree in this respect have no meaningful "opinion" of their own, and therefore cannot "consent." For this reason, freedom of speech has normally been considered to be in some sense intrinsic to the idea of democracy. But speech has also always been subject to controls, designed for various reasons, but in part to protect the constitutional order itself. How these controls are formulated is a matter of policy and legal improvisation within a particular constitutional tradition, and they in fact vary significantly between them and change in response to circumstances. It is this process of improvisation, as distinct from the project of identifying genuine democracy over the heads of the people themselves, that is the focus of the "Theoretical Preface."

What problems do constitutional thinkers concerned with repair and survival face, and how do they solve them? This is a large question that we will address only by pointing to the answer but in a way consistent with the Weberian and Kelsenian approach taken here. Weber was greatly concerned with controlling the bureaucracy as a central practical condition for a functioning democratic constitution that would fulfill the promises to the people who had sacrificed during the war. As his follower Karl Loewenstein put it,

> In Wilhelminian Germany, Max Weber had ample opportunity to observe how bureaucrats, conscious of and obsessed with power, arrogated to themselves the function of political decision-making and used it for their own ends. He did not accept the argument, popular at the time, that a responsible bureaucracy would meet the needs of the people of its own volition.
>
> (1966: 31)

The term "responsible bureaucracy" is a giveaway: it is the title of a major work by one of Weber's nemeses, Carl J. Friedrich, which expresses Friedrich's view of the best and indeed necessary form of government in the modern state (Friedrich and Cole, 1932).

It is a giveaway in another sense. It points directly to the relationship that Weber regarded as fundamentally problematic in the modern state: the relation between the bureaucrats and the people they are "responsible" to. Put in its broadest sense, this is an agency problem, where parliament is the principal, and the bureaucracy is the agent. Weber sought to augment the powers of parliament to investigate and to produce parliamentarians with the will and the following to control the bureaucracy. The relation between "the people" and parliament works the same way: the principals are the people, parliament, or individuals acting through electoral procedures, and parliamentarians are their agents.

As Karl Loewenstein observes, from the perspective of longer historical experience, Weber's advocacy of parliamentary power was "an incorrect conclusion from a correct premise" (1966: 31). "The legislative state of his time, which was directed primarily by the parliament, has been transformed into the present-day administrative state, which by necessity must be managed by the bureaucracy" (1966: 31). Weber was simply wrong in thinking that parliaments could control bureaucracies 1966: 34). At the time, Loewenstein himself thought that courts had successfully taken over the task of controlling bureaucracies (1966: 40). In this, he was also too optimistic: courts in the United States, under the doctrines of deference and standing, have largely abandoned this role, though they have recently fleetingly returned to it. Kelsen made a different point: that disciplining a bureaucracy and making it accountable might be better done through hierarchical authority than collegial bodies (Kelsen, 2013: 79–85). Both had similar concerns: that the realities of administration produced a gap between state action and both law and the people. This is the perennial problem of democracy, sometimes more salient than other times, but never absent.

Section I: Democracy and the Rule of Law: Principal Themes

Political practice differs from political theory in one place in particular: administration. How does administration fit into politics? The problem of the place of the administrative state in liberal political theory is the theme of the first chapter, "Democracy, Liberalism, and Discretion: The Political Puzzle of the Administrative State." Liberal political theory developed initially both as a rejection of the Continental administrative state and as an alternative to it; for Thomas Jefferson and Samuel Adams, officials were a curse to be mitigated. But later "democratic" thinkers took a different view: that the people were best served by a state with a radical degree of official discretionary power, and a minimum of legal constraint on their actions. This is a tension and inherent conflict: is government to be by the people or for the people? To some extent, the sheer existence of offices produces this tension. From a familiar, limited, civics point of view, there is no tension. The civil service, *Beamten*, bureaucrats, and minor government functionaries are subordinate to politics, are merely the human instruments of law, and therefore not part of politics at all. But the human instruments exercise discretionary power, the existence of which is a thorn in the side of liberal theory, which thinkers like Friedrich Hayek had trouble removing.

What is a "democratic" response to the conflict? There is much discussion today about "democratic values." Much of it, found in writers like Dahl and Jennifer Hochschild, is a rhetorical appropriation of the notion of democracy to validate policy preferences that the people themselves do not share, or to advance notions of representation and participation with solutions to the problems of agency that they do not share, and to install them through means that do not involve the normal methods of democratic persuasion, but through judicial or administrative practices.

Kelsen, in his discussion of representation (1955), was concerned with the metamorphoses from the people to legislation through electoral laws which specified different kinds of representation. Carl Schmitt expanded the discussion of representation to include monarchy and other forms of rule as "representation," but representation under a different ideology of representation. In administrative practice, a wide range of other means of representation exist and have taken on the role of representing group identities. In the United States, for example, many boards with review powers in relation to government agencies or agencies with government funding have mandates to include highly specific mixtures of individuals drawn from particular professional, ethnic, age, or other categories. Institutional Review Boards, discussed in Chapter 6, are an example of this, but the practice is pervasive. These are boards whose nominal role is to control administration. But as the chapter shows, they can also function to promote ideologies. They present the question, however, of "genuine representation." As with "genuine democracy," this is an inherently ideological notion. The claim that only women can genuinely represent women is a contestable doctrine at the primary level of political discussion. It and similar doctrines are grounded in real emotions, especially in relation to trust and solidarity. The tribal preference for misrule by "people who look like us" to competent rule by people who do not is a powerful political motivation in many contexts, especially trust-deficient ones. But these are not the only motives. The use of novel representational devices, such as mandated mixtures of individuals with specific different characteristics, is also often intelligible as an improvisational device in response to specific issues. Indeed, in the face of ethnic conflict, these can even be basic constitutional practices created through democratic legal means.

MacKinnon praises international organizations for the larger proportion of women represented in their offices compared to the proportion among elected officials ([2015]2016: 101). This is certainly a kind of representation, and one which appears as a solution to an agency problem: the problem of men mispresenting women. But it is in clear contrast to electoral representation: it is representation as defined by or for bodies with delegated powers. These organizations are normally characterized by their "democratic deficit." They are relatively immune from electoral democracy. Similarly, the judicial institutions that are tasked by MacKinnon with changing gender ideology are insulated from democratic processes. As a consequence, they are targets for elite projects which would not be democratically accepted. What they lack is reasonably direct accountability to the democratic citizen. The chapter that follows, "What Are Democratic Values? The Case of Accountability," is an attempt to explain this value, which is of special significance for the administrative state, and to locate it among the fundamental values in tension at the base of democracy.

Woodrow Wilson was a major ideologist of a conception of "democracy" in which the democratic (and legal) deficit was celebrated. In his case, it took the form of anti-populist ideology. Reconstructing this ideology is the theme of the next chapter, "The Ideology of Anti-Populism and the Administrative State," which connects it to the project of creating the largely autonomous administrative state itself, an ideology that has worked its way into the tacit understanding of the American elite. It nicely illustrates the trilemma of democracy, law, and administration. The discretionary power that Wilson was an untiring advocate of is increasingly important today, due to the sheer vastness and impenetrable obscurity of the decisions made and enforced by the administrative state and its agents, and complicated by such matters as the role of an expert authority. But the chapter points out not only the tension it produces with democracy in the sense of popular rule but also the tension within populism between the ends it seeks and the administrative means that these ends require.

Section II: Free Speech, Pluralism, and Toleration

This section is engaged with issues related to freedom of speech, which is normally taken to be a pillar and condition of democracy. In fact, it is regulated in multiple ways, by democratically arrived at laws and judicial doctrines as well as by administrative means. The history of tolerance precedes the history of democracy. But the history nevertheless holds some lessons about the cultural conditions that allowed for liberal democracy in the west and for the problem of sustaining these conditions in the face of value conflict. Political tolerance, supported by cultural tolerance, was a response to religious disagreement, which preserved the state from contestation by limiting the state's role in relation to religion. But both political and cultural tolerance has limits and like any value must be transformed by metamorphosis into a coercive legal system.

The first chapter in this section, "Religious Pluralism, Toleration, and Liberal Democracy: Past, Present, and Future," is a discussion of this history and the question of the conditions of maintaining toleration. Managing religious differences is one of the major problems for democracy: if democracy depends on coming to an agreement on intermediate values, conditions that are instrumental for people with divergent ultimate values, it is essential that the intermediate values at stake are shareable and sufficient to support a process of coming to practical agreement on laws. If they are not, if a group possesses an ideology with ultimate values that require intermediate ones that other groups do not share, one arrives at polarization. The group must either change its ideology or exclude itself from the possibility of compromise on the basis of common purposes and resist. If the group is a majority, it becomes a potential oppressor of the minorities it excludes: if it is a minority, it becomes alienated from the political process. This is why ideologization is a risk for democracy, to the extent that democracy depends on this kind of pluralism and pluralistic compromise.

The practice of toleration is a case of informal norms, supported by the practical experience of others, that leads to familiarity and trust. The limited government typically depends on informal norms of this kind, associated with various other non-legal and non-political beliefs, including religious beliefs. Kelsen speaks of the democratic mentality, which is not part of the legal meaning of democracy, but of the conditions for it, conditions which, it is hoped, also tend to be produced by it. He associates it with "the principle of toleration, and more especially the freedom of science, in conjunction with the belief in its possible objectivity" ([1933]1973: 102). But the absence of polarization, of the creation of intolerant minorities or majorities, is not something that mere participation guarantees. Nevertheless, there are policies that have the effect of promoting both tolerance and intolerance, such as the creation of common schools, which was closely connected to the idea of democracy in the American nineteenth century. And these are the kinds of improvisational enactments that serve to preserve a constitutional order. The goal of policy in a particular situation is often to improvise ways to support the maintenance of informal norms, in order to avoid the need for formal norms. But the metamorphoses involved in the enactment and enforcement of a policy carry the risk of unintended consequences and a distortion of the original purpose.

The difficulties of the metamorphoses of ideals or values into law, or quasi-law, are the subject of the next chapter, "The End of Clear Lines: Academic Freedom and Administrative Law." Academic freedom is a topic familiar to academics, and like "democracy" itself, it is encrusted with and depends on a mentality or culture of informal norms as well as a set of procedures that have legal effects. The German legal concept of academic freedom has tradition-ally been held up as a model because there the concept is metamorphosed into law. But even in German law, there were limits on such things as defa-mation (Goldberg, 2010). The American concept has only an indirect legal status. Nevertheless, it is entangled with administrative law and employment law in paradigmatically complex ways. This case study shows how radically the metamorphoses required in turning it into administrative law can transform a "right."

The place of academic freedom can be understood as a particular kind of principal–agent relation, in which the academic is given pay and a specific kind of freedom to act on behalf of the people who pay for the institutions that provide for academics, whether these are public or private. In the case of tuition paid by the student, the payment is direct and the activity has a market-like character, though normally one regulated by the administrative state in a variety of more or less direct ways. More typically, the principal is the state itself, which pays for the institution or the professor. In exchange, the institu-tional arrangements and the conduct of the professors are constrained formally or informally through acculturation and practice to assure the principal that the activities of the professors as they represent the institution, including speech, are limited to professional matters.

When a relation requires an informal "solution," such as "trust" or "respon-sibility," it is useful to ask what coercive relation it is a surrogate for, or what law would solve the same problem. There was an old American newspaper comic called "There oughta be a law." This is the *cri de coeur* of the person wronged by the failure of an informal procedure or the administration of the law itself, and a demand to improvise a law as a solution. Academic freedom is a value that itself is grounded in a relation of discretion, especially of self-regulation. It is traditionally associated with an unspecified, informal relation of trust and responsibility. Increasingly, however, academic conduct is sub-ject to formal rules that specify these relations. But like all extensions of state power in the form of administration, its regulation involves the creation of discretionary power and new opportunities for abuse, which produce the need for new legal improvisations to protect against it. In this chapter, the process is illustrated by the rise of administrative and administrative law constraints on academic freedom which have the effect of transforming the concept itself.

The core of the transformation is from a "rights" concept, in which free-dom was granted in exchange for a degree of political neutrality, to a concept in administrative law in which institutional procedures and individual actions and values are required to be "balanced" against other values affirmed by the administrative interpretation of the law. It is also a transformation that is taking place against a background where utility has replaced "truth" as a goal of science, and in which informal regulation of conduct within a community is being replaced by external regulation, in large part as a consequence of the instrumentalization of science. Rather than an anomaly, the changes described in this chapter illustrate the pervasive processes by which administration imposes a second metamorphosis of a value by interpreting the law in an enforceable way and by engaging in practices of enforcement that give an administrative meaning to the concept.

Section III: Fundamental Political Theory

Both Kelsen and Weber considered the diversity of values given and the condition under which democracy was compelled to operate. But there is always, even in democracies, a temptation to replace legally organized and limited discussion and contestation with ideological uniformity. This temptation is particularly acute for people who consider value conflict to be the result of error, regard it as a problem to be overcome, by revelation or reason, and regard toleration merely as a prudential response to value conflict. For them, "relativism" is a self-contradictory and self-undermining doctrine that is corrosive to the foundations of political order or a denial of its truth-revealing *telos*. One alternative view of the issue of value conflict points to the intrinsically irresolvable character of a certain class of value conflicts that are fundamental to politics. This strategy was Weber's. But it is found in a larger group of intellectuals and appears in a variety of forms and formulations.

In the chapter on "The Method of Antinomies," this strategy is traced through the thinking of a number of major political thinkers. The persistent and deep value conflicts that concern them are those which are irresolvable in a special sense: to achieve one value, in some respect, requires one, in a practical sense, to adapt or concede to the other. The paradigm case is the conflict between a conception of a society based on rules versus a society based on a commitment to a common end. Theoretically, each is possible. Practically, one cannot attain common ends without rules, and one cannot produce adherence to rules without their serving some common ends. There are many variations of this kind of binding between alternatives: the nemesis arises when a particular side of the antinomy is pushed too far in practice. If this kind of case is at the core of political traditions and accounts for the persistent struggles that characterize them, it is impossible to provide the kind of reductive account or critique of these traditions that a quest for a single organizing principle, such as justice, aspires to. It also exposes such reductions as ideologizations: partial perspectives that are persuasive only if they exclude considerations that are necessary to the practical application of their own core idea.

In the next chapter, "Decisionism and Politics: Weber as Constitutional Theorist," Weber's constitutional thinking is discussed, showing how it represented a revision of the utilitarian view of "ends" in the evolution of law in Rudolf von Ihering's *Zweck im Recht* [*Law as Means to an End*] to encompass the diversity of ends ([1877–1883]1924). An intermediate end, such as a dynamic constitutional order, can be widely shared among people who disagree on ultimate ends. This image of a "normal" yet dynamic modern political order is contrasted to the further development by Carl Schmitt of the absolutization of the element of decision: the sovereign who decides the state of exception, that is to say, decides whether the situation is normal and whether the normal legal order applies.

As should be clear from the "Theoretical Preface," the concept of intermediate ends, and their character as both value and fact, is essential to the discussion in this volume. What the concept of intermediate ends provides is an alternative to the idea of a coherent will of the people or the need for common values that amount to a coherent ideology. Yet this is also a case in which the inadequacies of the concept of values become evident. On the one hand, the term is meant to cover the vast relevant mental background to political choice and thought, including not only political culture and the tacit knowledge relevant to politics but also all the knowledge a person has and values, religious knowledge, traditions, and so forth. On the other hand, it also applies to the intermediate values that leaders can appeal to or invent. Democracy, the rule of law, efficiency, citizenship, and the nation are all values, intermediate for most people, interpreted differently by them. But new intermediate values, such as sustainability, are constantly invented. In all of these cases, there is the temptation to absolutize the value or to provide it with "philosophical grounding" which has the same effect.

Kelsen's strategy was to distinguish political fictions from the factual or operative content of law. In this way, he could produce a de-ideologized account of legal reality. The discussion of the rule of law parallels the discussion of democracy: in each case, theorists have attempted to derive inner principles which enable them to make normative judgments of actually existing legal and political systems. In the case of political systems, the judgments diverge from the choices made by participants under the legal order itself. In the case of the rule of law, the strategy is to find a hidden meaning in the concept of law that allows the critic to identify actual or "positive" law and obedience to it as inconsistent with the true "rule of law." The next chapter, "The Rule of Law Deflated: Weber and Kelsen," contrasts the "positivist" and value-free accounts given by Kelsen and Weber to those, such as Ronald Dworkin's (2013), which attempt to derive an overarching ideology from a particular formulation of the concept of law.

Dworkin cites cases where judges appeal to morality to support the claim that the law itself rests on a general morality. The chapter points to an alternative signaled by the role of an oath in judicial appointment: the oath of neutrality. This oath is sanctionable: it is an operative part of law rather than a fiction. But it is not an oath to a morality. It leaves open the choice of neutral means to resolve the kind of legal ambiguities that arise in any codification. Whether the appeal is to an ostensibly neutral and universal morality or to technical considerations of economics, the point is that it is, in the relevant circumstances, neutral, in accordance with the oath itself.

Sanctions are rarely if ever imposed. But there is a powerful informal basis for the subject of the oath and for a certain style of judicial conduct. The risk of embarrassment for having one's judgments overturned for poor legal reasoning is even greater. But the very existence of vast discretionary power poses a problem for democracy: possession of these powers makes their users a target for ideologization contrary to the opinions of the governed.

The issue of the nature of the rule of law relates closely to the problem of the metamorphosed legal concept of democracy. The rule of law and obedience to the law, as well as discretion employed in a manner consistent with popular or cultural understandings of fairness, dignity, decency, and so forth, are the instruments of democracy: to deviate from them under the influence of an academic theory about the true meaning of the rule of law is to repudiate the results of the democratic process itself in the name of "democracy." To advocate legal change through the democratic process on moral or ideological grounds is to act politically; to expound a theory that is designed to influence the discretionary choices of judges or administrators ideologically in the name of the true meaning of the rule of law but in violation of the sworn obligation of neutrality—or to treat judicial action as policy-making—is to circumvent the actual democratic process and obligations under the oath. The meaning of the law is something defined within the legal process itself, through legal means. The chapter explains what those means are.

Returning Discourse About Democracy to the People

Kelsen made, as we have noted, a characteristic distinction between the historical or decorative elements of law which he called political fictions and those which have actual legal significance, a significance signaled by the existence of sanctions attached to the law. This kind of thinking applied as well to his view of democratic ideology. He frequently appealed to the idea of natural psychological effects and aspects of states of affairs, also to distinguish them from the logical and factual implications of the coercive legal order itself.[3] Among these was the existence of ideological justifications for regimes. Kelsen considered this unsurprising and natural: "no regime," he wrote, "can wholly dispense with ideologies which vindicate and glorify it, even the democracies, or more accurately those who hold power in them" ([1933]1973: 104). But this is a psychological fact rather than a legal one or one constitutive of democracy or a potential clue to its essence. A "scientific" or realistic understanding of democracy should separate itself from its ideological justifications. The concept of natural rights is a good example, which Weber gave. As Weber says,

"It is after all, a piece of crude self-deception to think that even the most conservative among us could carry on living today without these achievements from the age of the 'Rights of Man'" (Weber, 1994: 159). But at the same time, he regarded the origins of the idea as religious and the extreme adherents to the doctrine itself as an instance of "fanaticism" and "fanatic advocacy" (Weber, [1968]1978: 6–7). Thus, he agreed with Jeremy Bentham that as an improvisation to protect against abuses by the state, or as Bentham called them "securities against misrule" ([1820]2012: 24), it is indispensable to modern liberty. But as a metaphysical doctrine, it is, as Bentham pungently put it, nonsense on stilts (cf. Schofield, 2003).

If we strip away these glorifications and vindications, what remains of the idea of democracy and the rule of law? The answer is simple: for Kelsen, the law is a social technology, a means to an end. "Democracy" is an end, but it is also a means to ends, the ends of the participants. It is distinguished from authoritarian regimes in which a ruler or ruling cadre decides the ends. It is a means by which the participants realize their ends in concert with others, according to legal methods of representation that they also participate in creating or approving and in revising. If the world was such that all people's ends cohered into a single common good accepted by all, and there was a world of fact that all accepted, politics would be unnecessary: we would have achieved what the Saint-Simonians dreamed of: the replacement of politics with administration. This, however, is easily confused with authoritarianism itself: if the authorities decide that the potential participants are unable to discern their own interests and must have them decided for them, we have an undemocratic regime.

But as we have seen, value conflicts do not disappear so easily. They are intrinsic to administration itself. But they are also present in the basic principal–agent relation that administration, understood as acting on behalf of the people, represents. In the metamorphosis of values into law, and law into administration, there is a constant tension that, in a democracy, is temporarily resolved, over and over, through legislative and constitutional improvisation. There is no permanent resolution to these conflicts and therefore no end to politics. Value conflicts, and the special value conflicts that are antinomies, in which the achievement of a given value is bound to the other, are ineliminable. But also ineliminable are the recurrent problems of the principal agent relation itself and the role of politics in devising solutions to them, solutions that are bound to circumstance and thus necessarily only temporary. Many of the supposedly constitutive values or essential features of democracy are such solutions: transparency, discussion, and the public sphere enable people to control and correct those who purport to speak for them. But these solutions are themselves subject to metamorphosis into law and contain their own value conflicts.

To reiterate from the "Theoretical Preface": where there is discretion, there is an agency relationship, and a need for protections against abuse, and trust. Much could be said sociologically and economically about the ways in which these discretionary relationships are policed. The preservation of the appearance of neutrality, supported by oaths, is a hallmark of liberal governance, and a paradigmatic case of controlling an agency relation. But it is easily betrayed. The sheer variety of means of assuring against betrayal extends through human relations and arises in every case in which the basic human relation of speaking for another or acting on their behalf arises. The assertion of expertise, backed by its own elaborate system of trust-assuring devices, is a key part of modern politics. Party membership and party discipline allow voters to trust people of whom they know nothing. Personal trust is important as well. But we must also ask why it is that trust is required and what trust is a substitute for. The differences between national traditions of administration are large, and each elicits its own variety of preferred means of assuring against betrayal. Yet betrayal, conflicts of interest, error, and so forth are endemic in these relations. Electoral politics itself, including leadership competition, may be seen as a mechanism for policing discretion. Repairing and preserving constitutional arrangements devoted to controlling the irreducible kinds of discretion that arise in governing, not surprisingly, are normal functions of actual political life.

There are many moving parts to this account of democracy, law, and administration. The chapters presented here each deal with particular parts, not the whole. Also, inevitably some important topics are left out: the role of expertise, for example. But the reader is owed at least an outline of what the whole would look like. In the next few paragraphs, we can outline the basic picture here, and how the parts fit together. Democracy, on the interpretation outlined here, is a collective agency relation. The power to replace the government, to amend its powers, and to set in place institutional controls on discretionary powers and their abuse, such as an "independent judiciary" and jury trials, as well as expert bodies, are among the many means by which the collective agent, the state, and its actual individual representatives, administrators, judges, the police, and other officials, can be controlled and compelled to follow the law. This agency relation is fraught with betrayal, distrust, and conflicting interests, as well as the constant fact of unintended consequences that need to be corrected for. Many of the mechanisms for controlling the individual authorized agents of the state are deterrents that are rarely employed.

This is the fundamental democratic fact: that elections, leader selection, and representation in legislation and in relation to official appointments are protections against abuse. The procedure itself, of majoritarian rule through legal mechanisms, such as law-governed elections, is imperfect, as are all the mechanisms to protect the people, the collective principal, from the authorized agents of the state. The processes of collective decision-making and "will formation" are themselves problematic and vary "culturally." Majority rule creates minorities: sometimes stable and oppositional, sometimes temporary. Managing the consequences of this fact is a fundamental problem for democracy: the twinning of democracy and "rights" in liberal democracy is a partial solution. This limits the power of majorities over minorities, in selected respects. The rights of assembly and freedom of speech serve as partial protections against both misrule and majority abuse of minorities. But there are other protections: majorities also have an interest in stability, among other things, that minorities can challenge, for example, through protest, and can exact concessions through these means.

The metamorphoses of desires and values into administrative action can be understood in terms of discretion, a term with two meanings. The first is legal: an ambiguity in the law gives the administrator the power to interpret. The second is political. Bureaucrats operate in terms of what Carl Friedrich called the rule of anticipated reactions: the limits to their power are what they can get away with without provoking a legislative or judicial reaction that would constrain them by clarifying or replacing the authorizing law or limiting their powers ([1937]1950: 49). The unwillingness of legislators and judges to micromanage bureaucrats except in extreme cases, and their willingness to defer to their "expert" advice, means that this is a considerable, indeed dominant, part of the distribution of power within the state. The potential for slippage between the "will of the people" and these results, and the fact that there is no "will of the people" other than the one artificially produced through electoral procedures, means that the notion is a fiction. Kelsen puts the point in this way: commenting on the phrase "the people's power has been transferred to the representative body," he notes that

> the last words [i.e., representative body] alone describe the political reality, and even this description is not completely free from ideological elements. It presupposes that the legislative power belongs—historically or by its very nature—to the people and has been transferred to parliament, which, obviously, is not true.
>
> (Kelsen, [1949]2006: 292–3)

The issue of discretion reveals the close connection between legal positivism and democracy. Unless, as legal positivism requires, the law is carried out as written, or as written but in the light of legislative intent, the legally structured expression of the will of the people is not being carried out. To have courts or administrators that operate according to their own judicial or administrative philosophy is to govern against the formal expression of the people. Such autonomous "philosophies" can nevertheless serve as guarantors of a certain kind of fidelity to the interests of the people. But they can also amount to an alternative to democracy in the formal sense which represents a distinct form of governance, akin to the Iranian model of "rule by the jurisprudent," and in this way serve as a vehicle of power for movements that cannot get their way in the liberal democratic sphere of free speech and leader competition.

The continuous and extensive fact of metamorphoses creates the opportunity, and even the necessity, of the use of discretionary power. This can be conceived of as "democratic" in the sense of tacit consent, as some theorists of public administration claim. Or it can be understood from the other, administrative side, as what the administrators can get away with by following the rule of anticipated reactions, using the coercive powers at their disposal, powers that themselves are limited only by this "rule," which is to say by what judges and elected officials, or the people in the streets or elsewhere, are willing and able to do to resist those powers.

Reactions reflect the "values," as we have used this portmanteau term, of the ruled. A response to unfairness or injustice as well as to negative consequences of an agreed policy produces a basis for legislative or leadership action and provides an incentive for action. The action takes the form of political improvisation, for example, in new law or new deterrent supervisory bodies. The means chosen normally reflect the pre-existing legal and constitutional machinery and build on them. These structures are kludges, too complex to replace, which are incorporated into the improvisations. But their significance can be transformed by the improvisations, such as an authorization of emergency rule which is extended beyond its original meaning.

Improvisation, in the face of the fundamental problem of agency, is the fundamental fact of democratic governance. To govern for the people is to control the metamorphoses of state action and their potential for abuse. But the concepts of abuse and success are valuative and subject to the fact of value pluralism and value conflict. These conflicts cannot be overcome by an appeal to the common good or a philosophical truth about justice: in the world of politics, it is simply the case that these are disputed or contested concepts, some of which involve irresolvable antinomies. Legal electoral devices are a means of making decisions in the face of conflict. But they too require some minimal, valuative, acceptance, as does the rule of law generally. There is no guarantee that this minimum will be met: these are fragile systems, and the maintenance of minimal agreement depends on sociological as well as political considerations, though policy can help or hinder the maintenance or development of the relevant conditions.

Notes

1   Richard Rorty provides a useful and similar discussion of these contrasts, as well as an account of Rawls' own apparent rejection of the idea that philosophy can instruct politics by providing a philosophical grounding for political preferences (Rorty, 2010: 211–26, 239–58).
2   The specifics of Weber's unusual view of democracy is not discussed here, but an account of them, Stephen Turner, "Weber's Countergenealogy of Democracy," will appear in a forthcoming volume edited Peter Gordon and Joshua Derman, *Max Weber at 100*.
3   The "coercive legal order" is part of Kelsen's endorsement of the delict-sanction theory of law, which he inherits from Blackstone's *Commentaries* ([1765–69]2016) and John Austin's *The Province of Jurisprudence Determined* (1995) (Kelsen, [1949]2006: 50–64).

References

Austin, John. *The Province of Jurisprudence Determined*. Cambridge: Cambridge University Press, 1995.

Baldwin, David A and Mark Haugaard. *Robert A Dahl: An Unending Quest*. London: Routledge, 2016.

Bentham, Jeremy. "Letter II: On the Liberty of Discussion in Public Meetings, 18th Oct., 1820," In *On the Liberty of the Press, and Public Discussion and other Legal and Political Writings for Spain and Portugal*, Edited by Catherine Pease-Watkin and Philip Schofield. Oxford: Clarendon Press, [1820]2012, 23–33. www.google.com/books/edition/On_the_Liberty_of_the_Press_and_Public_D/vF7zQG_wSE-MC?hl=en&gbpv=1&dq=Letter+II:+On+the+Liberty+of+Discussion+in+Public+Meetings,+18th+Oct.,+1820&pg=PA23&printsec=frontcover

Blackstone, William. *The Commentaries on the Laws of England*. Oxford: Oxford University Press, [1765–69]2016.

Caldwell, Christopher. *The Age of Entitlement: America since the Sixties*. New York: Simon & Schuster, 2020.

Calhoun, Craig, Dilip Parameshwar Gaonkar, and Charles Taylor. *Degenerations of Democracy*. Cambridge: Harvard University Press, 2022.

Codevilla, Angelo M. *The Ruling Class: How They Corrupted America and What We Can Do About It*. New York: Beaufort Books, 2010.

Dahl, Robert A. *How Democratic is the American Constitution?* 2nd edn. New Haven: Yale University Press, 2003.

Dahl, Robert A. *How Democratic is the American Constitution?* New Haven: Yale University Press, 2001.

Dahl, Robert A. *Polyarchy: Participation and Opposition*. New Haven: Yale University Press, 1971. https://archive.org/details/polyarchypartici0000dahl

Dworkin, Ronald. *Justice for Hedgehogs*. Cambridge: Harvard University Press, 2013.

Friedrich, Carl J. *Constitutional Government and Democracy: Theory and Practice in Europe and America*, revised edn. Boston: Ginn and Company, [1937]1950 (Previously published as *Constitutional Government and Politics*, 1937). https://archive.org/stream/in.ernet.dli.2015.64926/2015.64926.Constitutional-Government-And-Democracy_djvu.txt

Friedrich, Carl J. "The Role and the Position of the Common Man," *American Journal of Sociology* 49(5): 421–429, 1944.

Friedrich, Carl J., and Taylor Cole. *Responsible Bureaucracy: A Study of the Swiss Civil Service*. Cambridge: Harvard University Press, 1932.

Goldberg, Ann. *Honor, Politics, and the Law in Imperial Germany, 1871–1914*. Cambridge: Cambridge University Press, 2010.

Hamburger, Philip. *Is Administrative Law Unlawful?* Chicago: The University of Chicago Press, 2014.

Hamburger, Philip. *The Administrative Threat*. New York: Encounter Books, 2017.

Hochschild, Jennifer. "Robert Dahl: Scholar, Teacher, and Democrat," *Journal of Political Power* 8(2): 167–174, [2015]2016 (Reprinted in *Robert A. Dahl: An Unending Quest*, edited by David A. Baldwin and Mark Haugaard, London: Routledge, 2016, 11–18).

Ihering, Rudolph. *Law as Means to an End* [*Der Zweck im Recht*], translated by Isaac Husik of the 4th German edn. New York: Macmillan, [1877–1883]1924.

Jaccard, Don. "The Case of the Eleven-Inch Fish: A Study in Administrative Discretion," *Policy Perspectives* 7: 51–58, 1999.

Kelsen, Hans. *General Theory of Law & the State*. New Brunswick: Transaction Publishers, [1949]2006.

Kelsen, Hans. "Foundations of Democracy," *Ethics* 66(1): 1–101, 1955.

Kelsen, Hans. *The Essence and Value of Democracy* (translated by Brian Graf), Edited by Nadia Urbinati and Carlo Invernizzi Accetti. Lanham: Rowman & Littlefield, 2013.

Kelsen, Hans. "State-Form and World-Outlook," In *Hans Kelsen: Essays in Legal and Moral Philosophy* (translated by Peter Heath), Edited by Ota Weinberger. Dordrecht/Boston: D. Reidel Publishing Company, [1933]1973, 95–113 (Staatsform und Weltanschauung vol. 96 of *Rechtund Staat*, Tübingen: Mohr, 1933).

Koppl, Roger. *Expert Failure*. Cambridge: Cambridge University Press, 2018.

Loewenstein, Karl. *Max Weber's Political Ideas in the Perspective of Our Time*. Amherst: The University of Massachusetts Press, 1966.

MacKinnon, Catharine. "Dahl's Feminism," *Journal of Political Power* 8(2): 249–260, [2015]2016 (Reprinted in *Robert A. Dahl: An Unending Quest*, Edited by David A. Baldwin and Mark Haugaard. London: Routledge, 2016, 93–104).

MacKinnon, Catharine. *Toward a Feminist Theory of the State*. Cambridge: Harvard University Press, 1989.

MacLean, Nancy. *Democracy in Chains: The Deep History of the Radical Right's Stealth Plan for America*. New York: Viking Press, 2017.

Marini, John. *Unmasking the Administrative State: The Crisis of American Politics in the Twenty-First Century*, Edited by John Marini and Ken Masugi. New York: Encounter Books, 2019.

Oreskes, Naomi, and Erik M. Conway. *Merchants of Doubt: How a Handful of Scientists Obscured the Truth on Issues from Tobacco Smoke to Global Warming*. New York: Bloomsbury Press, 2010.

Parsons, Talcott. "Propaganda and Social Control," In *Essays in Sociological Theory*, Revised edn. New York: The Free Press, [1942]1954, 142–176.

Rawls, John. *Political Liberalism*. New York: Columbia University Press, 1993.

Rawls, John. "The Idea of Public Reason Revisited," *The University of Chicago Law Review* 64(3): 765–807, 1997.

Rawls, John. *The Law of Peoples*. Cambridge: Harvard University Press, 2001.

Rorty, Richard. *The Rorty Reader,* Edited by Chris Voparil and Richard J. Berstein. Malden: Blackwell, 2010. https://archive.org/details/rortyreader0000unse

Scharpf, Fritz. *Governing in Europe: Effective and Democratic?* Oxford: Oxford University Press, 1999.

Schofield, Philip. "Jeremy Bentham's 'Nonsense upon Stilts'," *Utilitas* 15(1): 1–26, 2003. https://doi.org/10.1017/S0953820800003745

Shils, E. "The Antinomies of Liberalism," In *The Virtues of Civility: Selected Essays on Liberalism, Tradition, and Society*, Edited by S. Grosby. Indianapolis: Liberty Fund, [1978]1997, 123–187.

Sowell, Thomas. *Race and Economics*. New York: David McKay Company, Inc., 1975.

Sykes, Charles. *A Nation of Victims: The Decay of the American Character*. New York: St. Martin's Press, 1992.

Tsebelis, George and Amie Kreppel. "The History of Conditional Agenda-Setting in European Institutions," *European Journal of Political Research* 33: 41–71, 1998.

Turner, Stephen. "The Pittsburgh Survey and the Survey Movement: An Episode in the History of Expertise" In *Pittsburgh Surveyed: Social Science and Social Reform in the Early Twentieth Century*, Edited by Maurine W. Greenwald and Margo Anderson. Pittsburgh: University of Pittsburgh Press, 1996, 35–49.

Turner, Stephen. "Weber's Countergenealogy of Democracy," In Peter Gordon and Joshua Derman, *Max Weber at 100*. Oxford: Oxford University Press, forthcoming.

Weber, Max. *Collected Methodological Writings,* translated by H. H. Bruun. New York: Routledge, 2012.

Weber, Max. *Economy and Society: An Outline of Interpretive Sociology*, 3 vols, Edited by Guenther Roth and Claus Wittich. Berkeley: University of California Press, [1968]1978.

Weber, Max. "Letter to Robert Wilbrandt," In *Collected Methodological Writings*, Edited and translated by H. H. Bruun. New York: Routledge, [1913]2012, 406.

Weber, Max. "Parliament and Government in Germany under a New Political Order," In *Political Writings*, Edited by Peter Lassman and Ronald Speirs (translated by Ronald Speirs). Cambridge: Cambridge University Press, 1994, 130–271.

Chapter 1

Democracy, Liberalism, and Discretion

The Political Puzzle of the Administrative State

Stephen Turner

"Democracy," in the classic sense, is a legal regime that operates with procedures that define the ways in which laws are made or changed through some form of majority rule. The procedures may specify a requirement for supermajorities to change certain fundamental, or constitutional, laws. For the purposes of discussions of liberal democracy as a functioning order, the relevant rights are those which are the conditions for democracy, understood as government by majority voting, normally with representation, based on discussion. Constraints on discussion, or interventions by the state to control or bias the discussion, that is to say, violations of the political neutrality of the state, are violations of the relevant rights. This was, essentially, the notion of democracy that was the starting point for the literature that this chapter discusses, on the relationship between democracy and the administrative state. As one of the key figures put it, "the term refers to any form of government in which the policy making authorities are chosen on a broad and substantially equal suffrage basis in elections that are free from direct government coercion." The author adds that under modern conditions this "necessarily embodies the principle of responsibility to public opinion" (Millspaugh, 1937: 64). But as we will see, this principle, as understood by the advocates of the administrative state, is not only different from the idea of democratic accountability but also hostile to it.

We can call this the narrow theory of liberal democracy. It does not involve notions like the will of the people, understood as something beyond and distinct from the expressions of that will through the procedures of the particular democracy, nor does it involve ends that are taken to be part of the full life or the full life of a community, such as social justice or economic equality. It leaves these to democratic decision. For the narrow theory, rights, social justice, and the like are the policy products or outcomes of the legal procedures and are created by the choices made through these procedures, such as a law establishing a legal right. What counts as "just" from the point of view of the narrow theory is itself the product of political decision, not something that can be used as a standard to judge it. The narrow sense allows for making "health care" a "right" through these procedures. But for the narrow sense, this too is a matter of democratic decision.[1]

DOI: 10.4324/9781003360810-2

The narrow conception is law-centered: it treats law as the expression of democracy and democracy as the product of legal procedures. It treats constitutional form as the product of legal democratic choice, rather than something to be measured against a philosophical standard of "genuine democracy." And, although the conception of democracy is narrow, it applies widely and equally to all legal orders that operate through legal procedures to express the choices of the people regardless of what those choices are. A "liberal" democracy is simply one in which the procedures reflect the freedom of individuals to choose, without state coercion or significant state limitations on the formation of opinion through discussion. A democratic choice to impose such restrictions is possible, but this would make the democracy an illiberal one. The critics of liberalism, such as Carl Schmitt, pointed out the inherent conflict between "democracy" and "liberalism" resulting from this possibility and argued that this unstable compound had long since collapsed: the government by discussion and public opinion of the eighteenth century no longer existed, public opinion was mere acclamation, and no one any longer believed that losing the vaunted freedom of speech would make any difference to political outcomes (Schmitt, [1928]2008: 275, 1985: 48–50). And the fear of the failure of these institutions has been a pervasive part of the history of democracy. During the democratic revival of the nineteenth century, the negative example of Florence was more potent, especially for Central Europe, than the example of the United States.

Conventional accounts of liberal constitutions, especially "liberal" ones, tend to ignore or obscure one large fact: the administrative state. There are, however, some revealing exceptions. The basic account of the "rule of law" comes from Albert Venn Dicey (Dicey, [1914]1962) and is expressly concerned with the developing administrative state of his own time in Britain, the late nineteenth and early twentieth centuries, and the example of the Continental administrative states that were already fully developed. Dicey's fear was that the administrative state, if it was not constrained by the common courts, would degrade into arbitrariness. As one commentator explains him, the essence of doctrine of the "rule of law, of which Dicey has, of course, given us the classic expression," is the "absence of arbitrary power of government officers and subjection of every man, including government officers, to ordinary law administered by ordinary tribunals" (Thach, 1935: 273). Others have noted the non-democratic character and origins of administrative law—in the royal prerogative (Hamburger, 2014) and in the royal bureaucratic powers of continental states that continued after the abolition of the monarchy. Carl Schmitt's thinking is particularly relevant here. Rather than attempting to derive the legality of administrative law from other forms of law, he points out that it is a separate constitutional principle, with its own distinctive form of legitimacy (Schmitt, [1928]2008: 93) and indeed argues that the modern bourgeois *Rechtsstaat*, what he calls the legislative state, presupposes the administrative state ([1932]2004: 12–13).

28   Stephen Turner

My concern in this chapter is with the administrative state but from the point of view of liberal political theory. I provide a basic introduction to the legal issues, but my concern is with the place of administrative discretion in liberal political theory. To address this will require turning the clock back to the point at which the institutions in question were being established. For reasons that will become apparent, this was largely an American discussion: it took the form of a debate over the relation of democracy to the administrative state. In Europe, as Schmitt, and, before him, as we will see, Woodrow Wilson noted, there was no such discussion. The administrative state preceded the "democratizing" impulse and accommodated it, sufficiently for the regimes in question to ignore the problem.

Administrative Law

Legal issues are critical to understanding the political problem of the administrative state, even if they are not sufficient. The distinction between law and administrative law works like this in the United States: "Under the U.S. Constitution, the government could bind its subjects only through the use of legislative or judicial power" (Hamburger, 2014: 3). This meant that "binding" had to be the result of a vote or an act of a court that was part of the judicial branch itself. This is law, as it is normally understood. However, the executive had its own powers, among them the denial of government benefits, and the implementation of regulatory regimes created in legislation, but which involved quasi-judicial and quasi-legislative powers, normally based on some form of licensure. This was nominally different. It was not about binding, and it was an assumed power of the executive not rooted in the constitution. But this acknowledged power gradually was transformed into something else—the power not only to make regulations with the force of law loosely based on actual law but also to adjudicate on the basis of these regulations in administrative courts or proceedings, and to enforce the results of these judgments, usually through sanctions involving the refusal of benefits or exclusion from licensed activities. The benefits in question might be those of participation in government grant programs, or broadcasting, which was licensed.

The constitutional status of the "state" as distinct from the judiciary and legislature is usually subsumed under the category of "the executive." But in practice, the administrative state, the actual carriers-out of the legal instructions of the executive and the other branches, has a great deal of autonomy. The legal basis for this autonomy is complex. Kelsen explains the discretionary power of courts in the face of ambiguous legislation in this way (Kelsen, 1955: 77–80). The ambiguities are legally meaningful: they represent a delegation of authority to decide the meaning of the law to the courts. The same principle applies to administration, and this produces some remarkable results. The number of "rules" in the form of enforceable regulations which administrative agencies make in interpreting the laws produced in the United States is 27 times the "laws" (Crews, 2017). And this is just the published regulations, which are supposed to go through a process of public review (a requirement that is often ignored). There are also directives that say, essentially, what the regulated body must do in order to prevent the regulatory agency from taking action against them. Together with the various forms of legal insulation against the political supervision of these administrative bodies, this produced a relatively autonomous branch of government.

These agencies are legally considered to be part of the executive, but they are protected from the elected "executive" as well as the courts, in various ways. Judicial review is rare and involves special constitutional courts that rarely act. In the United States, the situation differs, but the results are similar: judicial review is common, but agencies are deferred to under a doctrine enunciated in the Chevron case, and agencies are protected from suits by the legal interpretation of "standing," which limits accountability radically.[2] Agencies cannot be held to account by the public in court unless the plaintiff meets very rigorous tests of provable personal harm, tests that are rarely met. There is, in short, a high degree of autonomy in fact, and a high level of legal and procedural insulation that supports this autonomy.

An incidental consequence of the fact that administrative units in the executive can interpret their own regulations, adjudicate their own cases, and define their own procedures is that there is a larger role for discretion in enforcing them and a much more limited power of public contestation of them. Moreover, one major way of sanctioning institutions is the threat of denial of funds, which is both vague and difficult to adjudicate, if it is adjudicable in ordinary courts at all. The enforcement powers of the administrative state involve extraordinary discretion, allowing the state to threaten legal action to produce results that are not specified in regulations, and also permit vague regulation, such as letters of guidance which are not themselves regulations and therefore unchallengeable. In theory, these actions are subject to judicial supervision and legislative clarification, but the courts have generally "deferred" to executive agencies in the use of these powers, though on occasion have intervened, and legislative revision is fraught with the same issues of control of implementation as the original legislation, with the additional complication that regulation creates new interests by virtue of the fact that it creates an advantaged class of beneficiaries of the regulation, made up of people taking advantage of the opportunities created by it, which becomes a constituency for its continuation.

The American Reception of the Administrative State

The administrative state, and administrative law, regardless of questions in legal theory about its legal foundation, is a reality. What led to it? Is there an alternative? And what were the arguments for it in the first place? This is a lacuna in present discussions of liberalism: the focus is on the law and on the idea of politically limiting the expansion of the state and state power. To face the issues, we need to return to an earlier discussion, the discussion that took place during the birth of the American administrative state. As noted, there was no comparable discussion on the European continent: the administrative state was an institutional inheritance from monarchy and absolutism which theorists sought to control and curtail, but not to abolish. In the United States, in contrast, it needed to be invented, and it was, with the model of the European bureaucratic state in mind. It was these institutions that American reformers of the late nineteenth century admired and wished to create in the United States. The founders of the Columbia University School of Economics and Political Science traveled to Europe to observe the educational systems that supported these bureaucracies, in order to copy them (Hoxie, 1955: 21–3). John Burgess, the head and creator of this school, was a noted Germanophile. Albion Small, similarly, wrote his sole major work on the Cameralists, the German theorists of states administration whose writings started in the 1500s (Small, 1909). It was a tradition he took as a model for what social science itself should become: an administrative science. And although sociology, his nominal field, did not become one, the debate over administrative science, which became the field of public administration, and its relation to social science, formed a significant part of the subsequent literature.

Ironically, this vast literature has been forgotten, and the term "administrative state" is now being treated as an invention of the paranoid Right and a misunderstanding of the nature of the state itself. The issues debated in the period between the 1870s and the 1946 passage of the Administrative Procedures Act have been submerged, and the topic is instead reframed as a perennial one between those who believe the expansive state is our best, and most democratic, means for caring for one another and those who wrongly see it as oppressive (Eckart, 2017). The progenitors of this state, however, and the participants in the earlier debate, were under no illusions about its anti-democratic character, its reliance on discretion, the need to insulate officials from the law, and the conflict between this kind of state and the rule of law, and indeed they discussed it obsessively. The discussion began in earnest in the 1880s under the heading "Democracy and Efficiency," as a classic paper by Woodrow Wilson put it (1901), and in a second paper, "The Study of Administration" (Wilson, [1886]1941). The argument was couched in terms of "saving democracy." The ills of democratic politics were described in the most lurid manner by Wilson, in terms of decline from the early days of the Republic:

> Our later life has disclosed serious flaws, has even seemed ominous of pitiful failure, in some of the things we most prided ourselves upon having managed well: notably, in pure and efficient local government, in the successful organization of great cities, and in well-considered schemes of administration. The boss—a man elected by no votes, preferred by no open process of choice, occupying no office of responsibility—makes himself

Democracy, Liberalism, and Discretion 31

a veritable tyrant among us, and seems to cheat us of self-government; parties appear to hamper the movements of opinion rather than to give them form and means of expression; multitudinous voices of agitation, an infinite play of forces at cross-purpose, confuse us; and there seems to be no common counsel or definite union for action, after all.

(Wilson, 1901: n.p.)

The reasons for this "pitiful failure" include a standard list, which reappears throughout the long literature that followed. The solution is administrative reform. The principle of democracy, he insists, is not the problem; execution is: "What we have blundered at is its new applications and details, its successful combination with efficiency and purity in governmental action." The evils of the present administration are clear. "The poisonous atmosphere of city government, the crooked secrets of state administration, the confusion, the sinecurism, and corruption ever and again discovered in the bureau of Washington" (Wilson, [1886]1941: 485–6). The solution is professionalization: "Our theory, in short, has paid as little heed to efficiency as our practice. It has been a theory of non-professionalism in public affairs; and in many great matters of public action non-professionalism is non-efficiency" (Wilson, 1901: n.p.). The reasons for non-professionalism are not hard to find, though Wilson is careful not to say this directly. The reason is that Americans elect too many officials.

They give us so many elective offices that even the most conscientious voters have neither the time nor the opportunity to inform themselves with regard to every candidate on their ballots and must vote for a great many men of whom they know nothing. They give us, consequently, the local machine and the local boss; and where population crowds, interests compete, work moves strenuously and at haste, life is many-sided and without unity, and voters of every blood and environment and social derivation mix and stare at one another at the same voting places, government miscarries, is confused, irresponsible, unintelligent, and wasteful. Methods of electoral choice and administrative organization, which served us admirably well while the nation was homogeneous and rural, serve us oftentimes ill enough now that the nation is heterogeneous and crowded into cities (Wilson, 1901: n.p.).

The solution, elaborated by many American professors over the next 70 years, was to replace the system by which most offices were elected and involved short terms of office with a professional administration, meaning officials with tenure, a system of examinations, and to create (or at least pretend the existence of) the science of administration. The model was explicitly European—administration "is a foreign science . . . developed by French and German Professors" (Wilson, [1886]1941: 486). Wilson acknowledged that some modifications needed to be made to adapt the system to American tastes and recognized the dangers of pure bureaucratic rule. And this set up the basic conflict in the system, recognized by all its commentators, between a class of bureaucrats, insulated from direct political accountability and believing in its

32 Stephen Turner

own expertise, and the public which sought, with little success, to control it. As David Levitan put it, at the end of this period, "Unwise legislation may be mitigated somewhat by considerate and humane administration, but the citizen has no 'cushion' against arbitrary officialdom, often hidden behind the cloak of 'administrative necessity'." And Levitan offers what was to become the standard solution, which often took the form of a lament: "The real protection of the citizen lies in the development of a high degree of democratic consciousness among the administrative hierarchy" (1943: 357). It is apparent from the extensive literature on the education of public administrators that democratic consciousness went against the grain both of the systems of education that eschewed political theory and the hiring habits of administrative agencies, which preferred technicians to generalists. The theoretical solution to the problem of arbitrary officialdom was for the officials to voluntarily accept public opinion as a guide and limit and to cultivate public opinion.

Leonard White, a major thinker in the formative years of the discipline of public administration, put it thus:

> The problem, therefore, has gradually developed into that of finding means to ensure that the acts of administrative officers' shall be consistent not only with the law but equally with the purposes and temper of the mass of citizens. With the best of intentions, it is difficult for a conscientious administrator always to observe the limits placed either by law or by public opinion.
>
> (White, 1926: 419)

The reason for this problem with "observing limits" is that public opinion is backward: "The highest type of official will be in the advance guard of public opinion, and will concern himself to educate opinion to the standards which he knows should be applied" (White, 1926: 419). The official is

> always, in this account, "Chafing at the discrepancies between the opportunities for accomplishment which science has put in his hands and prevailing standards" (White, 1926: 419). One can see here, *in nuce*, the idea of a superior class directing the inferior masses both through administration and generating supportive public opinion.

With this, we arrive at the nub of the problem: either the official is a leader who imposes enlightened opinions and practices on a backward democratic public through regulation and subsidies, or the official defers to public opinion and to its expression in the electoral process and respects the checks on behavior in the law. The solution to this problem, on the side of the administrative class, was *not* to find a way to keep administrators in check, but to find a way to grant discretionary power for the officials to both lead and "render justice." This was, straightforwardly and self-consciously, an appropriation of ruling power

Democracy, Liberalism, and Discretion 33

from politics and the people to administration and the administrative class, and a violation of the political neutrality of the liberal state. But it was done, then as now, in the name of "democracy." The key to this solution was discretion.

Wilson was unambiguous on this—the way to make the system of professional administration work was to combine accountability with discretion:

> And let me say that large powers and unhampered discretion seem to me the indispensable conditions of responsibility. Public attention must be easily directed, in each case of good or bad administration, to just the man deserving of praise or blame. There is no danger in power, if only it be not irresponsible. If it be divided, dealt out in shares to many, it is obscured; and if it be obscured, it is made irresponsible. But if it be centered in heads of the service and in heads of branches of the service, it is easily watched and brought to book. If to keep his office a man must achieve open and honest success, and if at the same time he feels himself intrusted with large freedom of discretion, the greater his power the less likely is he to abuse it, the more is he nerved and sobered and elevated by it. The less his power, the more safely obscure and unnoticed does he feel his position to be, and the more readily does he relapse into remissness.
>
> (Wilson, [1886]1941: 497–98)

This was an expression of faith: give an administrator discretion and it would not go to his head but sober him up. It is difficult to imagine a more dubious psychological theory.

But Wilson, and many of the rest of the writers on this topic, had a fig leaf that allowed them to call this power democratic: to combine discretionary power with non-electoral legitimacy. While they worked to create a greater concentration of power, and more immunity from the courts and the law, they sought ways of legitimating their activities directly, for example, by experts speaking directly to the public, and to legitimate the bureaucracy on its own, so that, in Wilson's own words, "trust" could be established ([1886]1941: 494), and "docility" in acceptance of this new authority be generated among citizens ([1886]1941: 506). Accountability remains as part of the sales pitch, along with the goal of efficiency. According to Wilson, public opinion will do this job, because public opinion exists in the United States and is undeveloped in the Continent:

> The right answer seems to be that public opinion shall play the part of authoritative critic. But the method by which its authority shall be made to tell? Our peculiar American difficulty in organizing administration is not the danger of losing liberty, but the danger of not being able or willing to separate its essentials from its accidents. Our success is made doubtful by that besetting error of ours, the error of trying to do too much by vote. Self-government does not consist in having a hand in everything,

34 Stephen Turner

any more than housekeeping consists necessarily in cooking dinner with one's own hands. The cook must be trusted with a large discretion as to the management of the fires and the ovens.

(Wilson, [1886]1941: 498)

And his larger image of the legitimation of the administrative state shows why. But he does not explain how the administrator is to be held accountable or "brought to book."

There were many elements of this argument and many corollaries. One corollary was a sustained assault on the concept of the rule of law, and a search for alternatives that would free the discretionary administrative state from the legal traditions of the Anglosphere. The service state, it was routinely claimed, makes the idea of "the rule of law, of that lawyer-made bit that was forced between the teeth of the sovereign state in order that there be no Bastille and no *lettres de cachet* on, at least, British and American soil" irrelevant (Thach, 1935: 274).

The "rule of law, and all that it infers, is no longer found an effective means for, on the one hand, the satisfactory accomplishment by government of its necessary duties, on the other for the prevention of arbitrary action particularly on the part of administrative underlings."

(Thach, 1935: 274)

The reason for this is the necessity of discretion, which is a consequence of the necessity for "general" laws:

It seems too patent to need elaboration that the laws which emanate from the representative assembly must be steadily more, not less, general in character. That is to say, the terms used in the underlying statute must of necessity be of the character of standards, of norms, whose detailed content must be subsequently somehow filled in. The impossibility of detailed legislation with respect to most of the matters concerning which modern statutes must deal is apparent enough. On the one hand, the information, the special knowledge of a representative body cannot extend to technical details. On the other, the attempt to govern minutiae by the statute would result in placing administration in a hopeless straitjacket.

(Thach, 1935: 274)

The "hopeless straightjacket" would, of necessity, be loosened. And this led to a prophecy:

at this juncture we come all too forcibly face to face with a major defect of the rule of law, old style. In the United States it is always possible to attack the grant of ordinance power as in fact a grant of legislative power itself.

Democracy, Liberalism, and Discretion   35

But, to all realistic intents and purposes, such an attack will prove fruitless save in most extreme cases, for the good and sufficient reason that most such grants are plainly a necessity.

(Thach, 1935: 274–5)

This was, in effect, the response to Dicey and the liberal tradition: the courts are simply incapable of dealing with the issues of administration and will fail to do so. Thach, the author of these comments, acknowledges the legal point made by Hamburger, that the grant of legislative power is contrary to the rule of law. But he frankly states that the traditional concept of the rule of law, with its inevitable delay, is bankrupt:

The ancient formulae of the common law frequently fail to submit to equitable application in an industrial age. More and more it is being realized that justice can be rendered only by investing administrative officers and tribunals with discretion to render justice in accordance with the needs of the situation, unbound by precedent and unfettered by technical legal procedure.

(Pfiffner, 1935: 397)

The fetters of legal procedure were to be loosened in a variety of ways. One was to not be bound by precedent nor to give justifications for their actions that could be picked apart by lawyers:

For this reason administrative tribunals refuse to be bound by precedent. They publish no reasoned decisions upon which to predict future action. Such decisions as they do publish usually set forth a short statement of the facts supplemented by the decision reached.

(Pfiffner, 1935: 397)

This practice greatly limited the capacity of citizens to hold administrators accountable through the courts, even if they had access to them.

What discretion amounted to was impunity: officials, in the performance of their duties, were to be freed from personal liability for their actions, including criminal liability:

If the duty, in the performance of which the act causing the damage was done, is discretionary in character, the general rule is that executive and administrative officers may not be held responsible since the courts do not like to interfere with the discretion of the administration. Such discretionary action being of a *judicial* character, the officer is exempt from all responsibility by action for the motives which influence him and the manner in which such duties are performed.

(Thach, 1935: 278–279; original emphasis)

36 Stephen Turner

They would be free to harm people or deprive them of rights both by judgments and by issuing regulations, and except in extreme cases where they were found to be acting outside their official duties, were free of personal legal responsibility for doing so. It was consciously anti-democratic, in the sense that implementing such a system would deprive voters of the power to remove these officials directly.

Not only the voters but also the courts themselves would be limited in their power to police administrators:

> Granting that the original statute is constitutional and that the terms of the "completing" ordinances are within the four corners of the statute, the question is posed, shall the meaning of such ordinances in terms of the individual case be left to uncontrolled administrative agents?
>
> (Thach, 1935: 276)

The answer was an unambiguous "yes." And the rationale was no longer efficiency but the pressing need to "get things done":

> No one who believes in the orderly processes of government can maintain a brief for arbitrariness. On the other hand, the insistent demand on mod ern government is to get things done. The plain truth is that we can no longer afford the luxury of the law's delay. Administrative action is demanded in no uncertain terms. The possibility of delay, if nothing more, is an insuperable barrier to this solution of the problem.
>
> (Thach, 1935: 276–77)

The issue of delay was real, though, ironically, it became a central tactic of the administrative state to control activities of the market by "permitting" processes that required public comment, studies conducted by or under the control of the agencies. But the "if nothing more" of this phrase was also telling. There was of course much more, as the courts granted by substituting for strict adherence to the law and legislative intent a large element of purpose that the agency was allowed to discern on its own. With this, the state of laws became the discretionary state.

After 1946

The discussion of the role of discretionary power in democracy continued for 60 years from Wilson's initial defense of the administrative state. It was largely discontinued after the passage of the Administrative Procedures Act in 1946, which turned the issue into a legal and constitutional question. The major legal issue, which will not concern me here, involves delegation: the constitution forbids the delegation of legislative power from congress; the practice of administrative agencies in "interpreting" the law in the form of regulations is difficult to regard as anything other than legislative, even on Kelsenian grounds. My concern will be different: with the fate of discretion as a problem for liberal democracy.

The defenders of discretion reacted with undisguised hysteria to the passage of this act (Blachly and Oatman, 1946). The arguments they gave are of historical interest only: none of the things they predicted came to pass, for reasons they concede in their discussion: the requirement of the act was so ambiguous that they could be interpreted by the courts in a way favorable to the discretionary power of the agencies (Blachly and Oatman, 1946: 226). The major aim of the act was to provide for some transparency and public involvement in the rule-making process (Vermeule, 2015) and to provide for judicial review of agency actions. Both were systemically evaded, in large part because the courts themselves avoided these cases, in part because the transparency of these processes was turned into an agency-governed public comment system in which the public was simply ignored. The two parts were connected. The judicial response to the act assured that the public could be ignored, by gutting judicial control of the administrative state itself. The agencies, knowing they would not be held accountable, could treat public commentary as powerless. The legislative branch was not a factor: it rarely returned to the legislation it enacted to clarify ambiguities in a way that would constrain agencies.

The key judicial doctrines that eliminated judicial control were "standing" and "deference." These require some additional explanation, for they go to the heart of one of the issues that motivated Wilson and the early reformers: what they took to be the obsolescence of the doctrine of the separation of powers. The doctrine was effectively undermined by the creation of administrative law: this amounted to an appropriation of judicial power. It represented a fundamental constitutional change. But it was affirmed legislatively in the Administrative Procedures Act, and acquiesced to by the courts, in the form of these two doctrines, as well as many supporting decisions.

The doctrine of deference was a response to the question of "who decides" in the face of ambiguity in the law. The Supreme Court ruled that

> allowing a judicial precedent to foreclose an agency from interpreting an ambiguous statute . . . would allow a court's interpretation to override an agency's. Chevron's premise is that it is for agencies, not courts, to fill statutory gaps. The better rule is to hold judicial interpretations contained in precedents to the same demanding Chevron step one standard that applies if the court is reviewing the agency's construction on a blank slate: Only a judicial precedent holding that the statute unambiguously forecloses the agency's interpretation, and therefore contains no gap for the agency to fill, displaces a conflicting agency construction.
>
> (Shriver Center, 2013, 5.1.C.4.b. Deference to Agency Interpretation of Statutes: n.p.)

Ambiguity, or "gaps," in short, was to be treated as the agency's affair: courts would not intervene unless there was a judicial precedent that the agency had gone too far.

"Ambiguity," however, is also ambiguous. So court rulings on administrative law, and the use of its larger degree of discretion, introduces the element of "purpose" as, for example, in an opinion stating that "Title IX must [be] accord[ed] . . . a sweep as broad as its language."[3] The language of Title IX is simple and restricted to the prohibition of discrimination. The purpose was taken to justify actual discrimination in favor of previously discriminated against groups and to include under the heading of "discrimination" numerical differences between groups that resulted from individual choices and characteristics. The court ruled that actual discrimination was permissible because the action was related to the purpose rather than the text of the law.

The cases in which these precedents were established, however, were themselves limited to cases that were actually made subject to judicial review. The most powerful way that agencies preserve their discretion is to avoid review through the doctrine of standing. The basics of standing are contained in this test:

> In order to bring a claim in federal court, plaintiffs must demonstrate all three elements of standing: injury-in-fact, causation, and redressability. An injury-in-fact is an injury that is concrete, particularized, and actual or imminent. Proving causation requires plaintiffs to show that the injury is "fairly traceable" to the challenged action such that the challenged action has a "determinative or coercive effect" in causing the injury.
>
> (Yan, 2012: 596)

The tests exclude merely challenging agencies' abuses of discretion as a right of citizens: the plaintiff must meet the test of direct personal harm, a test that is usually understood to mean that even a hypothetical action by a third party that might be thought to intervene between the action of the agency and the harm invalidates the claim of causation. Thus, a policy that actually has, according to normal notions of causation, a profound effect on the injured party, is excluded on the grounds that a third party might have done otherwise. Profoundly casual actions of the sort social scientists routinely examine, those which affect the conditions of choice and therefore have predictable behavioral results are thus excluded, and the affected persons lack standing (Yan, 2012: 598). The arguments for this doctrine are the same as those we encountered in the democracy and efficiency debate: allowing agencies to be held judicially accountable would interfere with the agencies' efficiency, and agencies are more expert than the courts (Yan, 2012: 593).

Examples of agencies flouting the law, violating the principles of transparency to avoid judicial scrutiny, extending their authority, and threatening legislators are easy to find. What is more important to understand is that these are systemic issues. A footnote to one of the pre-1946 texts captures the problem for democracy that comes from discretionary power:

The aggressiveness of administrative officials in relation to expressions of public opinion through the initiative and referendum is well brought out by Coker, "The Interworkings of State Administration and Direct Legislation," in *Annals*, vol. 64, p. 122, at pp. 128–30, illustrating also how state officials under a centralized system may be tempted to use their powers over local subordinates to promote attacks upon measures enacted by the legislature against their opposition. In the national administration, compare the alleged attempt of agents of the department of justice to intimidate members of Congress conducting inquiries into the Departments of Justice and the Interior during 1924.

(White, 1926: 419n1)

These remain problems: there was legal opposition by the federal government to referenda against affirmative action (e.g., Mears, 2014). And the use of threats against legislators, implied or open, is the norm.

The Challenge to Liberalism

Why are these problems for liberalism, rather than mere problems of administration? Answering this question requires a return to fundamentals. Liberalism is inseparable from the idea of freedom from the authority of the state and of the restriction of the authority of the state. Democracy implies that the definition of these restrictions is decided through democratic procedures. Constitutionalism implies that these procedures be both rooted in the fundamental legal norms of the regime in question and that decisions about the application of these norms be governed by constitutional procedures as well, meaning, in practice, either judicial review or legislative or constitutional change. Discretionary power is inherently a challenge to liberalism and democracy: it represents a usurpation of state power beyond those agreed on through democratic procedures, in the name of purposes the state itself sets or discerns in the law on its own authority.

Donoso Cortes and Carl Schmitt were critics of liberalism for the failure of liberalism to come to decision, and defenders of state power against liberal restrictions. The leftist critics of liberalism in Britain in the 1930s made a parallel case, repeatedly, as did the New Deal defenders of administrative power against the courts. Schmitt's "decisionism" (2005) was a defense of discretion, and he asserted that discretionary power was more fundamental than law itself, because of the discretionary power of the executive to suspend the law and decide when the conditions for suspending the law had been met. The case for administrative discretion is a variant of this argument: the processes in which liberal discussion comes or fails to come to a conclusion are inadequate for the "needs" or "demands" of society. This means simply that within the agreed processes of decision-making based on discussion, no proposal has been sufficiently persuasive to lead to a decision. The necessity for a decision is not itself a matter of agreement within these processes. It is something higher— and often this "higher" necessity is presented as genuinely democratic, in as much as it reflects someone's view of what is best for society. The case for claiming that this kind of discretion is consistent with democracy is that there is some ultimate accountability, however indirect, in the form of elections of the legislature and executive, or in the acquiescence of the public to the state's claim to legitimacy.

If liberalism is, as Donoso Cortes claimed, government by discussion (Schmitt, 1985: 48–50), discretionary power is the antithesis of liberalism. To reclaim liberalism is to reclaim this power or limit it. And this produces a fundamental dilemma for liberalism. The expansion of discretion has occurred through the same liberal democratic means that were supposed to control discretion: the law as interpreted by the courts and the power of the elected executive and the legislature. At the root of the power of the discretionary state is the abdication of these restraining bodies. Part of the reason for this abdication is explained by the critics themselves: the inability of liberal discussion to come to decision, including the decision to restrain discretionary power.

The contemporary justification for this abdication is that the courts and the people should defer to experts, the experts in and employed by agencies—and not merely to decide through discussion to defer to experts on a case-by-case basis but also to accept the discretionary power of agencies as part of a general acquiescence to state power. And this means that the specific acts and rules produced by these agencies are not subject to discussion, except in an ineffective way. Nor is it helpful to refer to "experts" as a source of neutral authority: in the cases in question, matters of policy, value judgments that are controversial are mixed in not only with policy choices but in matters of acceptance of findings. The fact that agencies pay the people they take advice from, choose them, judge their advice or have their wards judge one another, and often conceal the data and methods the experts use to validate the agencies' choices, means that the communities of experts are subject to epistemic capture—to the induced dominance of a given expert opinion (Turner, 2001).

Schmitt argued that the conflict between liberalism and democracy would result in the democratic rejection of liberalism and the replacement of interest-based parties by totalizing parties. But he also believed as a corollary to this that liberalism would die, in effect, by its own hand, as a result of its failure to come to a decision to suppress the anti-liberal totalizing parties arrayed against it. But there are other ways for liberalism to die. The administrative state from its origins has aimed at making public opinion ineffective or undermining its independence, often in the name of leading it, educating it, or providing "justice," that is to say, something beyond mere "opinion." Its theorists understood that the best means of making public opinion and liberal discussion producing public opinion effective, and to put teeth into the idea of government by discussion, was the practice of voting for officials with real power. White observed, "As late as 1918 a well-known Democratic newspaper of Boston, opposing a constitutional amendment to extend the governor's term to two years, took up again the famous dictum of Samuel Adams, 'where annual elections end, tyranny begins'" (White, 1926: 438n1) (in fact, it is the words of Jefferson, in a letter to Sam Adams, recalling the maxim of the revolutionaries[4]). Perhaps, it is no longer the case that direct electoral means are the condition of effective liberal democracy, and there are better means. But if any are devised, they too need more teeth than is provided by the very indirect and mediated effect on the state of "public opinion" on its own. We know enough about the administrative state to know that it does not limit itself. Reclaiming liberalism, however, requires reclaiming control over the administrative state. The discretionary state, the *Obrigkeitsstaat* which German liberalism sought to replace with the *Rechtstaat*, is the antithesis of liberalism as well as of democracy. An uncontrolled administrative state, limited only by the need for a general sense of legitimacy, and what Wilson sought, a population trained in docility, is nothing more than a new *Obrigkeitsstaat*. And faith in the power of the discretionary state to do better than the electorally controlled state is the wedge for bringing it about, now as in Wilson's time.

Notes

1 The classic formulation of the narrow conception is Kelsen in the journal *Ethics* (1955).
2 *Chevron U.S.A., Inc. v. Natural Resources Defense Council, Inc.* 467 U.S. 837 *Chevron U.S.A., Inc. v. Natural Resources Defense Council, Inc.* (No. 82–1005) Argued: February 29, 1984; Decided: June 25, 1984 [*] www.law.cornell.edu/supremecourt/text/467/837 (accessed February 28, 2022).
3 *N. Haven, 456 U.S.* at 521 (quoting *United States v. Price*, 383 U.S. 787, 801 (1966)). https://supreme.justia.com/cases/federal/us/456/512/case. html (accessed 28 February 2022); see also *Dickerson v. New Banner Inst. Inc.*, 460 U.S. 103, 118 (1983).
4 Thomas Jefferson to Samuel Adams, February 26, 1800. The Thomas Jefferson Papers at the Library of Congress: Series 1: General Correspondence. 1651 to 1827 (25,884). www.loc.gov/resource/ mtj1.022_0124_0124/?st=text (accessed February 28, 2022).

References

Blachly, F. F., and M. E. Oatman. "Sabotage of the Administrative Process," *Public Administration Review* 6: 213–227, 1946.
Chevron USA, Inc. V. *Natural Resources Defense Council*, 467 U.S. 837, 1984. https://supreme.justia.com/cases/federal/us/467/837/
Crews, Clyde Wayne, Jr. "How Many Rules and Regulations Do Federal Agencies Issue?" *Forbes*, 15 August, 2017. www.forbes.com/sites/waynecrews/2017/08/15/how-many-rules-and-regulations-do-federal-agencies-issue/#594d24081e64
Dicey, Albert Venn. *Lectures on the Law & Public Opinion in England: During the Nineteenth Century*, 2nd edn. London: Macmillan and Company, [1914]1962.
Eckart, Kim. "Q & A: Sarah Quinn Lifts the Curtain on the 'Hidden State'," *UWNews*, 17 August, 2017. www.washington.edu/news/2017/08/17/q-a-sarah-quinn-lifts-the-curtain-on-the-hidden-state/.

Hamburger, Philip. *Is Administrative Law Unlawful?* Chicago: The University of Chicago Press, 2014.

Hoxie, R Gordon. *A History of the Faculty of Political Science, Columbia University.* New York: Columbia University Press, 1955.

Kelsen, Hans. "Foundations of Democracy," *Ethics* 66(1): 1–101, 1955.

Levitan, D M. "Political Ends and Administrative Means," *Public Administrative Review* 3: 353–359, 1943.

Mears, Bill. "Michigan's Ban on Affirmative Action Upheld by Supreme Court," *CNN*, April 23, 2014. www.cnn.com/2014/04/22/justice/scotus-michigan-affirmative-action/index.html

Millspaugh, A. C. "Democracy and Administrative Organization," In *Essays in Political Science*, Edited by J. M. Mathews. Baltimore: The Johns Hopkins Press, 64–73, 1937.

Pfiffner, J. M. *Public Administration.* New York: Ronald Press, 1935.

Schmitt, Carl. *Constitutional Theory*, translated by and edited by Jeffrey Seitzer. Durham: Duke University Press, [1928]2008.

Schmitt, Carl. *Legality and Legitimacy*, translated by Jeffrey Seltzer. Durham: Duke University Press, [1932]2004.

Schmitt, Carl. *Political Theology: Four Chapters on the Concept of Sovereignty*, translated by George Schwab. Chicago: University of Chicago Press, 2005.

Schmitt, Carl. *The Crisis of Parliamentary Democracy*, translated by Ellen Kennedy. Cambridge: MIT Press, 1985.

Shriver Center. "5.1.C Express Causes of Action, Administrative Procedure Act," *Federal Practice Manual for Legal Aid Attorneys*, 2013. www.federalpracticemanual. org/chapter5/section1c (accessed 28 February 2022)

Small, Albion. *The Cameralists: The Powers of German Social Policy.* Chicago and London: The University of Chicago Press, T. Fisher Unwin, 1909.

Thach, C. E. "The Inadequacies of the Rule of Law," In *Essays on the Law and Practice of Governmental Administration*, Edited by C. G. Haines and M. E. Dimock. Baltimore: Johns Hopkins, 1935, 269–286.

Turner, Stephen. "What Is the Problem with Experts?" *Social Studies of Science* 31(1): 23–49, 2001.

Vermeule, Adrian. " 'No': Review of Philip Hamburger is Administrative Law Unlawful?" *Texas Law Review* 3: 1547–1556, 2015. http://texaslawreview.org/wp-content/uploads/2015/08/Vermeule-93–6.pdf

White, L. D. *Introduction to Public Administration.* New York: Macmillan, 1926.

Wilson, Woodrow. "Democracy and Efficiency," *Atlantic Monthly*, 289–299, 1901. www.theatlantic.com/magazine/archive/1901/03/democracy-and-efficiency/520041/ (accessed 28 February 2022)

Wilson, Woodrow. "The Study of Administration," *Political Science Quarterly* 56(4): 481–506, [1886]1941.

Yan, Jerett. "Standing as a Limitation on Judicial Review of Agency Action," *Ecology Law Quarterly* 39: 593–618, 2012.

Chapter 2

Improving on Democracy

Stephen Turner

In the decades after John Rawls' *A Theory of Justice* (1971) and especially over the past 20 years or so, many books have been published with the same aim: to vindicate and explicate something that is usually called social democracy on philosophical or social science grounds. After the intense ideological rivalries of the twentieth century, this political ideal has become the default position of virtually all academic thinkers in relevant areas. A century that began with the frank acceptance of the irreconcilability of political value choices, and proceeded with extraordinarily intense ideological warfare, ended with a surprisingly broad, though loose, consensus. One could list such works as Philip Pettit (1997), Amartya Sen (2009), and Alan Gewirth (1978) as examples. And in sociology, one could give Pierre Bourdieu (Bourdieu, 2008; Wacquant, 2005) and Jürgen Habermas (2001) as more or less full members of this consensus.

The Consensus

The common element in the accounts that are directly concerned with vindicating this consensus is that they attempt to replace the terms of the earlier twentieth-century debate, especially the terms of the conflict between justice and freedom. These writers all reject the idea of freedom as non-interference or choice as inadequate or wrong; they all decry great wealth, the power of money or the power that money gives people, as a form of injustice; and all involve some idea of autonomy governed by reason.

The arguments needed to produce the conclusions are less stable than the conclusions: they know that freedom as non-interference is wrong because it comes to the wrong result, namely, a non-egalitarian (as well as vulgar and money-grubbing) society, but they differ in how to replace this notion of freedom. They use the language of rights, but only if it is extended to cover rights to well-being, and they acknowledge that there are collisions between these rights and the rights of classical liberalism, which they concede must give way, to some extent. They cannot bring themselves to be simply radical egalitarians, even if in their heart of hearts they think reason and justice dictate equality,

DOI: 10.4324/9781003360810-3

44 Stephen Turner

because they know that this outcome can only be produced by means that are visibly oppressive, and worse, undemocratic, in that they would never get the consent of people who have had the experience of freedom and a more or less meritocratic order. So, they are against something else: domination, a notion that can be extended to cover all sorts of humiliations, such as a lack of recognition of identities, as well as a lack of money.

Usually, these accounts come with some sort of motivating argument—something that serves to make it morally obligatory or at least a good thing that we actively support justice, even when it costs us to do so. Typically, these are anti-naturalistic arguments, in that the moral obligations go against the grain of what we would normally do or desire. Because the writers in this vein are concerned to avoid locutions like "forced to be free" and wish to portray the state as something other and better than a coercive apparatus, they want to find some sort of higher mode in which people do the right thing more or less voluntarily. The right thing is collective; the tension is between the collectively acknowledged good and the distorted private good, which is distorted because it is at heart a quest for something like autonomy and recognition but expresses itself in greed and power seeking, which are the things that need to be collectively controlled.

Each of these theorists operates with an analog to the idea of false consciousness: they are reformist because they think that current realities do not live up to the standards of genuine democracy or the decent society. They allocate the blame in various ways. One is electoral arrangements. These authors are not especially happy about normal democratic procedures, the machinery of courts, and the rule of law, unless it can be expanded to cover "social rights," dignity, and so forth. The boring procedures of voting and the like are different from, and perhaps inimical to, genuine democracy, which is about, or requires, equality of power, not a specific procedure. The ideas of deliberative democracy, according to Habermas, participatory democracy, and the like represent alternatives, but not alternatives with clear institutional or legal embodiments. But there are many other explanations of why "social democracy" has not happened: the media, the pre-existing culture (which is racist, patriarchal, antiegalitarian, suffused with false beliefs derived from religion, or scientism), a failed public sphere, or other sources.

Although these authors are sometimes portrayed as statist and do indeed argue for the expansion of the role of the state, they are not statists in the sense that they think the state can solve all the problems of a good society on its own. They want a social matrix in which the bad effects of competitiveness and striving are tempered, or replaced, by a regime of personal relations in which dignity is respected, autonomy is granted, and people trust each other—a decent society, as Avishai Margalit calls it (1996). All of the "social" goals involve more discretionary power for officials. These authors all embrace the idea of an activist, paternalist, benevolent state. Health care is often the model for the proper role of the state. Where it is done correctly, it combines dignity, compassion, paternalism, efficiency, the proper use of expertise, universalism, respect for autonomy, and sufficient provision with a rational allocation of scarce resources.

This is not to say that all is well with these accounts. They are studiously vague about how to match this vision of the state with the reality that many people will find such a state to be obnoxious, oppressive, and hostile. They are reluctant to draw lines in terms of legally enforceable rights: this simply reproduces the kind of adversarial culture that undermines trust and benevolence. In the cases of minority group rights and minority cultures, they are more sensitive. In these cases, paternalistic benevolence and oppression are hard to disentangle, at least from the point of view of the recipient, so they err on the side of protecting the culture of the minority group. For the dominant culture, however, matters are different: it needs to be reformed to accord with reason. And these writers tend to imagine, or pretend, that there is some sort of frictionless, perfect, administrative apparatus that enacts the good intentions of the state in a non-oppressive way. What makes these accounts "social" is that they are reluctant to rely on markets, except in contexts in which markets are demonstrably more efficient. The reluctance is nevertheless tempered by the recognition that the older idea of a state-managed economy, state ownership of the means of production, planning, and the like, failed to deliver on its promises and cannot be returned to.

Stein Ringen's book is very much in the mainstream of these writings. Where he is different is in his recognition of some sociological realities—families, for example—that are rarely mentioned in the usual approaches. He also attempts to engage, using data, the key issues that are commonly discussed in the abstract, such as the possibility of changing the opportunities for upward mobility through state intervention. And, in place of the motivating theory, he provides a shrewd discussion of the politics of reform: he recognizes that the "working class" has been replaced by the class of government workers and that the political possibility of reform rests on the involvement of the middle classes, who are pushed to the side of the rich by some reform strategies. He is also explicit, in a way that is rare in this literature, about the organizational and bureaucratic realities of the welfare state, the anti-democratic consequences of centralizing authority, and other topics that go beyond the considerations of justice and economics.

Ringen's Democracy

What do, or rather should, we want out of democracy? For Ringen, governments, or governance, should assure the possibility of a good life, or as he puts it "the freedom to find and live a good life." Mere liberty or "liberty as license" as he sometimes calls it is not enough. The good life involves self-mastery, reason, and meaningful choices. This not only depends on governance but also is potentially endangered by governance. So, governance should be both constrained, so as to avoid endangering the necessary freedom, and effective, so as to assure the conditions for it.

On the surface, this language sounds congenial to a more traditional liberal idea of freedom. But Ringen is not an enthusiast for liberal democracy as practiced, for example (and especially!), in the United States. He is an admirer of, and is well informed about, Scandinavian democracy, and much of the book reflects his attempts to work out what makes it work so well, and what threats there are to it. He approaches this problem in a more or less empirical way. He spends a considerable amount of effort trying to quantify or at least construct a kind of scale that reflects his preferences. He is critical of minimalist accounts of democracy, such as Guillermo O'Donnell's (2001), that provide criteria that distinguish advanced, established democracies from near democracies in the developing world. These accounts, Ringen argues, fail to differentiate between good and bad examples of advanced democracies and thus provide little in the way of guidance for the task of making existing democracies better.

In place of these criteria, he introduces a simple metric, based on data that he modifies a bit, to come up with eight basic differentiators (2007: 42–7). He gives these differentiators names to indicate what they are supposed to measure, but the basis is more interesting, because it sometimes produces odd results. The first is whether universal suffrage was introduced before 1940. Here the oddities are Australia and the United States, which fall in post-1940, presumably because the Aborigines in Australia and the Blacks in the American south were denied rights to vote, albeit never in a way that was sustained by the courts. The second is strength of the free press, measured by a Freedom House index number, in which France fails, and then a World Bank indicator of governmental effectiveness, which he corrects in the case of Korea, on the basis of his own work on the Korean welfare state. The next is "protection against the political use of economic power," which is made up of considerations involving financial scandals in politics, the use of "private" money for political campaigns, and corruption. A large political role for unions is, mysteriously, not an instance of the application of "economic power." After this, are two measures of "security": a UNICEF index involving child poverty (in which both post-unification Germany and the United States fail) and "public" health care expenditure relative to GDP. The final two are subjective: trust in government, measured by survey and allocated not on absolute values, but both on being above average and on increasing between 1990 and 2000, and then a combined measure: subjectively reported "experienced freedom" and a positive response to the question of whether most people can be trusted. The last two are combined to produce an index number. Only five of the 25 countries get points for this item. Overall, Norway and Sweden get perfect scores of eight, with Iceland next at seven, and New Zealand and the Netherlands close behind at six. The United States, southern Europe, and the third world bring up the distant rear with near-zero scores all across the list.

The indices are more interesting as a reflection of Ringen's way of thinking about democracy, which is strikingly weighted toward outputs—good governance understood in a particular way—and against inputs, such as democratic process, contestation, and public rather than bureaucratic power. When he does discuss inputs, he de-emphasizes actual electoral processes and praises other kinds of participation—demonstrations, union pressures, and so forth—that are outside the realm of public liberal discussion, to which he is strikingly averse. A traditional measure of democracy is whether power changes hands. Scandinavian democracy, tellingly, does poorly on this. Not surprisingly, it is not on Ringen's list. Most of the measures seem arbitrary: why choose the only measures for suffrage that make Scandinavia, a latecomer to universal male suffrage, seem like a leader? The trust measure is bizarre: the vast number of converging measures of trust that are normally used make the United States a high-trust country (Fukuyama, 1995: 255–66, 269–81, 335–42). The number that Ringen uses (in addition to above average reported trust), change in trust from 1990–2000, reflects the Clinton scandals in the United States, and doubtless similar events elsewhere. Why select a measure of trust that depends on transitory events? Nor does there seem to be any rationale for pairing subjective freedom and trust, other than that it helps make the rankings come out the way Ringen wants them to. Nor do they hold up very well as predictors: one suspects Ringen would like to take back his ratings of Iceland in the wake of its scandalous financial collapse.

The indices, however, are not simply arbitrary: they reflect some real and important preferences consistent with those he articulates in the book. But the preferences are decidedly odd in some respects, though they are consistent with the disdain for traditional views of democracy characteristic of the social democratic academic consensus. The traditional standard view of democracy is that the "purpose" of democracy is to enable people to resolve the problem of what the state should do. Democracy is a procedure for reconciling divergent opinions on this subject. Majority rule is a way of making these choices less oppressive: at least the majority agrees with them. The point of democracy is that the inputs of people's opinions, preferences, and desires are turned into the outputs of state action. State action that does not reflect these desires, opinions, and preferences, however worthy, is not democratic, and states that routinely ignore the formal processes by which preferences are expressed, namely, voting and public discussion, are not democratic.

The idea of consensus democracy is different: the consensus is one that allows bureaucracies to perform their good work on behalf of the people. What makes the regime "democratic" is that state action is "for" the people, rather than for some sort of special, private, economic interest.[1] Carl Schmitt, in his book on constitutional theory, made the point that European constitutions were ordinarily mixed (2008: 235–52): that the legislature, the executive, the bureaucracies, and the courts did not derive their legitimacy from the same sources, and that each had different histories, whose effects persisted. He

48 Stephen Turner

would have recognized the regimes Ringen describes as ideal as constitutional forms dominated by the pre-democratic forms of the monarchical administration, characterized by the predominance of administrative law and regulation rather than legislation, deferred to not because of the fact that they reflected popular opinion, but because they presented themselves as the custodian of the nation. Whether this kind of regime should be called "democratic" is an open question. Perhaps, it is best to simply treat it as a legitimate bureaucratic authority that derives its legitimacy from general consent, plebiscitary bureaucracy, to turn a Weberian phrase.

Ringen has no interest in what people want, except what they want as clients of the state. He is an advocate of empowering clients to have more choices and to have more voice about the services they receive, a tacit admission that even in the kind and benevolent governments he admires, they have little power. At the same time, he knows what people should want. The perennial problem is to give it to them and then make them accept it. Bureaucracies, he thinks, have a bias toward efficiency. They need more heart, and empowering clients is a way of producing this. But he is unapologetic about embracing "paternalism." For him, as the title of the book suggests, the issue is not process but what the right kind of democracy is supposed to produce. The model is a benevolent state, a high level of political consensus rather than contestation, trust, health care by the state, generosity to the poor, and a balance between efficiency and compassion. All these go together to make a good democracy. The state, because it is benevolent and trusted, would have the maximum of legitimacy. Disagreement is a sign of something gone wrong. Contention, suspicion of the state, and populist assertion against state elites would all be signs of state failure.

The last issue is the point at which the divergence in perspectives between Ringen and traditional democratic theory becomes most obvious. The usual "input" approach to politics would say this: a good democracy is one that reflects, with minimum distortions, but perhaps with agreed limits and stabilizing mechanisms, the wishes of the majority of the electorate, as expressed through a transparent procedure of voting and elections. Ringen has little interest in this, perhaps because, in the nations he favors, elections rarely change governments and are never contested on great and divisive issues. Classical liberalism depends on contention to bring out public issues, hold the state accountable, and so on. The point of freedom of speech, rights, the rule of law, and so forth is to protect people from the overweening state. One needs a contentious press and a contentious politics if only to keep the state honest and to reveal issues. Restrictions on the freedom of speech are looked on with suspicion, especially if they have the effect of increasing state control.

Ringen is having none of this: for him, the very existence of an opposition would be a sign of democratic failure. The good state is the one with a consensus politics with the right consensus. The fact that voters in the states he regards as inadequately developed democracies actually reject the kinds of measures he regards as the proper outputs of democracy just shows that

Improving on Democracy   49

these are inadequate states. His focus is so relentlessly on the state and what it provides that the traditional definition of democracy in terms of inputs and legal processes vanishes from his analysis. The public itself has no real political role: it figures only as a legitimating chorus for the state as it pursues the "democratic" ends he thinks states should pursue.

But the notion of consensus and his hostility to "economic power" hide some important things. For Ringen, the point of regulation and subsidy of political discussion is to get the right kinds of public discussion, meaning one uninfluenced by economic power. But economic power for Ringen seems to be defined simply to mean the influence of business money on political campaigns and lobbying. The fact, for example, that Swedish politics is dominated by a major union confederation which owns a controlling interest in the most important newspaper, is the main force in the party that has ruled with only slight interruptions for decades, and is well represented on government panels is apparently not an instance of economic power for Ringen. If one scaled up its membership to fit the population of the United States, this confederation would be a mind-boggling 66 million strong. This kind of overwhelming power would produce "consensus" even in the United States. Obama, who received the highest vote total in American history, had only 63.25 million votes.

The Good Life and the Good State

If mere egalitarianism is not enough of a goal for the good state, what is? Freedom, of course, needs to be restricted by any state. Freedom that produces poverty and inequality as a by-product needs to be corrected for. Libertarian conceptions of freedom have traditionally understood the kinds of constraints that the state imposes to achieve these corrections to conflict with freedom. Ringen devotes much of his discussion, as writers like Pettit have also done, to rejecting this account of freedom, and does so, like these other writers, in terms of Isaiah Berlin's discussion of positive and negative freedom in *Two Concepts of Liberty* (1958). Positive freedom, in the pejorative sense, is "freedom" to conform to the correct life; negative freedom is freedom from coercion and constraint. Positive freedom normally involves a certain amount of "forcing to be free." But once the forcing is done, the person subjected to it becomes genuinely free in a higher sense, autonomously choosing the life that fulfills their genuine purpose. The person with negative liberty, what Ringen calls liberty as license, is liable to fritter their life away, with their desires manipulated by others, incapable of genuine autonomy.

The good life, for Ringen, is the life of genuine autonomy—of *Bildung* or self-development, the Aristotelian mean, and so on. This life, he thinks, is wholly compatible with the good state, and the better state that democracy should aspire to would be the state that fosters this particular kind of good life. Freedom in the negative sense is beside the point. Berlin himself, he

50 Stephen Turner

argues, came to accept the necessity of some elements of positive freedom (Ringen, 2007: 186–8). The reasoning is something like this: the important thing is for people to be able to become what they want to become, at least if they want to become the right kind of person. How can the state foster this kind of good life? High taxation, which he thinks is absolutely essential (and whose decline he bemoans), is one way. If they want to become rich, they are out of luck. If they want to dominate others (at least on the basis of private power—bureaucrats are assumed to be either benevolent or efficiency conscious), they are also out of luck. But the state can and should eliminate artificial obstacles to people becoming what they should want to become. Capacities to pass on advantages to the next generation get in the way of this: if one gets an edge in competition as a result of one's parentage, the competition is not fair. So, equality of opportunity is a good in itself, not merely a lame substitute for real equality.

But can the state effectively change social outcomes? Haven't classes been stable despite the endless efforts of egalitarian governments to raise people up from the bottom? This would be a problem for "social democracy" if it was concerned solely with the distribution of wealth. But Ringen is an adamant opponent of the idea that classes are stable. Why this is an issue for him is obscure. If one is concerned with equality, and one accepts the equality of opportunity as a surrogate for equality that solves the problem of class by making it a product of effort and merit, one would be concerned with it. And if one is concerned with equality as such, one should be concerned with the concentration of wealth. If wealth begets political power, or is a form of domination as such, then one should be concerned that a high concentration of wealth in society represents evidence of domination in and of itself. But Ringen jettisons these old-fashioned notions in favor of agency ideas, particularly the idea of planning. Equal opportunities to get rich do not interest him: he wants the state to tax wealth away. So what is the point of talking about social mobility, which is not a measure of whether people can become what they wish to become or of their capacity to execute a life plan?

The United States, or at least a caricature version of it, is the negative to the positive of the Scandinavian state: unequal, with limited social mobility, cruel to the poor, and most importantly without a democratic political life, because of the influence of economic power. But oddly, when Ringen turns to the problem of improving good democracies by making them more responsive to their clients, giving people a stake in the government, and so forth, and even when he suggests ways to divert private wealth for the public good, his solutions resemble actual American practices, practices that the American Left generally disdains. Ringen recommends vouchers for parents so that they can control where their children are schooled. The use of vouchers (and the creation of state-funded alternative "charter" schools) is widespread in the United States and bitterly opposed by teachers' unions and egalitarians who think that parents will use the power of choice to get advantages for their own

Improving on Democracy 51

children. Ringen praises the recent Swedish practice of sending an account that tells what pension benefits one will get from the state and explains how they were calculated. He thinks this gives the beneficiary a sense of ownership and the sense that this is an earned social insurance benefit, not a gift of the state. Similar documents have been generated by the American social security system for decades, and for the same reason; to create the illusion of rights, when in fact the rights to the benefit may be taken away or modified at any time and are not backed by real savings, but only by the will of the state to tax. The American Left, however, wants to solve the problem of solvency for this system by going in the opposite direction from what Ringen suggests: turning it into a more traditional welfare system, including means testing, so that the relatively well-off do not benefit from their lifetime of "contributions." The idea that the rich should be forced to disgorge their wealth for the public benefit, which Ringen proposes to enforce by forcing the rich to put some of their wealth into foundations that must be used to fund public purposes—not merely the state's budget, but for social goods like education—is accomplished in the United States through tax benefits that encourage the rich to create foundations and give to university endowments, medical research, and programs for the poor. Notably, none of this appears in any of Ringen's calculations because, in the United States, these sources of money are "private."

Ringen loves high taxation, but he does not seem to grasp its economic consequences. He complains that the rich threaten to leave when taxes get too high, but he does not acknowledge the well-known fact that the rich are adept at keeping their wealth out of reach of the tax man, particularly the income tax man, even when they do not leave, and that in doing so, they put it to uses that have less economic benefit than it would have if it were invested. The Swedes, incidentally, appear to be world-class champions at this: the Gini coefficient for wealth (as distinct from the less meaningful measure for incomes, which vary across the life course) shows that the concentration of wealth in Sweden is still, after a century of high taxation, slightly greater than the concentration in the United States (Sanandaji and Gidehag, 2010). Ringen thinks that in objecting to high taxation, the middle classes are paranoid and that they need to be persuaded to ally against the rich to raise taxes. But the paranoia is well founded: salaries, the source of income for the middle classes, are easy targets for taxation, unlike the wealth of the rich.

Even in the case of Ringen's fears for democracy, his solution of giving more power to elected municipal governments, levels that are closer to the people, and his insistence on subsidiarity resemble actual American practice, in which there is public accountability, in the form of elected officials, at very low levels of authority, levels at which, in most of Europe and certainly in Scandinavia, are dominated by bureaucrats.

"Subsidiarity" is a gift of bureaucracies, usually to other lower-level bureaucracies. The primary device for producing accountability in municipalities and school systems in the United States is elections: the decision-makers at the local level are elected officials, not bureaucrats. This is a "democratic" solution that enables "responsive" solutions, vouchers for students, for example, to prevail over the wishes of public employee unions. But this solution does not appeal to Ringen, perhaps because he places so little value on the traditional idea of citizenship, and so much on the idea of the relation between the client of the state and the benevolent, kind, state patron.

Ringen comes close to, but does not directly ask, the question that has always be-deviled the academic consensus for "social democracy": if this form of state is so desirable, why do people vote against it? His discussions of the distorting political effects of economic power, the fears of the middle class that measures to expropriate from the rich will end up expropriating from them, and his gratitude for the historical accident that the Scandinavian welfare state was established when fear of poverty was overwhelming and before prosperity, and his suggestions for recruiting the middle classes to the cause of the benevolent state, all are indirect answers to this question. But these answers do not come to the point: perhaps, the desires people have for the state are inherently contradictory. People want benefits for which they do not wish to pay. Undisciplined polities, such as California, Greece, the United States, and many others, solve this conundrum by wishful financing.

The present crisis in public finance, both in Europe and in the United States, brings this problem back with a vengeance. Governments as diverse as those of Greece and California have been unable to manage the democratic pressures of powerful public employee unions and made financial choices that proved to be catastrophic in order to accommodate them. Iceland, the state which Ringen rates just below the very top in this scale, has been brought to its knees by the same crisis, revealing political ineptitude, bureaucratic incompetence, collusion with bankers, and a complicit, supine press. But Ringen may be right: perhaps, the paternalistic state, the legitimate bureaucracy which rules by consensus, or by a political cartel with powerful unions which are forced to be responsible because there is no countervailing power, is better able to manage these crises, and perhaps the state that keeps its eye on outputs will deliver the goods in the long run. A Left disciplined by the possession of overwhelming power would be the best way of maintaining social peace, popular acquiescence, and fiscal constraint. But perhaps, it is not: it could be that such states generate unsustainable demands on themselves, even in the most disciplined of political orders. And even the states he most admired have not always been so disciplined. The traditional view of democracy depends on no such bets: the people perform the inputting, through regular competitive elections, and are responsible for the outputs. The "consensus" that Ringen celebrates is a result of intermediating institutions that muffle these inputs and add their own. He should be more concerned than he is that the bets underlying his ideal of democracy more closely resemble those underlying regimes that no one considers democratic.

Note

1 This same binary opposition is found in the writings of Bent Flyvbjerg, along with the same blindness to the fact that state bureaucracies are themselves political players (Turner, 2008).

References

Berlin, Isaiah. *Two Concepts of Liberty*. Oxford: Clarendon Press, 1958.

Bourdieu, Pierre. *Political Interventions: Social Science and Political Action*, translated by D Fernbach. London: Verso, 2008.

Fukuyama, Francis. *Trust: The Social Virtues and the Creation of Prosperity*. New York: Free Press, 1995.

Gewirth, Alan. *Reason and Morality*. Chicago: The University of Chicago Press, 1978.

Habermas, Jürgen. *The Post National Constellation: Political Essays*, translated and Edited by M Pensky. Cambridge: The MIT Press, 2001.

Margalit, Avishai. *The Decent Society*. Cambridge: Harvard University Press, 1996.

O'Donnell, Guillermo. "Democratic Theory and Comparative Politics," *Studies in Comparative International Development* 36(1): 7–36, 2001.

Pettit, Phillip. *Republicanism: A Theory of Freedom and Government*. Oxford: Oxford University Press, 1997.

Rawls, John. *A Theory of Justice*. Cambridge: Harvard University Press, 1971.

Ringen, Stein. *What is Democracy For? On Freedom and Moral Government*. Princeton: Princeton University Press, 2007.

Sanandaji, Nima and Robert Gidehag. "Is Sweden a False Utopia?" *New Geography*, 2 May, 2010. www.newgeography.com/content/001543-is-sweden-a-false-utopia.

Schmitt, Carl. *Constitutional Theory*, translated and Edited by J Seitzer. Durham: Duke University Press, 2008.

Sen, Amartya. *The Idea of Justice*. Cambridge: Harvard University Press, 2009.

Turner, Stephen. "Balancing Expert Power: Two Models for the Future of Politics," In Nico Stehr. *Knowledge and Democracy: Is Liberty a Daughter of Knowledge*? New Brunswick: Transaction Publishers, 2008, 119–141.

Wacquant, Loïc. *Pierre Bourdieu and Democratic Politics: The Mystery of Ministry*. Cambridge: Polity Press, 2005.

Chapter 3

What Are Democratic Values? A Twenty-First-Century Kelsenian Approach

Stephen Turner and George Mazur

"Democratic theory" is the core subject in the large area of social and political thought today. Why, one might wonder, is there a problem of democratic theory at this point in history at all? Democratic practices are enshrined in the constitutions of all the major countries of the world. The justifications of democracy have been around for centuries. What else is there to say? This is the question that Robert Dahl himself asked, in the book that marked the beginning of the rebirth of this topic, *A Preface to Democratic Theory* ([1956]2006). The question is closely connected to Kelsen, or rather to Kelsen's reception or lack of reception in the United States during this same period (Scheuerman, 2014).

There is a simple, reductive, answer to this question. Most of what passes for democratic theory is, implicitly or explicitly, concerned with justifying, expounding, or elaborating the conditions for democracy of a particular kind. The kind of democracy being justified is "social" democracy. This "democratic theory" is disillusioned about natural rights, skeptical of the ability of democracy as presently embodied in actual constitutional orders to deliver social justice or even democracy itself without a strong state assuring welfare and mediating class conflict, and generally regards actual liberal democracies of the past as inadequate and failures because they did not do so (e.g., della Porta, 2013 and Ringen, 2007).

Social democracy needs a theory because it contains elements that liberal democracy and its theory neither countenanced nor was, in some important respects, consistent with. Moreover, as an ideal as yet unrealized, social democracy has elements that may not be consistent with one another. The task of ironing out these potential inconsistencies, and replacing the elements of classical conceptions of liberal democracy that are not reconcilable with the "social" of social democracy, provided a forum for saying what did remain to be said.

The demand for such a theory, or the interest in having one, came at a particular moment. The end of the Second World War ushered in the age of the welfare state understood as a democratic welfare state. The vogue for general planning in the 1930s, the New Deal in the United States, were responses to

DOI: 10.4324/9781003360810-4

and alternatives to the ideal of socialism. But the ideal of socialism substituted "fraternity" or solidarity for notions of the democratic process, and specifically for "liberal" notions of the democratic process. The new model, after the war "for democracy," was a hybrid, a natural extension neither of socialism nor of liberal democracy. Nevertheless, these regimes proved to be popular. They were thus democratic in a particular sense: they grew out of actual compromises between people with different views and attained majority support through established procedures.

Democratic theory was a means of making it an extension of liberal democracy in theory as well as in fact, and also to legitimate the compromise intellectually, in the hope of providing a new ideological basis that would resist the ideologies of Left and Right of the past. Dahl's own thinking grew out of what one might call the "problems of liberalism" tradition, which was concerned with the many internal and practical contradictions and anomalies of the liberal idea.

Most of these arose from the conflict between freedom and the need to protect the liberal order from the consequences of the exercise of freedom, from Voltaire's "no freedom for the enemies of freedom," to Kant's denial that there was a conflict between genuine freedom and obedience to the state. But on the Left, the largest strand of this tradition was the conflict between the ideal of political equality and the reality of economic inequality, which was taken to undermine and nullify the claims of liberal democracies to be genuinely democratic or even to provide for genuinely liberal discussion.

The issues here defy easy summary but are epitomized by the conflict between the means necessary to produce the conditions for liberal democracy and the limitation on state power that is central to liberalism. Liberalism is characterized by its preference for indirect means, and therefore for law that structures interests and opportunities rather than commands actions. The primal form of equality for liberalism is equal treatment under the law. The stance of the liberal state with respect to interests, opinions, moral stances, and religion is neutral. The idea of the Rule of Law is underpinned by this idea of neutrality. Social democracy regards this preference as an obstacle to achieving the substantive reality of equal political participation, which is held to require substantial rather than nominal equality—the equal right of the rich and the poor to sleep under bridges.

The Left was faced with the practical problem of the inability of the proletariat to bring about a full socialist revolution. The Left had little interest in or patience with the dogmas of liberalism, most of which involve freedom. They were ambivalent at best about the "rule of law," seeing property rights in particular as a serious constraint on the powers of the social democratic state to bring about the reforms that socialist parties desired. Constitutionalism was regarded similarly. The language of rights was treated with suspicion, and only used when it could be extended to cover rights to human well-being, as it was in the negotiated language of the UN Charter, which transformed "rights" into

56 Stephen Turner and George Mazur

a Leftist usage. This set the stage for the project of "democratic theory," to which we now turn. But before examining this project, it is necessary to consider the thinking of Hans Kelsen.

Kelsen's Response

These accounts face a basic issue: they are contrary to democracy itself. They express ideals that their advocates wish were the ideals of the electorate, but which are not: the electorate agreed to a bargain when they accepted the welfare state, but have failed, for the most part, to accept the theory. The rise of populism, both the envy populism of the Left, and the freedom and accountability populism of the Right, are better indicators of the underlying beliefs of the voters. The center finds ever-shifting compromises between Left and Right. The democracies we have are democracies that have been democratically arrived at, or ratified, or accepted through the acceptance of revisions over long periods. They represent the "will of the people" through the legal means that have been democratically established for doing so. But they nevertheless have a basis in the idea of democracy itself.

The root meaning of democracy, as Kelsen pointed out, was the rule of the people. And one can ask whether the procedures that have been democratically adopted have become inimical to the rule of the people. But this is not normally how these critiques have been constructed. Rather, they assume something like a theory of false consciousness in which the voters fail to understand their own interests and thus accept both a system of voting and a set of rulers that amounts to a failure of "democracy" in the theoretically preferred sense. With this, we come to a key metaphilosophical distinction: between teleological and non-teleological accounts of democracy, with some roots in neo-Kantianism, in the distinction between constitutive and regulative. If one defines democracy in such a way that it does not fully exist, one has a "critical" basis for evaluating actual regimes and a guideline for achieving democracy. The signs of such a conception are in terms like "genuine," "substantive," and "real." The model for this line of argument is Babeuf: democracy means equality, genuine equality is equality of incomes, and therefore only a regime that enforces this is genuinely democratic. But one can translate the same thinking in dozens of similar ways, merely by substituting the defining terms for democracy, for example, by defining it in terms of undistorted communication, or service to the people, or non-domination, or a long list of welfare state goods, as in the writings of Stein Ringen, or for that matter in terms of human rights. Each of these concepts places the concept outside the process of political decision.

What was Kelsen's response to this line of thinking? His account of democracy was an attempt to distinguish the essentials from the incidentals. And there was a good reason for doing so. The construction of "democratic theory" also purported to identify "essentials" or "fulfillments of the concept of democracy" that were lacking in actual democratic regimes. So, the issue turns into a metaphilosophical one: how does one determine essentials or fulfillments, and more importantly, from the perspective of the problem of authority, of who determines them. Kelsen provides a non-teleological, minimalist alternative definition, nicely summarized in the introduction to the English translation of *The Essence and Value of Democracy* ([1929]2013). The fundamental principle—the genuinely essential one—was this:

> democracies are predicated on the idea that coercive legal norms are only legitimate to the extent that those who are subjected to them have contributed to making them, while all other political regimes are predicated on a principle of "authority."
>
> (Urbinati and Accetti, 2013: 5–6)

"Contributed" is a minimal concept, but it has an important implication. To "contribute," there must be means of contributing. And Kelsen adds to this by defining this further by the requirement that those who are subject to coercive legal norms are also able to contribute to their revision.

If we take this minimal definition as a starting point, we can then inquire into the status of other aspects of democracy. We can ask what is essential, what is contingent, and what are the conditions of different forms of democracy, such as liberal democracy, and ask, especially, what the relation between liberalism and democracy is, and where freedom in general has a place in democracy. Kelsen has a concept for the features of democracy that are practical requirements or necessities for democracy. Some of them are universal. Others are requirements for particular ends chosen politically. Thus, "For Kelsen, on the other hand, 'formal' and 'substantive' democracy are 'inseparable from one another', inasmuch as the former constitutes the only available means for realizing the latter" (Urbinati and Accetti, 2013: 7). This is a universal consideration. The necessity is causal: there is no other way to cause contributions to the revision of coercive norms without a procedure.

Freedom, however, is a different matter, but there are important parallels. If one believes in natural rights, rights outside of any political order, which limit the validity of the claims of law or of the people, one must also consider that the actualization of such rights is inseparable—not conceptually, but practically—from a legal order. The same goes, as Kelsen was at pains to explain, for natural law: the term does not describe a coercive order, but must be implemented by one, at which it is no longer "natural," but artificial and human. The slogans of natural rights and natural law are nevertheless important. They can be implemented by legislation into a coercive order, at which point they become rights and law, but in the sense of civil rights and law, the rights and law of the particular coercive order are in question. So, one can have a democratic commitment to such rights, but not as part of democratic theory itself, because the idea of such rights is contrary to the basic principle of democracy, for reasons that will become apparent. What counts as "free" is a matter of political choice. In this respect, Philip Pettit's principle of non-domination, his substitute for freedom as non-intervention (Pettit, 1997), is a valuable pointer: what different groups consider to be inappropriate state action regardless of how they are supported by law produced by democratic procedures will vary from society to society, and from group to group. They will also vary from individual to individual. Pettit assumes that we can always refer to the question of what counts as domination to the common knowledge of a group, though he acknowledges that this creates a problem of minority groups within a political order whose common knowledge differs from that of other groups. It is of course a contingent fact that there is such "common knowledge" or that particular groups possess it. If they did, it would be democratic for the coercive legal order to abide by it. But as a practical matter, this too requires a procedure, and there is no procedure for converting common knowledge, or even recognizing it, apart from the ordinary procedures of voting and representation, delegation of authority, and so forth. Thus, this consideration returns us to procedures.

Procedures, however, involve the same dilemma: they can be justified on higher principles or justified as democratic choices. To justify them on higher principles is by definition to justify them on other than as democratic choices, unless these "principles" are converted into democratic choices by being chosen through democratic procedures by those who contribute to the making of the coercive rules under which they live.

Majority rule and the procedures that enact it have some important advantages: it "ensures that more individuals are in favor of the existing social order than opposed to it at any given time" (Urbinati and Accetti, 2013: 11). And there are two constraints that favor it:

> Anything less would mean that the will of the state could from its very inception conflict with more wills than it agrees with. Anything more would make it possible for a minority, rather than the majority, to determine the will of the state by preventing an alteration of that will.
>
> (Kelsen, [1929]2013: 31)

Why does this matter? It is difficult to see how either alternative could be regarded as "democratic." Both alternatives imply minority rule: the first by beginning with minority rule; the second by allowing a minority to prevent change. But if these constraints are temporary and revocable by procedures that are agreed on through other temporary and revocable procedures, we can approximate a situation in which "more individuals are in favor of the existing social order than opposed to it" over the long run, rather than at any given time, and generate consent for a legal order that involves constraints on the revision and enactment of laws—perhaps greater consent than any order which submits to a procedure of immediate majority rule.

We can begin with the term of the day: "democratic values." This is a sufficiently confused concept that it requires a ground-up analysis. We can start with the minimal definition of democracy given by Kelsen. To live in a democracy requires one to submit to one's peers, to give up one's freedoms—for example, under legislative authority. Acceptance of this condition is the central, and perhaps, the only specifically democratic value. But the burdens of this value are so great that it is not, in pure form, a value that anyone will accept without reservations. So, democracies invariably seek a compromise that limits the power of peers. And typically, this takes the legal form of constitutional limits on democratic power: democracy in chains. "Democratic values," in short, in their extreme form, are always in tension with individual wills, as Kelsen would put it. So, another value is implied by the first value: to place oneself under the control of one's peers requires the abandonment, or at least the subordination, of those values which conflict with this value, meaning those values that exclude, as a matter of principle, submission to the will of particular peers.

To put this in positive terms, it requires what Kelsen explicitly calls relativism. Kelsen says that Relativism is the only philosophy consistent with democracy. This relativism has seemed by many to be a bizarre conclusion. By itself, it appears not only to undermine the idea of a philosophy aiming at one or another form of genuine democracy—Babouvism or its variants—as anti-democratic, which is already implied by the argument that democracy requires that the people choose the ends of the state, but also to undermine any value commitments. But relativism is a meta-philosophical doctrine about the rational equality of ultimate value choices. It does not preclude any ultimate value choice, as long as it accepts this, combined with the acceptance of the relativity, or the equal rationality, of all such choices.

Relativism about ultimate values, however, is not the same as relativism about all values. There are many intermediate values, and politics for the most part is about such values (Turner and Factor, 1987). These might include such things as national greatness or government efficiency, both of which have an effect on the achievement of the ultimate values of individuals but are not themselves such values—though they might be for some very unusual people or people in unusual circumstances, such as the battlefield. And with intermediate values, there are non-relativistic considerations, of causal possibility, of achievability, and of conflicts with other values. This is the domain Kelsen treats as "sociotechnical" considerations.

If we add the sociotechnical consideration that the achievement of democratic rule in the sense of contribution to the revision of the legal order requires its own procedures, we can add some other values, notably the value of adhering to the procedures themselves. The first and most obvious is the value of acting in accordance with the procedures—obedience to the rule of law, in short. So, the appropriate "democratic values" for a given political order will be one that respects, at least as a starting point for revision, the particular compromise that occurs in particular legal orders: a respect for procedures, and for the procedures that have been democratically chosen. We can call this "constitutional consent."

60 Stephen Turner and George Mazur

And although it falls short of immediate "democratic consent" to revisions of the law, there are many other practical obstacles to a pure system of democratic consent which produce more serious problems which this kind of consent may protect against. Most of these problems become evident in a complex social order, with mass participation, and a powerful state. And with this complexity comes a more complex division of political labor, and the need for values that correspond to this division of labor. Kelsen assumes the existence of a judicial function, and an executive or administrative function. And these involve distinctive values and expectations: a judicial ethic and an administrative one. The actual values of the holders of particular positions may vary significantly from one regime to another, and within ministries, according to the position in question.

Socio-Technical Means

Kelsen's category of socio-technical means carries much of the burden of his argument, but it needs both scrutiny and revision, and also extension beyond its main object, the defense of the party system, to the administrative part of the state. The key to his discussion of these "means" is that they are on the fact side of the fact–value distinction, following Weber on value neutrality. A few of Kelsen's arguments in this category can serve as examples:

> It is a well-known fact that, because he is unable to achieve any appreciable influence on government, the isolated individual lacks any real political existence. Democracy is only feasible if, in order to influence the will of society, individuals integrate themselves into associations based on their various political goals. Collective bodies, which unite the common interests of their individual members as political parties, must come to mediate between the individual and the state.
>
> (Kelsen, [1929]2013: 39)

Several things need to be said about the form of this argument. In the first place, it is a factual argument that depends on context, not a direct implication of the notion of democracy itself. There might be a technological or organizational means better than parties for individuals to achieve influence on governments. One obvious one is through lawsuits, a means so powerful that governments find ways to restrict them, through such doctrines as sovereign immunity or, in the United States, judicial conventions about "standing" that allow bureaucracies to avoid accountability, or the doctrine of qualified immunity, allows criminal acts by persons acting for the state to be subject to lower legal standards than persons acting privately. But another is through the claim of expertise—which has its own complex implications for the concept of democracy. These turn out to be closely related.

What is directly implied by the concept of democracy, as distinct from being a socio-technical means? Consider the following more or less standard view of the necessity of certain kinds of liberal discourse for democracy, expressed as a democratic value:

> freely forming one's convictions (often by confrontation with the reasoning and convictions of others) and knowingly bringing those convictions to bear on political decisions (often by trying to get others to change their convictions) (Cohen, 2001: 72–3; Dworkin, 2002: 202–3).
>
> (Kolodny, 2016: 9)

Moreover,

> it isn't enough to cite the value of forming convictions about policy. One can have ample, fully resourced opportunity for forming convictions about policy without any opportunity to influence policy in light of those convictions.
>
> (Kolodny, 2016: 9n15)

This freedom to form convictions and affiliations can be taken as a condition of political participation and therefore an implication of the core democratic value. And this condition implies its own values, which can be added to the list of "democratic values." It is the condition of being open to persuasion and therefore to self-skepticism and self-doubt. We can call this value "epistemic humility." Without it, there is no point to government by discussion, the kind of opinion formation discussed earlier, because there would be no point to discussion. Democracies can of course survive fundamental disagreements about values, if they are not comprehensive, i.e., ideological. Thus, particular values, the right to abortion, for example, can be subject to democratic decision, as long as the participants accept the fundamental democratic value of acceptance of the authority of the people and place it above these values, even if they do not accept the values themselves as "relatively" valid. But more commonly, there is an agreement to limit political decision-making—to restrict the state so as to prevent it from making such choices—so that these value conflicts do not become "political."

Accountability

What democracies also require, which Kelsen may have assumed would simply follow from the procedures by which the will of the people would be expressed, is accountability: the coercive power to enforce this will over officials as well as representatives. This must be said to be as essential to the concept of democracy as a condition of meaningful political participation. Without it there is no point to persuasion or the making of policy: the state could do as it pleased. It is this value that is at the core of the "democratic deficit" of the EU and the rage against the regulatory state in the US.

Where does accountability fit into the scheme of democratic values? Is it derivable from, or an extension of, a fundamental or essential value, or is it part of a socio-technical means? If the fundamental value here is acceptance of subordination to one's peers, and majority voting according to rules, through parties and representation, is a socio-technical means, or a procedure to implement the value which is optional, in the sense that there may be others that also work, it seems as though there is a natural division. The essential principle of subordination to one's peers applies universally within a democracy—to officials, experts, citizens, children, and so forth. We may agree to exemptions from this principle, as we do when we establish rights, but to do so is a political act.

Making this distinction sheds some light on recent writing on democracy and also on the role of democratic procedures in relation to officials and official discretion. Consider this statement from the conclusion of Donatella della Porta's *Can Democracy be Saved?*

> If really existing democracies suffer from a "vast underutilization of political resources" (Offe, 2011, 461), an increase in the participatory and deliberative qualities of democracy can help to overcome it. To the question, then, "Can democracy be saved?," the answer could therefore be optimistic, but the (ever-mutable) solutions require changes in conceptions and practices of democracy as much as in our ways of looking at them. Delegation and majority voting no longer work in the face of more and more defiant citizens and complex, global problems, which require local as well as specialized knowledge. An image of democracy as a market perniciously pushes for individual egoism when collective commitment is called for instead. Conceptions and practices of democracy as participation and deliberation can help to address democracy in this "era of defiance" (Rosanvallon, 2006).
>
> (della Porta, 2013: 189)

This is to say that the older arguments for parties and representation no longer work and that, in the face of popular resistance and problem complexity, the solution is a different socio-technical means, using "participation and deliberation."

Do "complex, global problems, which require local as well as specialized knowledge," get resolved by "participation and deliberation"? This is a socio-technical problem, and the bias of the literature, including Kelsen's writings, has been on the democratic character of policymaking. But the kinds of problems della Porta mentions are precisely the kinds that involve experts—with local as well as specialized knowledge. And the relation participants have and can have with these experts violates core democratic values. The relations involve deference to, and trust of, people recognized as superior: an aristocratic rather than democratic set of values. "Deliberation" with superiors is inherently unequal. Yet complex problems normally are addressed by experts, groups of stakeholders assembled to negotiate solutions, experts interacting with locals, and so forth. These efforts typically seek legitimation for their superior knowledge rather than "collective commitment." The goal is acquiescence and treating the results of the experts' proceedings as matters of fact to be dealt with. They fall into the category of "authority." Collective commitment, in contrast, is something else.

How does this kind of policy-making structure, which is the norm in modern states, relate to democracy? This is a crucial question for democratic theory. In the first place, it renders most of the discussion of the public sphere irrelevant: these discussions are between people who are insulated from democratic accountability as Civil Servants, experts from universities or corporations, who further insulate themselves by acting collectively, through internal bodies that distribute responsibility in such a way as to void individual responsibility. Where do "democratic values" fit in here? Kelsen remarks that "[h]e who in his political desires and actions is able to lay claim to divine inspiration or otherworldly enlightenment may well be right to be deaf to the voices of his fellows" (Kelsen, [1929]2013: 104). Experts assert authority—epistemic authority—on the basis of this-worldly enlightenment, but are equally deaf to the voices of their fellows who lack expertise. If democratic values are the condition of democracy, claims of expertise are themselves in conflict with them: epistemic humility is the opposite of claims to the kind of expertise that relates to policy or to implementation.

One might think that the fact–value distinction would help here: to be an expert is to be on the side of fact alone. But of course not only policies but also socio-technical means of governance come with values—to go from facts to a policy requires values. So, these discussions can never be on the side of fact alone, and in practice, are shot through with valuative considerations, including considerations about how much risk to take in accepting given knowledge claims.

The apparent attraction of deliberation is this: it achieves both commitment and a result, without reference to an agreement on procedures, like majority rule voting, which seems like an arbitrary convention when related to truth or wisdom, and which legitimates a policy indirectly, by reference to the convention, while deliberation seems to hold the promise of providing both rational justification and commitment without reference to a convention and thus without submission to the wishes of others. But collective commitment is a fantasy or a horror. The point of democracy is the convention of submission to the majority in the face of disagreement.

There is a reason that deliberation does not actually happen in the real world in the way that participatory democracy envisions. People are not competent to participate in deliberation and do not wish to. And the phrasing by della Porta contains its own explanation: complexity. Complexity can be dealt with by deliberators in think tanks coming up with proposals that politicians can adopt.

But parties and individual politicians no longer can serve this purpose, precisely because mastering a variety of complex issues is beyond their capacities.

So what kind of democracy is possible in the face of complexity and expert knowledge? A more plausible model, involving accountability, would be this: experts, stakeholders, and so forth do the work of generating policy proposals, which are then ratified by representatives. The role of democracy in this process is to hold the representatives accountable. To put this in terms established by Jon Elster, the role of democratic procedures in these cases is as a "security against misrule." Elster focuses on juries and other secondary bodies that oversee and correct for decision-makers (2013). This is an indication not of the decision-free character of these processes, but rather the reverse: that they are so clearly discretionary that protection against misrule is necessary.

How do these processes relate to the core value of democracy? "Contributing" to the creation of the coercive order under which one lives, and submission to one's peers, is an ongoing process, for Kelsen. So, the processes of accountability are part of this as much as policy formation or what Habermas calls collective will formation. And in the face of complexity, they are the most important part: it is only when the unintended consequences of policies made to deal with complex problems are revealed and apparent to non-experts that the public can make a meaningful contribution. And it is routinely the case that policies affect different groups differentially and in unanticipated ways. Thus, the mechanisms of correction—protests, removal from office, and prosecution for abuses of discretion—become more important than the mechanisms of policy creation, from the point of view of democracy and democratic values.

The urgent problem for modern democracies is with the excesses of the administrative state, a practical socio-technical necessity, and the expert or the bureaucrat who is part of this apparatus who lays claim to a this-worldly enlightenment of a kind that entitles him to be deaf to the voices of his fellows. And this may be the best argument for democracy—as the ultimate security against misrule. It is only this role of democracy that can address the problems that arise when an insulated organ, such as the judiciary, subject to an indirect and weak form of democratic accountability, declines to serve the purpose it was designed for, namely, to curb administrative overreach. But the threat of ultimate accountability mitigates the necessary delegation of authority to courts or regulatory agencies. To strengthen democracy, it is this power that needs to be enhanced. The phenomenon of populism and protests are intelligible precisely because they reflect the failures of multiple bodies, parliamentary parties, courts, ministries, and so forth, in the face of complexity. Rather than "threats to democracy," they are ways of giving voice to a demand for accountability, which is a part of the core or essence of "democratic values." The idea that the "norms of democracy" require deference to these bodies is, as Kelsen would say, as he did of the criticisms of political parties, "an ideologically veiled resistance to the realization of democracy itself" (Kelsen, [1929]2013: 39).

References

Cohen, Joshua. "Money, Politics, and Political Equality," In *Fact and Value*, Edited by Alex Byrne, Robert Stalnaker, and Ralph Wedgwood. Cambridge: MIT Press, 2001, 47–80.

Dahl, Robert. *A Preface to Democratic Theory*. Chicago: University of Chicago Press, [1956]2006.

della Porta, Donatella. *Can Democracy Be Saved?: Participation, Deliberation and Social Movements*. Cambridge: Polity, 2013.

Dworkin, Ronald. *Sovereign Virtue*. Cambridge: Harvard University Press, 2002.

Elster, Jon. *Securities against Misrule: Juries, Assemblies, Elections*. Cambridge: Cambridge University Press, 2013.

Kelsen, Hans. *The Essence and Value of Democracy*, Edited by Nadia Urbinati and Carlo Invernizzi Accetti and translated by Brian Graf. Lanham: Rowman & Littlefield, [1929]2013.

Kelsen, Hans. *Vom Wesen und Wert der Demokratie*. Tübingen: Mohr, 1929.

Kolodny, Niko. *Democracy for Idealists*. Berkeley: Kadish Workshop in Law, Philosophy and Political Theory, Joshua Cohen and Veronique Munoz-Darde, University of California Berkeley, 2016.

Offe, Claus. "Crisis and Innovation of Liberal Democracy: Can Deliberation Be Institutionalised?" *Sociologický Časopis/Czech Sociological Review* 47(3): 447–472, 2011.

Pettit, Philip. *Republicanism: A Theory of Freedom and Government*. Oxford: Oxford University Press, 1997.

Ringen, Stein. *What Democracy is For: On Freedom and Moral Government*. Oxford: Oxford University Press, 2007.

Rosanvallon, Pierre. *La Contre-Démocratie. La politique à l'âge de la défiance*. Paris: Seuil, 2006.

Scheuerman, W. E. "Professor Kelsen's Amazing Disappearing Act," In *Émigré Scholars and the Genesis of International Relations*, Edited by Felix Rösch. London: Palgrave Macmillan, 2014, 81–102.

Turner, Stephen and Regis Factor. "Decisionism and Politics: Weber as Constitutional Theorist," In *Max Weber, Rationality and Modernity*, Edited by Scott Lash and Sam Whimster. London: Allen and Unwin, 1987, 334–354.

Urbinati, Nadia and Carlo Invernizzi Accetti. "Editors Introduction," In *Hans Kelsen, The Essence and Value of Democracy*, translated by Brian Graf. Lanham: Rowman & Littlefield, 2013, 1–24.

Chapter 4

The Ideology of Anti-Populism and the Administrative State

Stephen Turner

Introduction

The people, the state, and expertise form an unstable triad, and relating the three in a coherent way, either institutionally or theoretically, is ultimately not possible. Finding a way of dealing with these relations nevertheless is a problem that needs to be solved and re-solved. The theorization of the problem goes back to Plato's *Republic* and the "solution" of making philosophers kings. The example of the Republic is revealing, but one might also take the long European tradition of the three orders, those who pray, those who work, and those who fight (Duby, [1978]1980). Unstable triads are mythogenic: making sense of their relations requires fictions, or myths, which legitimate arrangements, and these may temporarily stabilize what is inherently unstable, as Plato used the myth of the metals, and as Aquinas used a hierarchical natural law. As one would expect, the particular need for constructing myths of this kind will vary according to the circumstances, including the inherited institutional structures. What needs to be justified will differ.

Harvey Mansfield defined populism, by which he meant populism as a political idea, as the belief in the virtue of the people. "A populist let us say is a democrat who is satisfied with his own and with the people's virtue" (Mansfield, 1996: 7). Populism is thus based on a myth as well. But it is a myth whose role is primarily negative: it does not constitute an order but rejects one in the name of the people. Actual rule requires more. But to deny the myth of the superior wisdom of the people is to threaten the democratic idea itself. And this poses a special problem for ostensibly "democratic" regimes. The need for rulers requires its own "democratic" myths, such as the theory of representation. But the myth of the people constrains these myths.

Mansfield follows his line on the populist with another: "This distinguishes him from a reformer who is satisfied with his own virtue but not with other people's. Giving over government to the people is not the same as lecturing them" (Mansfield, 1996: 7). Progressivism took this tack. The progressives of the early twentieth century wanted the support and enthusiasm of "the people" and envied populism for this. But they wanted to lead the people themselves.

DOI: 10.4324/9781003360810-5

And they asserted themselves not in the name of people's interests and wishes, but in the name of expertise. Progressivism was to be the alliance of experts and an aroused "people" (Turner, 1996). And this followed an emerging practice of social movements based on expertise, notably the prohibition movement, which employed the techniques presently associated with climate science under the heading alcohol science (Okrent, 2010; Turner, 2001, 2014), through this and other movements, became the third leg in the modem triad. And anti-populism came to take the form of a set of assertions about expertise and governance. My concern here will be the genealogy and significance of these assertions, and their function as governing myths.

The anti-populist, who is, unlike the populist, not satisfied with the people's virtue, faces a fundamental problem: to deny populism is to deny democracy, or a founding element of the democratic idea, that the people should be, and are the best, governors of themselves. Thus anti-populism, if it pretends to be democratic, cannot overtly deny the myth of the people. But the need for rulers and for the justification of their rule creates an opportunity to redefine the democratic idea, to create an appropriate counter-myth that enables the people to have a place, but not to rule. Anti-populism consists of myths and fictions of this kind, which can be identified in history.

Calling them myths is not to discount them. As W.I. Thomas and Dorothy Swaine Thomas said, "[if] men define situations as real, they are real in their consequences" (Thomas and Thomas, 1928: 571–72). But it is to call attention to their role in discourse. My concern in what follows will be with the role they play, though it will be evident that many of the concepts at play in these discussions diverge from the thinking and experience of the people involved, and that these divergences are the source of the instability of the solutions to the triadic relation between people, state, and expertise. I will try to cut through some of these myths, by explaining the issues that gave rise to them.

The Problematic Idea of "The People"

The place to begin, with populism, is with the pure democratic idea itself. Classically, it means rule by the people, the demos. But we are accustomed to adding disclaimers and qualifications, or specifications, to this idea: that expressions of the will of the people must take the form of laws and procedures, such as election laws and laws governing representation; or from a liberal perspective, that genuine democratic will formation requires free individuals with freedom of speech and various individual rights; or from the Left, that substantive equality rather than mere formal equality is required for meaningful democratic participation. These additions function as temporary stabilizers to the relations between the three elements. But they each have their own difficulties and are mythic on their own.

The critics of the concept of "the people" are correct in one respect: the construction of the concept in different contexts has varied enormously, and there is no continuity between the various manifestations of the concept, which arise situationally and create unities in response to particular concrete issues. Where there is a commonality between populisms is in the targets of their antagonism. Populism is intrinsically a denial of the special superiority of rulers and elites.

This conflict has taken multiple forms in the history of government and in the history of political thought. Indeed, one can think of government as a scheme of reconciling the two: of adjusting the relation between the wishes of the ruled and the superior power of the ruler necessary to achieve political goods.

"Democratic" solutions require some sort of democratic backstop. Democratic accountability through the direct election of officials is one such means; the discretionary power of administrators coupled with a general sense of the beneficial character and hence legitimacy of their actions is another. These correspond to the shoe-wearer and the shoemaker, respectively. And the latter solution has long been intertwined with the problem of expertise, for the simple reason that the main claim for the need for discretionary power is that desirable governmental actions require expertise that the public lacks. But this is not an unproblematic solution to the problem of triadic balance: indeed, it depends on its own fragile myths.

We tend to think of the problem of democracy in terms of modem democratic theory, which pertains primarily to liberal democracy, and its conception of the people. But there is a long separate history of rule by the people, *il populo*, and people's parties in Europe, which is the subject of extensive discussion by Weber under the heading of "non-legitimate domination" (Weber, [1921]1966) reaching back to the Greek notion of democracy itself. These parties and these constitutional forms were separated by several centuries from the political alignments of Europe in the nineteenth century at the time of the rise of the People's Party in the United States, the source of the term populism itself.

The American People's Party—what I will call Populism with an upper-case P in what follows—differed from these earlier parties in an important respect. Expertise was not a major component of the earlier historical conflict between the people—who in the case of *il populo* were a fixed social class—and the governing elite, also a fixed social class. Expertise was even then part of the claim of the elite to rule. The conflict is as old as Aristotle, who compared the expertise of the shoemaker to the needs of the customers whose foot was pinched. But expertise as an independent source of authority, expertise other than expertise about ruling itself, was a new element. The Populists challenged not only the elites but also an economic dogma supported by expert opinion.

Expertise not only adds complexity to the relation between rulers and ruled but also stabilizes this two-element relation by adding a third leg. To claim expertise is to add a legitimacy claim. To claim to be acting in accordance with expertise is even better: it displaces the authoritarian character of the relationship onto a neutral third source. To have the third source accepted as neutral and authoritative is better yet: it means that consensus between the three elements

The Ideology of Anti-Populism and the Administrative State   69

of the triad has been achieved and that there is no room for conflict. The exercise of discretionary power no longer needs democratic accountability. The people accept the experts, and the administrators merely use their discretion in accordance with their expertise. Both those who exercise power and those it is exercised upon accept the legitimacy of the expert. And the expert never exercises power: the neutrality of the expert raises expertise above politics.

Populism, by asserting the superior wisdom of the people, rejects the identification of power and expertise. But in doing so, it calls into question the notion of democracy itself. If governments are legitimated by experts, what, exactly, is the point of democratic accountability? What role do "the people" have other than to obey, or perhaps to occasionally ratify the system of governance as a whole? This no longer seems to be democracy. It is, rather, paternalism.[1] But explicit arguments for paternalism, or elite rule, cannot be squared with the rhetoric of democracy: "the people" still need to have an active role for a regime to be democratic.

As a consequence, anti-Populism takes an odd form: as an alternative account of democracy itself that developed in the course of the campaign against Populism. My main concern will thus be with explaining anti-Populism as an ideology, an ideology that gets concealed, in a Foucauldian way, in subsequent practice. As I will show, anti-Populism is a product of a particular ideological need: to reconcile practices derived from absolutism with the claim to be a "democracy." As it happens, this is a need that is continually renewed, as new extensions of governmental practice rooted in the traditions of royal bureaucracies need to be justified, and new forms of "Populist" ' resistance to these practices need to be rejected. Claims about expertise play a large role in this reconciliation.

Populism is democratic in a specific sense: it is a reassertion of popular control as a remedy for the perceived failure or injustice of normal political and administrative practice, especially failures of representation and abuses by bureaucrats. In response to failures of representation, populists endorse referenda, plebiscites, constitutional amendments, or direct elections over mediated ones, depending on the system they are trying to circumvent. Populist movements happen when political parties, traditional leaders, elites, and politics as usual fail to deliver the expected goods, or fail to accord with the popular sense of reality, or are perceived as untrustworthy and corrupt.

What is typical in such cases is conflict with elites, and elite failure, as well as a rejection of the workings of the political system itself, particularly the parties. Populisms thus normally operate in conflict, with, or as an alternative to, parties, and commonly rely on charismatic leaders, or else create an alternative party, or attempt to take over an existing party. Populist tendencies are prone to co-optation and typically do not outlast the situations that produced them, though they do represent a reserve of general sentiment against elites and particular ruling groups that can be activated in new situations. They differ from ideologies and ideological parties in that they are situational rather than analytic, in the sense that they have concrete targets and grievances rather than a developed analysis of political life that is extended to new situations and refined and elaborated. This accounts for many of the distinctive features of populist movements, especially the preference for leaders who promise to act decisively, in contrast to normal "politicians," and their hostility to "politics as usual."[2]

Populisms are situation-driven rather than analysis-driven, or to put it differently, driven by specific crises or grievances, rather than by a permanent ideological viewpoint, though these movements of course have an analytic component. The situational character of Populism also bears on another important contrast. It is necessary to distinguish two aspects of governance, sometimes known as input and output legitimacy, but normally treated as the distinction between representation or legislation and administration, or between democracy as government by the people or government for the people. Traditional parties and normal politics are concerned with representation and legislation. Populism typically arises in situations in which there are larger failures, failures which extend beyond normal political processes, and therefore beyond mere legislation within existing political practices. They typically seek reform of these practices, such as the role of lobbyists.

The antinomy of Populism is elite rule. Elites rule through particular strategies and fail through typical issues. Elite solidarity is essential to elite rule; division among the elite is a typical cause of elite failure (Shipman et al., 2018). Elites rule through alliances between the elite and a significant non-elite group. The most stable of these alliances have been with the middle classes, normally under an ideology of meritocracy, property rights, and support of business, an alliance that is played off against the demands of the excluded group, the poor. But an upstairs-downstairs alliance is always possible, and the upper hand the elite has in dealing with the non-elite segments of society depends on its ability to choose alternative groups to ally with. Thus pluralism favors the elite because it provides more opportunities to change alliances. Populism, in contrast, must produce enough unity in the population to effectively counter the elite, and must therefore transcend differences between segments of society in the name of the people. Both Left and Right populisms are anti-pluralist, as a simple consequence of the dynamics of elite alliance-making: neither kind of Populism could succeed if the elite used its alliance-making power to divide the movement. To the extent that elite rule depends on manipulating and shifting alliances with non-elite groups, as is the norm (Shipman et al., 2018), an attack on pluralism is a threat to elite rule as a political system itself.

The distinction between situation and analysis driven has other consequences. Zizek captures this distinction in thinking by contrasting Marxism to Populism: [For] a Populist, the cause of the troubles is ultimately never the system as such but the intruder who corrupted it (financial manipulators, not necessarily capitalists, and so on); not a fatal flaw inscribed into the structure

The Ideology of Anti-Populism and the Administrative State 71

as such but an element that does not play its role within the structure properly. For a Marxist, on the contrary (as for a Freudian), the pathological (deviating misbehavior of some elements) is the symptom of the normal, an indicator of what is wrong in the very structure that is threatened with "pathological" outbursts (Zizek, 2006: 556–57; see also Laclau, 2005).

The Marxist, in short, needs an analysis, or a theory, about the system; the Populist needs only villains, such as "the 1%." Zizek goes on to, in effect, reject the populists' target, the elite, characterizing the "pseudo concreteness of the figure that is selected as the enemy, the singular agent behind all threats to the people" (Zizek, 2006: 556). His is, therefore, a kind of Left-wing anti-populism. What makes Right-wing Populism "dangerous" is that the villains it identifies include not only the elite but also groups that are excluded from the populist's conception of the people, and therefore populism undermines "pluralism." The excluded groups are necessarily small, however, because the populist's strategy must be to break the alliances of the elite with subgroups and absorb them into "the people."

Populism is a response to the failure of ordinary political processes and is therefore hostile to business as usual. Parties intervene between the "people" and the state, in the course of electoral processes, so they are often understood as part of the obstacle to electoral control by "the people" in the situation of the time. In the American case, the solution was to form a new party. This failed, yet the issues raised by the populists were taken up by the extant parties.[3] Weber himself admired Gladstone for being able to go over the heads of the party leaders and speak directly to the people and took this as a model for democratic control of the bureaucracy, which he saw as the preeminent danger to human freedom. This positive view of demagoguery points to something important: that the expression of non-elite opinion may be channeled in a variety of ways, dependent on the local political circumstances. Demonstrations, or manifestations, are a standard tactic in Europe, but less effective in the United States. Charismatic leaders may represent the popular opinion, either on the Left or on the Right. These forms of expression are independent of the views being expressed. What is common to them is that they are responses to the imperviousness of the existing political order.

The common theme of Populisms is accountability to the people, electoral accountability where possible, but through other means if necessary. Anti-populism is an attempt to restrict accountability. And here the claim of expertise becomes relevant. Experts are by definition not directly accountable to the public, but to their expertise, or their expert community, or collectively, as members of an expert class, or as part of an expert institution. Bureaucracies, notoriously, displace responsibility to rules that the bureaucracy interprets for itself and conceal decision-making by distributing its contributory elements to multiple officials none of whom have complete responsibility and by protecting officials from personal liability for actions. So, there is a sense in which expertise and bureaucracy have an elective affinity, which is actualized as a

72 Stephen Turner

means of avoiding accountability to "the people." One is an organizational and the other an epistemic means to the same end. Not surprisingly, they play a large role in the ideology of anti-populism.

Real Populism

American Populism of the late nineteenth century is the source of the term and the model for the category. Some thinkers, eager to associate populism with fascism, either deny it was a genuine case of Populism or alternatively insinuate that it was a nascent form of fascism. My own reason for choosing the American late nineteenth and early twentieth centuries is simple. It illustrates issues that are submerged, for historical reasons, in cases of recent Right-wing European populism, which are nevertheless illuminated by the American case. My concern will be with the co-eval phenomenon of the American administrative state, and its justifying theory, which was explicitly anti-populist and becomes solidified in a vast subsequent theoretical literature in public administration. For historical reasons that will become apparent, the parallel European literature on this general topic lacks the degree of explicit theorizing on the relation of democracy to the administration that figures in the American discussion.

The major difference was this: the Continental administrative state did not need to be justified or explained in relation to democracy; it already existed prior to the many gradual steps toward "democracy." The American form had to be created and was created through borrowing from, and reflecting on, Continental models. This meant that there was an explicit analysis of the administrative state and its relation to democracy, one which happens to have produced a specific intellectual tradition and body of practice, in which the issue of democracy is central. Much of the discussion focused on legal and constitutional issues, a topic I will not pursue here, but they may be briefly summarized. The People's Party in the United States invoked the original democratic impulses of the ordinary people as expressed in the American founding, and especially in the thinking of the anti-federalists, such as Sam Adams, that officeholders should be voted on every year, thus maximizing electoral accountability. From a comparative perspective, the fundamental constitutional feature of the American government was rule by elected officials at all levels of administration, a practice that never emerged in Europe. It was this feature, and the complaints about such things as machine politics, that produced the negative view of American democracy that dominated European perspectives in the late nineteenth century, and is also central to the narrative of anti-populism.

The Populist movement arose in response to the world wheat price crisis of the 1880s, which coincided with the rapid expansion of cities, the world economy, and consequently the demand for capital, creating a crisis for credit that affected much of the capitalist world. Here the claim that the people had superior wisdom, an element not directly addressed in the UN definition, was

The Ideology of Anti-Populism and the Administrative State   73

important. There was an expert consensus on this, at least in the United States among economists and the elite, for strong currencies and the gold standard and against the radical expansion of money supplies. The platform of the People's Party of 1892 is the standard source for their views, though the movement, and the idea of reversing the turn to the gold standard, preceded it. This was the source of their key anti-elitist social analysis:

> Silver, which has been accepted as coin since the dawn of history, has been demonetized to add to the purchasing power of gold by decreasing the value of all forms of property as well as human labor, and the supply of currency is purposely abridged to fatten usurers, bankrupt enterprise, and enslave industry. A vast conspiracy against mankind has been organized on two continents, and it is rapidly taking possession of the world. If not met and overthrown at once it forebodes terrible social convulsions, the destruction of civilization, or the establishment of an absolute despotism.
>
> (National People's Party Platform, [1892]1966: 91)

The platform, and the movement itself, went far beyond this, and in ways that are typical of populisms generally. The core of their position was an account of the situation:

> The conditions which surround us best justify our co-operation; we meet in the midst of a nation brought to the verge of moral, political, and material ruin. Corruption dominates the ballot-box, the Legislatures, the Congress, and touches even the ermine of the bench. The people are demoralized; most of the States have been compelled to isolate the voters at the polling places to prevent universal intimidation and bribery. The newspapers are largely subsidized or muzzled, public opinion silenced, business prostrated, homes covered with mortgages, labor impoverished, and the land concentrating in the hands of capitalists. The urban workmen are denied the right to organize for self-protection, imported pauperized labor beats down their wages, a hireling standing army, unrecognized by our laws, is established to shoot them down, and they are rapidly degenerating into European conditions. The fruits of the toil of millions are boldly stolen to build up colossal fortunes for a few, unprecedented in the history of mankind; and the possessors of those, in turn, despise the republic and endanger liberty. From the same prolific womb of governmental injustice we breed the two great classes—tramps and millionaires.
>
> (National People's Party Platform, [1892]1966: 90)

The aim of the movement was "to restore" popular rule, and in this respect, it was a form of identity politics *avant la lettre*, but the identity was discussed not in the language of class, but in terms of "the plain people," who were identified with the founders.

74   Stephen Turner

[We] seek to restore the government of the Republic to the hands of "the plain people," with which class it originated. We assert our purposes to be identical with the purposes of the National Constitution; to form a more perfect union and establish justice, insure domestic tranquility, provide for the common defense, promote the general welfare, and secure the blessings of liberty for ourselves and our posterity.

(National People's Party Platform, [1892]1966: 92)

The Populist movement allied itself with the Knights of Labor, the largest union of the time, and the Knights, whose "identity" was so broad as only to exclude bankers, were ultimately supplanted by trade unions. There were, however, exclusions that followed from their account of the situation. The Knights and the trade unions generally were also opposed to unrestricted immigration, and for the same reasons. The party platform reflected this:

That we condemn the fallacy of protecting American labor under the present system, which opens our ports to the pauper and criminal classes of the world and crowds out our wage-earners; and we denounce the present ineffective laws against contract labor, and demand the further restriction of undesirable emigration.

(National People's Party Platform, [1892]1966: 95)

Their attitude to the state was, however, paradoxical. On the one hand, they wanted an increase in government power:

We believe that the power of government—or in other words, of the people—should be expanded (as in the case of the postal service) as rapidly and as far as the good sense of an intelligent people and the teachings of experience shall justify, to the end that oppression, injustice, and poverty shall eventually cease in the land.

(National People's Party Platform, [1892]1966: 92)

But they did not want the creation of an unaccountable administration or massive bureaucracy.

Thus in a platform item calling for government control of the railroads, they qualified this demand by asking for an amendment to the Constitution by which all persons engaged in the government service shall be placed under a civil service regulation of the most rigid character, so as to prevent the increase of the power of the national administration by the use of such additional government employes [sic].

(National People's Party Platform, [1892]1966: 93)

This may seem to be a contradictory demand: more government action without more power for the national administration and more bureaucrats, and

The Ideology of Anti-Populism and the Administrative State   75

less money in the hands of the state. But their suspicions of state power were foremost. They held that "the money of the country should be kept as much as possible in the hands of the people," and thus demanded "that all State and national revenues shall be limited to the necessary expenses of the government, economically and honestly administered" (National People's Party Platform, [1892]1966: 94).

These demands were made in the larger context of a demand for greater electoral control, for example, for the popular election of senators, and the imposition of one-term limits for the President and Vice-President, and for the secret ballot. The theme is clear: democracy requires the maximization of electoral control of the state and a state that is responsive to the demands of the people as expressed in voting, with as little mediation as possible by professional politicians. But the situational aspects of the demands were epistemic: they were rejections of the guiding, and often "expert," opinions of the elite.

The Enemies of Populism

Woodrow Wilson, writing in the nineteenth and early twentieth century as a professor, the only American president with this background, provides a complete intellectual articulation of anti-populist thinking. The basic elements are these: the people cannot be trusted to perform certain tasks, such as voting for administrators. But they can be led, by opinion leaders, which gives them the illusion of choice, to accept what they are given, and administrators can be given actual discretionary power, and a great deal of it, under the fiction that what they do is not "politics" but pure administration, and that political choices determine the ends which administrators seek. The justification for this arrangement is that the people are rather stupid, and administrators possess knowledge and expertise that the amateurs who get elected to the excessive multitude of democratically accountable offices do not. Moreover, the electoral process needs to be radically curtailed: it is corrupted by political machines and the like. So, the vast number of political offices needs to be reduced, by centralization, thus eliminating the need for local, independent, politically accountable officeholders. The administrators who will replace them can be trusted and are accountable to the public because their responsibilities are well-defined, despite the lack of an electoral method, or indeed any method but trust, of holding them accountable. Pluralism means that there are no "people" left for them to be democratically accountable to, as there once were, so the ideal of democratic accountability in the present leads instead to corruption and incompetence. Hallowed political ideas, such as the separation of powers and the rule of law, need to be discarded. Similarly, for the rule of law, it is inefficient to have the courts and lawyers in a position to correct and supervise administrators. They need a wide zone of discretionary power, and this needs to include powers to regulate of the sort normally thought to be part of legislation. This arrangement "saves" democracy, but saves it from itself: it not only produces better results but also limits the domain of democracy to the range of things that opinion leaders of a kind resembling the British aristocracy, responsible but also benignly concerned with the general good, can exercise their influence over.

The temporal and logical order of this argument matters. It was not an argument of the form "we have the relevant expertise, and are prevented from using it by an ignorant public, and therefore need positions of authority which are free from electoral supervision, which we can be trusted to use correctly." Instead, it took the form of "the public is ignorant, officials need to be protected from them, they can be trusted if they are given a free hand, and then they can develop the expertise to act." It is more an argument *against* the people than an argument for the alternative. Obviously, this was not, so to speak, an argument that could be made as part of an open political agenda. It needed to be disguised as something else. And the disguise came in the form of a variety of claims about the inadequacies of the electoral process. Wilson's solution was, invariably, to limit electoral accountability. And this directly clashed with Populism.

The novelty of Populism was that the case for the people no longer rested on the virtues of the Yeoman Farmer. Now, it rested on the falsity of the beliefs of the elite, particularly with respect to the Gold Standard. The anti-Populists seized on this. This was a matter on which the elite claimed overwhelming expert support. Wilson's own animus against Populism verged on the hysterical, despite his professorial language.

> There could be no better illustration of this than the constant re-argument, *de nova*, of the money question among us, and the easy currency to be obtained, at every juncture of financial crisis, for the most childish errors with regard to the well-known laws of value and exchange. No nation not isolated like ourselves in thought and experience could possibly think itself able to establish a value of its own for gold and silver, by legislation which paid no regard either to the commercial operations or to the laws of coinage and exchange which obtained outside its own borders. That a great political party should be able to win men of undoubted cultivation and practical sense to the support of a platform which embodied palpable and thrice-proven errors in such matters, and that, too, at a great election following close upon protracted, earnest, frank, and universal discussion, and should poll but little less than half the votes of the nation, is startling proof enough that we have learned to think, for the most part, only in terms of our own separate life and independent action, and have come to think ourselves a divided portion of mankind, masters and makers of our own laws of trade.

(Wilson, 1901: 294)

This represents an early appearance of an appeal to expertise and a complaint about its lack of effect on the voting masses. Wilson concedes to at least some

The Ideology of Anti-Populism and the Administrative State   **77**

of his opponents the Jeffersonian virtues of cultivation and practical sense. But "practical sense" now becomes an insult: this did not protect them from childish errors.[4]

The solution was to be found in reforming basic political institutions, under the pretext of "efficiency," with the effect of eliminating electoral accountability, the basic aim of Populism. But the pretext was not based on an attack on the governance of big cities. As Woodrow Wilson expressed the complaints motivating him:

> Our later life has disclosed serious flaws, has even seemed ominous of pitiful failure, in some of the things we most prided ourselves upon having managed well: notably, in pure and efficient local government, in the successful organization of great cities, and in well-considered schemes of administration. The boss—a man elected by no votes, preferred by no open process of choice, occupying no office of responsibility—makes himself a veritable tyrant amongst us, and seems to cheat us of self-government; parties appear to hamper the movements of opinion rather than to give them form and means of expression; multitudinous voices of agitation, an infinite play of forces at cross-purpose, confuse us; and there seems to be no common counsel or definite union for action, after all.
>
> (Wilson, 1901: 291)

These were, so to speak, Populist complaints against the existing system and paralleled the People's Party platform's strictures against rail lobbyists. But Wilson and the Populists had diametrically opposed solutions. Wilson believed that what was needed was elite rule, based on the model of the English aristocracy. Ever the Anglophile and secret Germanophile, Wilson used a German source to describe it.

> Until 1888, influential country gentlemen, appointed justices of the peace by the crown upon the nomination of the Lord Chancellor, were the governing officers of her counties. Practically every important matter of local administration was in their hands, and yet the people of the counties had absolutely no voice in their selection. Things had stood so for more than four hundred years. Professor Rudolph Gneist, the great German student of English institutions, in expounding English ideas of self-government as he found them exemplified in the actual organization of local administration, declared that the word *government* was quite as emphatic in the compound as the word *self*. The people of the counties were not self-directed in affairs: they were governed by crown officials. The policy of the crown was indeed moderated and guided in all things by the influence of a representative parliament; the justices received no salaries; were men resident in the counties for which they were commissioned, identified with them in life and interest, landlords and neighbors among the men whose public

affairs they administered. They had nothing to gain by oppression, much to gain by the real advancement of prosperity and good feeling within their jurisdictions: they were in a very excellent and substantial sense representative men. But they were not elected representatives; their rule was not democratic either in form or in principle. Such was the local self-government of England during some of the most notable and honorable periods of her history.

(Wilson, 1901: 295)

This was elite rule *on behalf* of the people, not self-government. And it provided Wilson with the model he developed for saving "democracy." The problem was to find a class of people who fit this model of representation and to give them power. The new class was an invented one: administrators who would be granted vast discretionary power.

The Case for the Administrative State

The argument he developed was an attempt to discredit elections and sanitize and justify administrative power and discretion. Expertise played a role in this argument, but not a simple one. Wilson's argumentative strategy was clear: to limit elections and to limit electoral control of "administration," which is conceived in such a way as to replace offices under electoral control and to centralize power so as to eliminate them. The present system, he thought, gives

so many elective offices that even the most conscientious voters have neither the time nor the opportunity to inform themselves with regard to every candidate on their ballots, and must vote for a great many men of whom they know nothing. They give us, consequently, the local machine and the local boss; and where population crowds, interests compete, work moves strenuously and at haste, life is many-sided and without unity, and voters of every blood and environment and social derivation mix and stare at one another at the same voting places, government miscarries, is confused, irresponsible, unintelligent, wasteful. Methods of electoral choice and administrative organization, which served us admirably well while the nation was homogeneous and rural, serve us oftentimes ill enough now that the nation is heterogeneous and crowded into cities.

(Wilson, 1901: 296)

This brings together two ideas: that democracy requires homogeneity and that heterogeneity requires administrative power. What this power was supposed to be was extensive and discretionary, but apolitical. "Administrative questions are not political questions. Although politics sets the tasks for administration, it should not be suffered to manipulate its offices" (Wilson, [1887]1941: 494). It requires no electoral accountability, but trust, and organization that inspires trust:

The Ideology of Anti-Populism and the Administrative State 79

> *Trust is strength* in all relations of life; and, as it is the office of the constitutional reformer to create conditions of trustfulness, so it is the office of the administrative organizer to fit administration with conditions of clear-cut responsibility which shall insure trustworthiness.
>
> (Wilson, [1887]1941: 497; italics in original)

But this has a specific meaning: "large powers and unhampered discretion seem to me the indispensable conditions of responsibility" (Wilson, [1887]1941: 497). The two are supposed to go hand in hand:

> If to keep his office a man must achieve open and honest success, and if at the same time he feels himself intrusted with large freedom of discretion, the greater his power the less likely is he to abuse it, the more is he nerved and sobered and elevated by it. The less his power, the more safely obscure and unnoticed does he feel his position to be, and the more readily does he relapse into remissness.
>
> (Wilson, [1887]1941: 498)

So, to advance efficiency required a different political model, and to be "democratic" required not just the pretense of political neutrality and subordination to the goals set in the political realm, but a claim about expertise. This represented a fundamental change in the very idea of representative government, which Wilson candidly admitted, and it was a change that directly implicated the populist idea of the wisdom of the people, which Wilson demoted to "the opinion of the street." Only the right opinions should count, and they should arise in a particular setting, controlled by bureaucrats.

> Representative government has had its long life and excellent development, not in order that common opinion, the opinion of the street, might prevail, but in order that the best opinion, the opinion generated by the best possible methods of general counsel, might rule in affairs; in order that some sober and best opinion might be created, by thoughtful and responsible discussion conducted by men intimately informed concerning the public weal, and officially commissioned to look to its safeguarding and advancement,—by discussion in parliaments, discussion face to face between authoritative critics and responsible ministers of state.
>
> (Wilson, 1901: 290–91)

The error of the past was clear to Wilson, and it was shown in the misinterpretation of the concept of self-governance. "We printed the *SELF* large and the *government* small in almost every administrative arrangement we made; and that is still our attitude and preference" (Wilson, 1901: 296; emphasis in the original). This simply did not work.

We have found that even among ourselves such arrangements are not universally convenient or serviceable. They give us untrained officials, and an expert civil service is almost unknown amongst us. The aim of this response was to save democracy from itself, from electoral control, and from the opinion of the street, though the creation of an efficient and expert administrative state.

(Wilson, 1901: 296)

What is distinctive about Wilson's writing, and that of such figures as John Burgess, who founded the Columbia University School of Economic and Political Science (Hoxie, 1955) precisely for the task of creating a class of professional bureaucrats, is this: it relied on European models, and the protagonists were Francophiles, Germanophiles, and Anglophiles, but provided a "democratic" rationale for practices with a constitutional origin in either royal centralization or absolutism. The model was state bureaucracy, or what was openly called by Wilson, in the parlance of this pre-Bolshevik time, "state socialism." As Carl Schmitt pointed out, in Europe, bureaucratic rule was a constitutional form that stood on its own, and European constitutions were mixed constitutions, with different elements that depended on different forms of legitimacy, of which this was one (Schmitt, [1932]2004, [1928]2008). In the American setting, bureaucratic powers of the sort that were normal on the Continent raised constitutional issues, particularly over the doctrine of separation of powers, which forbade administrators from legislating, and conflicted with the practice of judicial review, which empowered the courts to oversee regulation. What Wilson hankered after was the Continental model. So, he had to overcome resistance to the idea that it was incompatible with democracy.

We have supposed that there could be one way of efficiency for democratic governments, and another for monarchical. We have declined to provide ourselves with a professional civil service, because we deemed it undemocratic; we have made shift to do without a trained diplomatic and consular service, because we thought the training given by other governments to their foreign agents unnecessary in the case of affairs so simple and unsophisticated as the foreign relations of a democracy in politics and trade, transactions so frank, so open, so straightforward, interests so free from all touch of chicane or indirection; we have hesitated to put our presidents or governors or mayors into direct and responsible relations of leadership with our legislatures and councils in the making of laws and ordinances, because such a connection between lawmakers and executive officers seemed inconsistent with the theory of checks and balances whose realization in practice we understood Montesquieu to have proved essential to the maintenance of a free

The Ideology of Anti-Populism and the Administrative State   81

government. Our theory, in short, has paid as little heed to efficiency as our practice. It has been a theory of non-professionalism in public affairs; and in many great matters of public action non-professionalism is non-efficiency.

(Wilson, 1901: 291)

For efficiency, the system—democratic self-government—needed to go or to be limited drastically. An area needed to be carved out that was free of the system of checks and balances between the branches, within the executive, that allowed for discretionary power free from direct electoral or judicial supervision.

> Our success is made doubtful by that besetting error of ours, the error of trying to do too much by vote. Self-government does not consist in having a hand in everything, any more than housekeeping consists necessarily in cooking dinner with one's own hands. The cook must be trusted with a large discretion as to the management of the fires and the ovens.

(Wilson, [1887]1941: 498)

The people would be given some say in the new model, but only on the terms granted by administrators, terms based on expert knowledge of "the best means." "Let administrative study find the best means for giving public criticism this control and for shutting it out from all other interference" (Wilson, [1887]1941: 499). Shutting it out of interference, judicial or political, was the goal.

The myths here are multiple, and they make up a more or less coherent whole. The "less" in the coherence is itself valuable: the various parts can be substituted for or need not even be mentioned in contexts where they are taken for granted, so this does not look like an ideology. The key idea is the incompetence of the people to govern themselves, and the consequent need for the delegation of authority to administrators, who possess expertise that is beyond the ken of the people. These administrators needed no supervision: merely by being given responsibility and discretionary power they would become paragons of apolitically. Without democratic control, and free from the interference of lawyers and courts, the government would become efficient. By giving up democratic control, and accepting the pale substitute of trust, "democracy" would be saved. No one needs to believe these myths. They simply need to be embodied in practice: political parties need to ignore the discretionary actions of administrators and thus give their tacit consent. Courts need to invent doctrines that enable them to deny relief to those who are injured by these acts. Politicians need to pass political problems off to "experts." Experts need to claim and thus take questions out of politics, with the tacit or explicit consent of politicians.

Populism and Democratic Theory

Wilson caught Populism in a basic practical contradiction: it wanted more government, but without bureaucrats, and without giving up electoral control. In a sense, this problem is a variant of the classic problem of the conflict between liberalism and democracy, in which a democratic vote can eliminate the freedoms that are a condition of a functioning democracy. The wishes of the people may lead them to what amounts to a practical contradiction. But these issues are intrinsic to democracy itself, in its original and core meaning. So is the problem of minorities:

> democracy as a majoritarian system of rule inevitably favors majorities over minorities, whether these are minorities of interest, opinion, or ethnicities with different opinions or interests than the majority. Much of the mythology of democracy involves the papering over of these hard facts.

Anti-populism is, like liberalism itself, anti-democratic. But liberal anti-populism relied on liberal means—on the rule of law and on constitutional restrictions on the state itself—to tie the hands of "the people." Liberalism is based on fear of the people. Left anti-populism or progressivism is also anti-democratic. It denigrates the people: the notions of false consciousness, misrecognition, and so forth are anti-democratic in the guise of anti-populism. But the guise is important; it allows anti-democratic ideas to be presented as "saving democracy," or true democracy, when it is in fact a means of expanding the power of the state, and its discretionary power, which can then be used for "progressive" ends.

Weber famously praised Gladstone for his ability to break out of the constraints of the party and speak directly to the people and promoted a constitutional design that was intended to maximize the possibility of this kind of leadership. He thought of this as the only means to control the bureaucracy, which parties would not do. Just as Weber viewed the fundamental form of democratic rule as plebiscitarian and wished to amplify plebiscitary possibilities and forms, the American populists endorsed "the legislative system known as the initiative and referendum" (National People's Party Platform, [1892]1966: 95). The point of anti-populism was to prevent the use of these means and restrict accountability even more—to the point that it was anti-democratic in the name of democracy.

Notes

1 This, in fact, is what writers like Philip Kitcher (2001) actually argue for.
2 Left Populism makes the same gestures, but in academic circles, at least there is a model of democratic transformational change in which structures and societal norms are dissolved in a moment of collective fusion, i.e., without leadership; see Wolin (1993, 1996).

The Ideology of Anti-Populism and the Administrative State   83

3   But not completely. Some issues were ignored or restructured. And populist senti-
    ment remained a distinctive feature of local politics in many places, a half-century
    after the movement itself expired; see Key (1949).
4   It is worth noting that in three decades, the gold standard was dead, on a worldwide
    basis.

References

Duby, G. *The Three Orders: Feudal Society Imagined*. Chicago: The University of Chi-
    cago Press, [1978]1980.
Hoxie, R. G. *A history of the Faculty of Political Science, Columbia University*. New
    York: Columbia University Press, 1955.
Key, V. O. *Southern Politics in State and Nation*. Knoxville: University of Tennessee
    Press, 1949.
Kitcher, P. *Science, Truth, and Democracy*. New York: Oxford University Press, 2001.
Laclau, E. *On Populist Reason*. London/New York: Verso, 2005.
Mansfield, H. "Was It Really a Myth? The Persistence of Individualism in America,"
    The Times Literary Supplement, 9 February, 1996 (Retrieved from The Times Liter-
    ary Supplement Historical Archive). www.the-tls.co.uk/archive/.
National People's Party Platform. "The Omaha Platform: National People's Party Plat-
    form," In *A Populist Reader: Selections from the Works of American Populist Lead-
    ers*, Edited by G. B. Tindall. New York: Harper and Row, 90–96, [1892]1966.
Okrent, D. *Last Call: The Rise and Fall of Prohibition*. New York: Simon and Schuster,
    2010.
Schmitt, C. *Constitutional Theory*. Durham: Duke University Press, [1928]2008.
Schmitt, C. *Legality and Legitimacy*. Durham: Duke University Press, [1932]2004.
Shipman, A., J. Edmunds, and B. S. Turner. *The New Power Elite: Inequality, Politics
    and Greed*. London/New York: Anthem Press, 2018.
Thomas, W. I., and D. S. Thomas. *The Child in America: Behavior Problems and Pro-
    grams*. New York: Knopf, 1928.
Turner, S. "The Pittsburgh Survey and the Survey Movement: An Episode in the His-
    tory of Expertise," In *Pittsburgh Surveyed: Social Science and Social Reform in the
    Early Twentieth Century*, Edited by M. W. Greenwald and M. Anderson. Pittsburgh:
    University of Pittsburgh Press, 35–39, 1996.
Turner, S. *The Politics of Expertise*. New York: Routledge, 2014.
Turner, S. "What is the Problem with Experts?" *Social Studies of Science* 31(1): 123–
    149, 2001.
Weber, M. *The City*. New York: The Free Press, [1921]1966.
Wilson, W. "Democracy and Efficiency," *Atlantic Monthly*, March, 1901. www.theat-
    lantic.com/magazine/archive/1901/03/democracy-and-efficiency/520041/.
Wilson, W. "The Study of Administration," *Political Science Quarterly* 56(4): 481–
    506, [1887]1941.
Wolin, S. "Democracy, Difference, and Recognition," *Political Theory* 21(3): 464–483,
    1993.
Wolin, S. "Fugitive Democracy," In *Democracy and Difference: Contesting the Bound-
    aries of the Political*, Edited by S. Benhabib. Princeton: Princeton University Press,
    31–45, 1996.
Zizek, S. "Against the Populist Temptation," *Critical Inquiry* 2(3): 551–574, 2006.

Part I

Free Speech, Pluralism, and Toleration

Chapter 5

Religious Pluralism, Toleration, and Liberal Democracy

Past, Present, and Future

Stephen Turner

The problem of the role of religion in contemporary politics is so deeply bound up with the history of the body of modern political thought that is at the basis of liberal democracy, that some discussion of this history is almost inevitable whenever the issue of religion and politics arises. One view of the history of liberalism, and indeed of the modern state, is that the edicts of toleration issued by the French monarchy during the French wars of religion (and subsequently revoked) were the kernels from which the modern secular state grew. Historians of these events are at pains to insist that the creation of such a state was the farthest thing from the minds of the monarchs and ministers who issued these edicts, and this is certainly true (Holt, 1995). They were pragmatic steps designed to bring about peace between the Protestants and the Catholics or to give the Church time to convert the Protestants back by peaceful means.

Peace in itself, however, was not the aim of the kings and ministers, but a means to an end. The end was to protect the French state from the consequences of religious civil violence. It was believed, probably quite correctly, that a state which failed to suppress extensive civil violence would cease to have authority and lose its power to command in the eyes of its subjects. More generally, it was feared that the state would perish in the violence that sectarian antagonism unleased. This was not an idle fear, given that foreign armies and private armies with powerful military leaders rapidly emerged in the course of the civil violence that we call the French wars of religion. The leaders of the factions and the army they represented, together with foreign allies, could very well overwhelm the powers of the monarch, as indeed they did in England in Cromwell's time.

For political theory, the situations in which the state is assessing the conditions for its own survival and acting with its remaining powers to assure its survival are politics at its ultimate defining point. Declaring a religiously motivated action to be forbidden on the grounds of state interest is a method of dealing with a certain class of problems. Edicts of toleration, supported, if need be, by force, are a political means to the end of survival. The idea of toleration is a part of the technical machinery of the modem state, and in what follows, the technical uses of toleration and a series of similar devices will be the focus of the discussion.

DOI: 10.4324/9781003360810-7

88 Stephen Turner

Toleration and Liberalism

The connection between this technical method and liberalism is quite direct. Liberalism and parliamentary democracy rely on and would not be possible without at least the availability of this and other methods of eliminating certain kinds of issues from the realm of politics. Toleration proceeds by criminalizing or forbidding certain classes of religiously motivated action against people with particular beliefs. Other techniques, I will show later, are available to liberalism; criminalization is an infrequent method in modern settled regimes. Nevertheless, it is used, and it is the possibility of criminalization and the use of state force to suppress religiously motivated action that is at the root of the more benign techniques that are ordinarily used.[1]

Modem states typically use two other techniques, each of which has a similar effect, which is to say, each removes the topic from the arena of politics and puts it into another category. The two techniques we may call "neutralization" and "establishing." They appear to be opposites, but in political terms, they serve similar purposes. The United States employs, with respect to religion, the technique of neutralization. The state attempts to be neutral between religions and more recently between religion and irreligion. The First Amendment is the embodiment of the Constitution's commitment to state neutrality with regard to religion and serves many of the same purposes as the edicts of toleration during the French wars of religion. The state, by refusing to establish any particular religion or to be biased toward any particular religion, assures that certain religious disputes, that is to say, disputes between religions, do not get expressed in the arena of politics. In theory, there is no incentive for a religious leader to become involved in the politics of a religiously neutral state for specifically "religious" purposes because the politics of the religiously neutral state are limited to nonreligious matters. One could not, except indirectly, advance the cause of one religion against another through a state that in its constitutional rules forbade the state to act preferentially toward a religion.

Curiously, establishing a religion has, under the right circumstances, similar effects. The establisher of the religion is the state, and the state sets the limit on what the religion can do politically. In the city of Uppsala, there is a striking bit of symbolism that underscores this relation. The city has a royal castle surrounded by cannons. Below the castle is a major cathedral beside the residence of the bishop. One of the cannons is aimed more or less directly at the bishop's residence. It was explained to me that this was intended as a constant reminder that the church was politically subordinate to the state. The effect of establishing a church, then, is not merely to state a preference for one church over others, but to remove the church as an independent political agent.

The church, acting within its domain, was "established" and free to govern its own affairs. But the domain was set by establishing power which simply delegated a particular domain of freedom to the church. This delegation has the effect of removing the business of the church from political consideration and as a result of the Supreme Court decision, has involved the claim of privacy, and it is curious, but not entirely surprising, that the religious Right and the feminist Left disagree on the issues but agree on the principle that there is no natural fact of privacy that limits state action and also on the principle that the limitation of state action to that which is subject to rational public persuasion is a limitation which runs contrary to their own deeply held beliefs. Both, in some forms at least, are thus fundamentally opposed to liberalism as an idea on the grounds that liberalism leads to fundamentally immoral results and that morality is not on the table to be negotiated in the public realm.

Mechanisms for Removing Issues From the Political Domain

I have now run together a quite complex series of ideas that will need some disentangling, but let me simply suggest how they could be disentangled and go on from that to a discussion of the more general problem of the future of liberalism in the face of these kinds of conflicts. The notion of privacy is deeply rooted in Western civilization. The idea that the state cannot forbid one to defend one's life, the right of self-defense, is ordinarily held to be a right that no legitimate legal system ought to abrogate, except under special and well-justified circumstances, such as criminal punishment or military orders, the cases in which we have chosen to sacrifice our human rights for the more limited but more secure benefits of civil rights. Nevertheless, as these exceptions suggest, these rights are not absolute and are not clearly fixed historically. The right of self-defense, notoriously, has shrunken from a right to protect one's belongings against any threat or apparent threat to a much more limited right to protect one's person against imminent destruction (Fletcher, 1978).

The limits of the private realm, to put it simply, are decided politically. The other devices of liberalism I have listed here are equally a matter of politics, even though the political decisions we make with respect to these devices are unusual ones. They are not temporary compromises constantly up for renegotiation but compromises that become givens of the political discussion itself, at least for a time. They are taken to be not open to continuous challenges in the course of political discussion. All of them, including such basic decisions as the one to accept the results of scientific opinion on matters deemed scientific (and decisions about what is to be deemed scientific), are political. But they are political in a special sense. They require a much higher threshold of acceptance in order to serve their fundamental discussion-limiting role. It may be, for example, that the flat-earth society has adherents and that a large number of Baptists reject evolution. But we do not therefore treat these as topics for political discussion and take away from scientists the role as neutral arbitrators that we usually grant them.

Let me briefly review the argument to this point. Liberalism requires reasoned persuasion in public discussion and liberal parliamentary democracy does this with representatives who are open to reasoned persuasion. The realm of issues that can be processed through reasoned discussion is limited. Consequently, there needs to be a means, or several means, by which reasoned discussion is protected from the effects of, or the need to make decisions about, issues that cannot be made subject to reasoned persuasion. Some issues obviously may remain unsettled and not require a decision. They can be relegated to the "private" realm, and we can agree to disagree about their morality, recognizing that we are unable to agree on civic action with respect to them. Or we can disagree about whether to disagree, but keep this disagreement from affecting the discussion of other issues. The problems arise with issues that must be settled, but cannot be settled through the reasoned persuasion of representatives, and with unsettleable disagreements that cannot be separated from the rest of the discussion.

The devices by which such issues are removed from public discussion operate in different and specific ways. Issues do not come, so to speak, pre-labeled in categories like "open to rational resolution" and "not open to rational resolution," or even "religious" and "nonreligious." A considerable portion of the law on these matters in fact assumes, for example, that religion is a natural and unproblematic category so that the courts can easily determine that what the state is establishing or failing to establish is in fact a religion. As I have suggested, parallel to the case of science, the decision of what constitutes a religion or religious action is a political decision, though it may be made by courts, and, similarly, decisions about what is criminal and what is not are political decisions.

The case of bigamy among Mormons is a case in point; the criminalization of the consumption of alcohol during Prohibition is another. Prohibition involved a constitutional amendment. The admission of Utah to the Union also involved a decision that required more than mere majority rule. These mundane constitutional facts reflect a much more fundamental fact that holds for all of these techniques of flushing unsettleable disputes from the political system or protecting public discussion from these unsettleable disputes, and that is this: the agreements that allow for the use of these techniques require a much higher level of consensus than ordinary political discussions. If we agree that something is a private matter, for example, if we agree to disagree on the morality of something, we agree to remove it from political discussion. But people can refuse to agree to disagree and insist that the issue remains a matter of political discussion. It takes more than a majority vote to deal with this kind of refusal to disagree. The use of the authority of science, for example, in expert testimony in courtrooms and to settle disputes involving the appropriate regulation of pollution, involves a general consensus as to what science is and requires a general respect for science. As I have suggested, this need not be absolute, but it must be pretty overwhelming in order for us to remove scientific issues from the political realm and treat them as facts to be taken for granted by the state and by political discussion.

Making Formerly "Private" Issues "Public"

Religion has played a prominent and dramatic role in challenging or establishing these "high-threshold" matters of consensus. Issues like abortion arise and have destructive effects on public discourse primarily because they involve these borderline disputes which the system of rational persuasion and compromise cannot handle and which then need to be removed from public discussion by some "high-threshold" means. In itself, abortion is the sort of issue that might be left unsettled for a long period, and the question of its publicness or privacy might be discussed for a long time. However, abortion and many of the other unsettled issues do not ordinarily exist on their own and are separate from other questions. They are connected to and often come to represent cultural stands or religious understandings of life and thus raise a special problem for liberal discussion, especially when the viewpoints they are connected to are viewpoints that it has been agreed are not the proper part of public discussion or civic action, such as particular sectarian religious beliefs. If one's opponents on a given issue are characterized as evil, for example, it will become impossible to hold serious discussions with them on other issues.

Religion also has a positive role to play in forming new "high-threshold" consensuses in which formerly private issues become matters for public discourse. But in the case of liberal democracy, it has been a somewhat problematic role. The nineteenth-century consensus on what divided public and private with respect to religion was itself rooted in religion, in the saying of Jesus to "render unto Caesar that which is Caesar's," and particularly in Protestant notions about individual conscience and the individual character of a relationship to God, which could be used as the basis for a kind of mutual respect of private life and belief. "Rooted in" does not mean "determined by," for the same religious ideas sometimes allowed for much in the way of intrusion by religious authorities. In the Reformation, the idea of reform was meant to entail the reform of society as well as religion, and thinkers like Calvin and John Knox, when they attained power, had no scruples about persecuting those they believed to be sinners.

I suspect that there was a kind of flattening of denominational differences with respect to these issues in the nineteenth century in the United States. The Great Awakening was a moment at which many Americans changed their denominational affiliations to affiliations that they found to be more consistent with their religious feelings. The westward expansion led to the creation of religious communities with members from diverse denominational backgrounds. The shuffling of denominations helped to strengthen the political commonalities of American Protestantism by bringing together in the same churches persons with divergent but not irreconcilable attitudes toward authority and toward such things as public/private distinctions.

To the extent that there are close connections between religious ideas over which there is no consensus and political disputes which because of their connection to these religious ideas are not processable through reasoned persuasion, religious pluralism is a threat to liberal democracy.

One need only look at truly sectarian societies, such as Ulster, to see what happens when religious identity defines political loyalty. If the mechanisms for flushing religiously motivated issues out of the public domain cannot work, and cannot work because they require a high-threshold consensus which religious groups or other groups are actively attempting to undermine, then the mechanisms necessary to the preservation of something for liberal democracy to be about will break down and eventually the appearance of public discussion and persuasion becomes sham. Public life becomes instead a domain for expressive politics and stand taking. Political violence, in the form of arson, assassinations, and killings of opponents, not infrequently follows close on the heels of this kind of expressive politics.

But expressive politics sometimes works: the protests against the war in Vietnam made the war into a political issue rather than a test of loyalty. Opposition was not only, so to speak, decriminalized, the opponents carried the day once the war became a political issue. As a political issue, it had to be settled, and it was—in favor of the protesters. The civil rights movement, in its integrationist phase, worked in a similar way: the formerly accepted fact of segregation in the southern states was moved from the margins of politics, from the status of an issue that people had agreed to disagree about, to the status of an issue that could be addressed through civic action. Religious leaders and religious appeals had a prominent role in both movements, of course. In these cases, then, the process of removing issues from the public realm worked in reverse: formerly "private" topics were made into public topics, subjects for civic action, and more importantly, subjects for public discussion and persuasion. In the case of the abortion issue, the process of moving the issue into either a status in which we agree to disagree or a meaningful political discussion has not yet worked, but this is the point of the effort: to persuade people that it is, or is not, a proper subject for political discussion and civic action.

Religious Pluralism and the Schoolhouses of Liberalism

We now arrive at a somewhat peculiar set of puzzles, partly raised by the facts, and partly raised by the interpretations placed upon them by others. The first is this: is religious pluralism compatible with liberal democracy? One answer based on fact is that it is not, and the present experience of Islamic societies, the fact of sectarian violence in Ulster, and the long history of religious warfare in Europe show that it is not. Liberal democracy, this history suggests, requires in practice an established church or its de facto equivalent, and not merely toleration. Nineteenth-century America probably represents, at least in retrospect, the de facto equivalent of an established church. Protestant sects agreed to treat the differences between them as matters of no concern to the state and agreed on the dividing line between religion and the state. But they also agreed on a great deal about what else was of concern to the state and what was not. Without a religiously based consensus of this sort (which may, as it has in the United States, become part of the secular understanding of the relation between religion and politics), it is difficult to see how the mechanisms of removing unsettleable disputes from politics could work, and why politics would not inevitably degenerate into sectarian civil war.

The problem arises in part as a result of the theories we use to think through the problem of the character of religiously motivated politics. If religions are incompatible worldviews, we have no reason to suppose that liberal politics in the sense I have discussed here is possible if it is conducted between persons who hold these incompatible views. By definition, worldviews have premises that are beyond the reach of rational persuasion. Put simply, if we take these accounts of the relation between religion and politics seriously, liberal democracy is incompatible with liberal democracy, unless the religious conceptions in question happen, by happy accident, not to produce the kinds of conflicts that liberal democracies cannot resolve. Yet liberal democracies have not, for the most part, collapsed into sectarian civil violence. Civil violence motivated by religious conflicts has indeed occurred and did in the United States in the case of each of the three movements discussed earlier. But the authors of civil violence were marginalized and treated as criminals. It did not lead to massive sectarian counter-violence or to a descent into political sectarianism of the sort found in Ulster or the French wars of religion. In what follows, I will try to explain why. Part of the explanation is simple. Secularization, in Europe, has relegated the problem to conflicts between the secularized public and religious minorities, whose conduct becomes, by wide consensus, a police problem. The American situation is somewhat different. But to understand this difference, it is necessary to locate it in a somewhat broader picture of the social and political implications and relations of religion.

One of the most striking differences between political orders is to be found in the nature of the "political" experiences available to people outside of politics. An influential view of the French Revolution traced the rise of the revolutionary representative bodies to a long tradition of debate within Masonic lodges (Furêt, 1981). Whatever the ultimate validity of this interpretation, it fits with a fact that is obvious to anyone who has looked at the development of social and political institutions: practically operating political forms, such as functioning parliamentary democracies, are not isolated or anomalous institutions but function in much the same way as other bodies in the same society. In American life, for example, there are literally thousands and thousands of voluntary organizations each of which makes decisions and has a structure of elections, representation, compromise between interests, the articulation of common goals, and so on and so forth that directly parallels the structure of the national political system and the various smaller political units. One's "political" experience in the United States is thus not at all limited to voting but is likely to include participation in the PTA, Little League, and so forth.

It will also include, of course, experience in church politics. Indeed, one can hardly underestimate the importance, in the nineteenth century and before, of church polity both as a schoolhouse of democracy and as a source of conflicting political habits and attitudes to authority. The former names and some present names of denominations are the names of their form of church polity; the grex, the flock, is the political authority for Congregationalism, just as the presbytery and episcopate are for Presbyterianism and Episcopalianism. If one observed the situation at independence, one might have predicted that the various denominations, each with a different relation to authority, and some quite used to exercising state powers, would produce a political collision. For various reasons, notably, the revulsion against things English and the willingness of the religious leaders of New England to give up some of their political authority, the collision did not occur (Bryce, [1888]1910). Religious groups gave up their political powers, and religious tests for office were abolished. In the nineteenth century itself, a kind of homogenization of attitudes toward the public/private sphere emerged. Perhaps, this was in large part a consequence of the fact that people with different denominational origins came to worship together and more importantly to participate in the decision-making processes of churches together. In any case, Protestants with different denominational origins were thrown together in various ways, both within church polities and within the public realm. And they were forced to become more cognizant of differences, and, given their own religious ideas, were led to regard the differences as legitimate matters of conscience and thus "private." Why is this significant? The collision that should have happened did not. The theory of religions as incompatible worldviews with irreconcilable political implications would have predicted that the religious diversity of nineteenth-century America would have collapsed the public realm, the realm of reasoned persuasion of representatives essential to liberal democracy, into sectarian conflict. The public/private distinction would never have developed because the propriety and application of the distinction are themselves subject to religiously rooted disagreement. Yet a functioning consensus on the limits of religion in politics did develop.

This nineteenth-century history suggests a process by which such consensuses do develop. People acting together for common purposes, religious or secular, must come to some sort of accommodation of the fact that they hold beliefs that differ if they are to work together and live together. They do so by accepting the legitimacy of differences and relegating the differences to the "private" realm. And they protect the public realm and the possibility of reasoned persuasion in the public realm from the consequences of the fact that people have different religious views by doing so. The important fact about this process of the mutual recognition of religious legitimacy is that it is nonpolitical. It is a basis for tolerance in something other than the political need of the state to suppress civil violence.

As I have suggested, this mechanism serves the purposes that liberal democracy requires, of moving unsettlable topics off the political agenda by underwriting agreements to disagree. The problem with this mechanism is that there is no guarantee that it will work. But there are conditions that increase the probability of it working and conditions that make it less likely to work.[2] Residential and communal segregation, for example, limits the number and kinds of cooperative ventures that teach the lessons of toleration. But serious political purposes relating to the society as a whole require going beyond local religiously segregated communities and going beyond sectarian limits. Thus, we arrive at a paradox: religiously motivated attempts to transform society in a particular image, at least in the United States, compel their adherents to cooperate with and build coalitions with others whose religious views differ. And this holds even when, and perhaps especially when, the particular policy or political aim, whether it is the prohibition of abortion or civil rights, is in the pile of issues that lie outside the domain of ordinary rational persuasion and have been removed, by agreement, from the continuing conversation of liberal democracy. So, these movements tend to become schoolhouses of toleration, though quite unintentionally.

The pro-life movement is a case in point. Who would have imagined, 50 years ago, that a coalition would emerge between the Catholic Church and Protestant fundamentalists in which large numbers of the laity and clergy of each group would cooperate on a continuous basis in a common public endeavor? Yet this is precisely what has happened, and as a consequence, the lesson of toleration—the mutual acceptance of religious legitimacy—has been learned by both sides. The tactical necessity of cooperation, in short, has had consequences of the same kind as occurred in nineteenth-century Protestantism. This new tolerance does not resolve the issue at hand. But it changes the conditions under which future issues become located in relation to the conversation of liberal democracy, for it assures that some differences on which we have agreed to disagree will remain "private," under the umbrella of religious differences mutually recognized to be legitimate alternatives. And it may also lead to alterations in the scope of what is accepted as public, for example, in rewriting the limitations on public subsidy of "religious" schools.

Into the Next Century

The lessons of political toleration with which I began this discussion were very painfully learned. They can certainly be forgotten. But they are less likely to be forgotten in a society in which the habit of toleration is learned and sustained in the "political" experiences of individuals in such organizations as the PTA and

98 Stephen Turner

Little League, and even, paradoxically, in such movements as the right-to-life movement. The sheer fact of religious diversity, indeed, provides a kind of assurance that the lesson of toleration will always be there to be learned and relearned. In the private realm, little can be accomplished by relying only on the religiously like-minded because the number of truly religiously like-minded in an era of religious pluralism will always be small. Thus, in a way, pluralism provides a kind of protection against the potential for sectarian political fanaticism of its various elements. But this is true only in societies in which there is a vital sector of intermediate institutions such as the PTA, or social movements, in which these lessons can be learned. In those societies without such institutions, such as those of the Islamic world, or societies in which such institutions are religiously differentiated, such as Northern Ireland, the habits of toleration are not learnable and the more brutal lessons of civil war must be taught instead.

Liberal democracy, as I have suggested, is more fragile than state authority. It requires effective mechanisms for moving issues in and out of the realm of political discussion. Religious motivations have played a large role in this process of moving issues from public to private and from private to public. But the religious motivations have, so far at least, been altered by the experience of cooperation in such a way that no issue has yet been forced onto the political agenda that ends the possibility of the rational persuasion of representatives. Because of the process of "privatization" and mutual recognition of religious legitimacy between political allies, religious diversity is a kind of protector of liberal democracy, for it assures that no sectarian movement can succeed without shedding much of its sectarian intolerance.

Notes

1   In United States in the nineteenth century, there was a clear instance of the state suppression of the religious practice of bigamy by the Mormons. Criminalization, of course, is not a mere matter of passing laws. It must represent, as it did in this case, a strong or, as I am calling it here, "high-threshold" consensus.
2   The curious history of the Catholic Church's response to these necessities in twentieth-century America reflects the recognition of the hierarchy that membership in voluntary organizations would lead to toleration, and large efforts were made to create Catholic alternatives to these organizations, such as the Knights of Columbus as a Catholic alternative to the Masons, or Catholic enclaves within them, such as Catholic Boy Scout Troops. These efforts were helped by residential segregation in large cities. But in the end, the efforts were fruitless and the laity accepted the nineteenth-century Protestant consensus on the public/private distinction and indeed on the role of conscience, thus making the American Church and American Catholicism into a source of considerable anxiety to the Vatican.

References

Bryce, James. *The American Commonwealth*, 2 vols. London/New York: Macmillan and Co. [1888]1910. https://oll.libertyfund.org//title/mcdowell-the-american-commonwealth-2-vols

Fletcher, G. P. *Rethinking Criminal Law*. Boston/Toronto: Little, Brown and Company, 1978.

Furêt, François. *Interpreting the French Revolution*. Cambridge: Cambridge University Press, 1981.

Holt, Mack P. *The French Wars of Religion, 1552–1629*. Cambridge: Cambridge University Press, 1995.

Nussbaum, Martha. *Times Higher Education Supplement*, 2 February, 1996, 17–18.

Polanyi, Michael. *The Logic of Liberty: Reflections and Rejoinders*. Chicago: University of Chicago Press, 1951.

Price, Don K. *The Scientific Estate*. Cambridge: Belknap Press of Harvard University Press, 1965.

Schmitt, Carl. *Political Theology*. Cambridge: MIT Press, [1934]1985.

Schmitt, Carl. *The Crisis of Parliamentary Democracy*. Cambridge: MIT Press, [1926] 1985.

Chapter 6

The End of Clear Lines
Academic Freedom and Administrative Law

Stephen Turner

In this chapter, I will focus on the legal structures and quasi-legal regulatory structures that relate to academic freedom, in addition to the basic theory that applies to them. My aim is to explain (1) how changes in them affect academic freedom, (2) the legal properties of the new constraints under which those in the academy operate, and (3) the differences between this current situation and academic freedom as it has traditionally been understood. The primary issues I will be concerned with are discretionary legal and administrative power and the way that regulations, as implemented by universities, have expanded this power, as well as the enlarged role of contract law and employment contracts as protections of academic freedom. Academic freedom is undergoing a redefinition in the face of new legal circumstances. Its two traditional dimensions are the higher education institutions' autonomy from the state and the individual freedom of scholars. It was traditionally thought that independence from the state and the existence of strong faculty governance were the best guarantors of academic freedom (Tiede, 2015). The American Association of University Professors (MUP) fought for both. Academic freedom, however, is increasingly restricted by regulations implemented by universities, which can take the form of institutional review boards, research misconduct tribunals, and Title IX enforcement. Because many federal regulations governing institutions of higher education are themselves vague and broad, the specific rules created by these institutions are a result of discretionary power over academics that is inimical to the traditional notion of academic freedom as a well-defined right. The idea of university autonomy, similarly, has undergone important changes. It has been significantly compromised as a result of federal regulation of a kind that did not exist in the first half of the twentieth century. One effect of intensified federal regulation is self-monitoring within higher education institutions (often with the assistance of an internal bureaucratic office) that seeks not only to conform to these externally imposed rules but also to invent local variations that expand on them.

DOI: 10.4324/9781003360810-8

The Basic Legal Situation

There are several kinds of law that interact in cases of academic freedom: (1) statutory law, or law created by legislation; (2) constitutional law, which authorizes or limits the power of legislatures; (3) case law, which is created by judges through decisions that become precedents for other judicial decisions and follow legal or constitutional principles; (4) contract law, which bears on academic freedom, because the relation between professors and their university is defined by an employment contract; and (5) administrative law, which is the "law" created by bureaucrats that specifies and interprets legislation, as well as regulates the actions of the government itself and (indirectly) the actions of bodies, such as universities, that are expected to conform to administrative regulations. Many federal regulations compel institutions of higher education to produce their own internal regulations and leave them open to sanctions if they do not.[1] Theoretically, these directives are grounded in actual statutory law. But the interpretation of the law by the agencies, and by the organizations implementing their own regulations, often strays far from the text and the original intent of the law. The procedures that directly govern faculty members are those of the university itself. The ones to be discussed here, involving equal opportunity, research misconduct, and a review of research to conform to ethical standards, are responses to federal administrative law—i.e., to the law contained in directives, definitions, and "letters of guidance" provided by federal agencies-and are motivated in part by the threat of litigation or a withholding of funds. The procedures for implementing the directives in different academic institutions typically meet neither ordinary legal standards of predictability, transparency, or the equitable treatment of persons, nor are they required to do so. In law, they are viewed as an extension of the rights of employers to govern their employees as they see fit. But the contractual relation between universities and their employees itself has limits, and one of the features of the present situation is that these boundaries are being reached, making employment law the new arena for academic freedom issues.

The historical legal strategy of the MUP, in its attempts to define academic freedom, was to delineate it as a contractual relation between higher education institutions and individual faculty members, in order to offer protections beyond those of ordinary employment law. The goal was to provide a definition of academic freedom that mimicked the form of law itself, rather than merely specifying an ideal. This meant establishing clear distinctions that could be appealed to by the MUP to condemn and sanction universities and colleges for administrative actions inconsistent with academic freedom. Clarity in these distinctions served various purposes: it assured the credibility of the actions; provided guidelines for university administrators; protected the MUP from charges of partisanship and inconsistency; and, perhaps most importantly, linked the notion of academic freedom to the legal idea of due process and the value of legal certainty. Thus, this framework also aligned with one way in which courts decide cases—by striking down laws that are "unconstitutionally vague."

But the AAUP does not enact law, and its definitions are not law. The strategy was to assert certain rights for faculty, yet these were rights that went beyond anything codified in law. By describing correct standards, the AAUP could establish what Continental legal theory calls "customary law." Actual courts could defer to these standards in the name of normal and accepted practice when the term "academic freedom" appeared in employment contracts or handbooks. The AAUP standards thus served to provide a definition of the concept and of standard practice with a quasi-legal meaning (i.e., a bright-line rule) and the marks of legality in its own processes (a quasi-judicial process of inquiry). In addition, they carried the mark of law: a regime of sanctions applied by the AAUP itself, in the form of notifications to the scholarly community that a university was not in compliance.

The basic idea of the AAUP statements on the academic freedom of individuals (as distinct from the academic freedom of institutions from state interference), which have undergone only minor revision, is that:

> Teachers are entitled to full freedom in research and in the publication of the results, subject to the adequate performance of their other academic duties.
>
> Teachers are entitled to freedom in the classroom in discussing their subject, but they should be careful not to introduce into their teaching controversial matter that has no relation to their subject.
>
> College and university teachers are citizens, members of a learned profession, and officers of an educational institution. When they speak or write as citizens, they should be free from institutional censorship or discipline, but their special position in the community imposes special obligations. As scholars and educational officers, they should remember that the public may judge their profession and their institution by their utterances.
>
> (AAUP, 1940)

This definition had two elements: (1) professional autonomy, or freedom of teaching and research within the limits of the professional activities of the faculty member, and (2) freedom of speech and action as a citizen outside the classroom. In the past, virtually all academic freedom issues, including those that motivated the original formulations of these principles in 1915 (AAUP, [1915]2015), fell into two categories: governance issues involving the freedom of colleges themselves (e.g., those regarding the interference of governing bodies) and the rights of academics as citizens (particularly issues of freedom of speech).

Citizen speech had a problematic legal status. Standard employment law does not protect free speech in the broad sense envisioned by the AAUP standards. Public speech deleterious to the interests of the employer can be sanctioned by employers, more or less at their discretion. They are free to protect their interests, as they understand them, by firing employees within some reasonably limited notion of harm. This contractual right overrides the freedom to speak guaranteed by the First Amendment and directly conflicts with the right to be "free from institutional censorship or discipline," as asserted by the AAUP. This special academic right is something the courts have never directly established, though there are no clear cases rejecting it, either. None of the standard First Amendment cases in employment law concerns professors.

A few, notably Pickering (1968), relate to teachers.[2] In cases involving professors, courts have typically evaded the issue by deciding the cases on other grounds, for example, by pointing to the violation of a different rule to which the professor was bound as part of the employment relationship (Svrluga, 2017) or rejecting the action of the university on the grounds that it was in violation of the employment contract.

In one recent case involving extramural speech, a jury trial found for the university against a fired tenured professor who, on a blog, asserted a conspiracy theory about the Sandy Hook shootings. The institution successfully argued that he had lied to them about his "use of university resources" for his blog and "repeatedly and intentionally refused to file mandatory disclosure forms that require all professors to reveal outside work and activities that could affect their work or the university." Though the trial showed that this policy was inconsistently applied, the professor lost the case (Ramadan, 2016; McMahon, 2017). The greater bureaucratization of higher education institutions and the vast expansion of rules of this kind pose new risks for faculty. These rules provide multiple occasions for their violation and many issues of interpretation. Under the law, employers have wide discretion in interpreting their own rules. The proliferation of vague language in them creates greater discretionary power for administrators, who can use them against faculty members they choose to punish while avoiding overt challenges to academic freedom.

The core of academic freedom, freedom within the classroom and in professional writing, has no direct constitutional standing and no basis in federal law. It does, however, have an indirect existence in employment law. The courts acknowledge it as a "good" that is distinctive to the academic setting and indirectly affirm it as the basis of the contractual understandings governing academics; the thought being that the meaning of an employment contract is determined in part by normal practices in the field in question. But there is sometimes a more direct and stronger legal basis. To the extent that professors are protected, this occurs under the heading of employment law: for doing their job according to their employment contract, as other types of employees are. State law and state university charters also sometimes guarantee academic freedom, and faculty handbooks asserting academic freedom have intermittently been held to be legally binding.

104 Stephen Turner

Employment cases have not, however, produced a body of case law. Case law is limited in this area, for a simple reason. Academic lawsuits that come before courts and juries tend to produce surprising results because they are handled in terms of non-academic understandings of the same practices. Those in the professoriate avoid court cases because they are typically advised that juries react to suits where an employee disobeys an employer by affirming that one should do what the boss says. Precedent-establishing legal cases involving academics are thus rare. Ordinarily, out-of-court settlements are negotiated. Partly, this is to avoid litigation expenses. In addition, it is because the courts have not been terribly respectful of standard academic practices that are consequently unpredictable when cases involving them arise, which poses a risk for both sides. For example, in dealing with publishers, one ordinarily signs a document asserting that one holds the rights to the book or paper one is publishing and that the work was not done "for hire," which would mean that the rights would belong to the employer. A decision involving Brown University, however, addressed this question (Foraste, 2003), and the judge found that academic publication was "for hire"—contrary to the documents academics routinely sign for publishers. The practice did not change, though some problematic legal documents were created by universities to release these rights to the professorial authors—but not without reserving for themselves final authority over the disposition of the work in question.

The California Oath Case

The University of California loyalty oath controversy was the most important academic freedom case of the twentieth century in the United States. It can serve as a baseline for understanding what has changed in the legal atmosphere of the university. The case began with two incidents that fell under the second area of academic freedom defined by the AAUP. Three professors were fired from the University of Washington in January 1949 for having Communist sympathies: Herbert Phillips, Joe Butterworth, and Ralph Gundlach (Lange, 1999; Schrecker, 1999). The UCLA Graduate Student Assembly received permission to host a debate featuring Phillips ("Prelude to Controversy," 1949). He was invited to speak at the Los Angeles campus of the university, which was not then a separate institution, as the Berkeley and Los Angeles faculty were nominally one unit. When the invitation was made public, members of the institution's Board of Regents moved to stop it.

The California state constitution "required [the University of California] to be free of all sectarian or partisan influences" (Gardner, 1967: 15). This is a formulation of a fundamental principle of liberal democracy: the political neutrality of the state. The rules implementing this provision were understood by the provost to mean that controversial views could be presented, but only if both sides were represented. Despite the fact that the event was structured as a debate, the Regents expressed concern that the university was being used

The End of Clear Lines   105

for propaganda purposes (Gardner, 1967: 24). In response, the administration was led to "strengthen" both the prohibitions against using the university as a platform for propaganda and the existing loyalty oath. Accepting the oath was already a condition of employment for all state employees.

The oath became the issue. Faculty who were opposed rejected the addition to the existing oath, which was an affirmation that the oath-taker did not believe in and was not a member of an organization advocating the overthrow of the US government. The Communist party was the only relevant example of such an organization (Gardner, 1967: 26). The initial skirmish over the oath involved a graduate student instructor. In response, the body representing these non-faculty employees called for the elimination of political tests for appointments. The objections of the faculty, however, hinged on tenure and focused on the slogan "academic freedom does not exist where the right of tenure is not inviolate" (Gardner, 1967: 121). There was also a due process objection because refusals to sign the new oath could lead to firings "without the Regents ever bothering to investigate whether these men are in fact communists or otherwise disloyal" (Gardner, 1967: 122).

The controversy ended with a long-delayed censure of the administration by the AAUP (Gardner, 1967: 208–10), and a court case in which the California Supreme Court ruled that the Regents had invaded the authority of the legislature by its actions. The court ordered the Regents to appoint the non-signers of the new oath who had already signed the oath required of all state employees (Gardner, 1967: 242–44). The principles at stake in this case were eventually affirmed in a decisive federal court case (Keyishian, 1967), in which the court ruled that requiring faculty to sign a document asserting that they were not and had not been Communists was a violation of First Amendment rights and was also "vague and overbroad." This case produced the standard text on which legal appeals of academic freedom have since relied:

> Our nation is deeply committed to safeguarding academic freedom, which is of transcendent value to all of us and not merely to the teachers concerned. That freedom is therefore a special concern of the First Amendment, which does not tolerate laws that cast a pall of orthodoxy over the classroom . . . The classroom is peculiarly the "marketplace of ideas." The nation's future depends upon leaders trained through wide exposure to that robust exchange of ideas which discovers truth "out of a multitude of tongues," [rather] than through any kind of authoritative selection.
>
> (Keyishian, 1967)

This is a succinct formulation of what we might dub the "liberal theory of academic freedom,"[3] and the participants in the oath controversy also adhered to it; namely, scholars were independent and beholden only to truth and their conscience in the pursuit of truth. As autonomous scholars, they were protected by the inviolability of tenure and free to make their own choices in the face of

106 Stephen Turner

the actual diversity of thought in a competitive marketplace of ideas (at a time when the research was not yet grant dependent). The customs of the university, such as tenure and non-sectarianism, were to serve to protect this freedom. Although the issues in this controversy were complex, they involved statutes and bright lines, such as the inviolability of tenure and due process. The acts of the administrators were simple and objective: the Regents threatened dismissal for failure to sign a piece of paper.

The First Amendment and Employment Law

The liberal theory of academic freedom was thus endorsed by the courts in the *Keyishian* case cited earlier. The courts, however, did not create a novel right to academic freedom but instead appealed to the First Amendment as the source of the right to reject the loyalty oath. The First Amendment has also played a role in many subsequent cases, but it is not as helpful as might be expected, because, in general, one gives up many of one's rights in an employment relationship, including much of one's free-speech rights. There is case law in the instance of state institutions, and it is clear: "Statements public employees make as part of their official duties are not protected under the First Amendment; thus, it does not protect employees who make them from disciplinary actions" (Norman-Eady, 2006). The concern motivating this ruling comes from the consideration that "without some control over employees' words and actions, a government entity could not provide services efficiently or effectively." Nonetheless, there is an important exception to this general rule. Speech that does not impair services is protected if it is in fact speech as a citizen "about matters of public concern" (Norman-Eady, 2006). The difficulty with this rule comes in drawing a line between citizen speech and speech related to duties.

The controlling case law is itself surprisingly narrow in its view of citizen speech. The *Garcetti* case involved a deputy prosecutor who was fired for concluding, as part of his duties, that an affidavit was flawed and testifying for the defense after the district attorney decided to prosecute the case anyway. The employee claimed that his speech was protected citizen speech because it met the test of public concern. The court ruled against this claim. Truth was not a defense. Justice Stevens, in a dissent, commented that this meant there was no protection for speech that "is just unwelcome speech because it reveals facts that the supervisor would rather not have anyone else discover" (Garcetti, 2006; Kaplin and Lee, 2013: 384–85).

Would *Garcetti* apply to professors who are state employees? There is no definitive case involving professors that would protect those who made public statements against the positions taken by a university. Moreover, there is little ground for thinking that an exception would be made. Employment law would protect professors from arbitrary actions by their university in violation of the contract with them as employees, but not from punishment for opposing the will of, or doctrines endorsed by, that institution. We will see an example of the use of this power in a later section (on Title IX). Although such power is not extensively invoked, there are few limitations on its use, and that, in itself, has a potentially chilling effect on speech. There is no clear line between "public" speech critical of a university's policies and speech that is disruptive of that institution's mission and, thus, punishable.

Administrative Law and Academic Freedom

Administrative law is law made in the form of rules and other authoritative pronouncements by bodies that are part of the executive branch and by judicial interpretations that modify these rules. It is not law in the sense of incurring judicial penalties. The penalties are administrative, based on the idea that an agency can regulate bodies with whom they have a contractual relationship. For example, universities enter into this type of relationship by accepting federal funds, directly or indirectly, such as through governmental loans to their students for tuition.

The rules implement and specify the legislation on which they are based. The core laws relating to higher education institutions include Title IX (the federal law against sex discrimination, which is implemented through regulations that universities are required to create); federal law relating to the responsible conduct of research (which is governed within the academy by institutional review boards); and laws against research misconduct (which are further specified by university regulations and dealt with by procedures the institutions create). Each will be discussed in the following.

Federal agencies implement these laws by developing rules that are more specific than the initiating legislation. There is a legislative basis for this practice in the 1945 Administrative Procedure Act, which specifies formal procedures for rule making and public input and requires a degree of transparency. Agencies may have their own court-like, quasi-judicial structures to try cases involving these rules. The legal basis for this activity is the judicial finding that agencies have "the power to construe" legislation. There is, however, no direct constitutional basis for this kind of law or power, and, indeed, sub-delegation of legislative powers is forbidden by the constitution. The courts have evaded this restriction by claiming that the agencies, in their rule making, are merely defining terms in the law. The grounds for permitting agencies to construe the law are that the legislature, by failing to be specific, grants discretion to the agencies to do so (Strauss, 1989: 22–23). This is itself an oddity-traditional legal thinking that ambiguity in the law grants discretion to the courts. Thus, in the US context, the doctrine of deference amounts to a grant by the judiciary of their authority to agencies. We can leave aside the vexing question of whether judicial recognition and deference to these agencies are constitutionally justified (Hamburger, 2014, 2017), or whether the administrative law "courts" are genuine courts, but it is important to note that there is a fundamental issue here over the nature and legitimacy of authority. Judicial deference to the agencies, except in cases of clear failures of due process or other egregious errors, is a revocable judicial choice, not a constitutionally specified feature of the power of agencies or the executive branch.

The body of rules in administrative law today exceeds the body of federal legislation by a factor of ten. Yet the published rules are only part of the story. There is much more law making by agencies in the forms of "guidance," definitions, and authoritative interpretation of the statutes themselves. These activities are not subject to the restrictions on rule making, and the mere fact of selective enforcement of the rules requires the bodies subject to them to infer "the law" from the practices of the agency. Statute law is subject to legal construction, based on the explicit language of the statute, and, if this fails, on legislative intent. The courts, however, have treated administrative law differently, by introducing the element of "purpose." The discretionary power of agencies to issue rules in accordance with the supposed purpose of the legislation was affirmed in an opinion stating that "Title IX must [be] accord[ed] . . . a sweep as broad as its language" to realize its goals of eliminating discrimination and promoting equal opportunity (North Haven, 1982; see also Dickerson, 1983). In the case of Title IX, which merely forbids discrimination, the effect of agency and court decisions is to warrant precisely the opposite of the law. "Affirmative action" (the result of an additional executive order), which evolved, after litigation, into discrimination in the name of "diversity"—a doctrine unmentioned in the law—can be used to justify the favorable treatment of historically disadvantaged groups.

Universities are obligated to regulate themselves by issuing rules and implementing those devised by the agencies. They are granted discretion, however, in constructing their own regulations to enforce the rules, in accordance with the purpose of the law. A higher education institution is not limited by the law-it can introduce its own, more restrictive rules as part of its rights as an employer. The attitude of universities, to quote one official at my own institution, is that federal regulations are "the floor," or the minimum, and there may be compelling interest in going beyond the minimum in constructing the regulations within a university that academics must follow. This means that university policies implementing the law and the administrative extensions of the law may vary substantially from one university to another and, like administrative law itself, create their own quasi-legal procedures for appeal, sanction, and the like. The role of a federal agency in relation to these internal university regulations becomes one of reviewing policies for conformity to the agency's construal of the law.

Courts may play a role if the approved policy conflicts with other explicit rights, including contractual rights that are part of the employment relationship. One place in which policies based on Title IX have come into conflict with academic freedom concerns anti-harassment policies. In the 1980s and 1990s, courts invoked the principles of free speech and academic freedom to protect the constitutional free speech rights of public university professors and students against encroachments by overly broad anti-harassment policies. For example, in a case brought by a biopsychology graduate student who was concerned that theories he wished to explore could be labeled as "racist" or "sexist" under the policy, a federal court found the University of Michigan's sexual harassment policy to be unconstitutionally vague and overly broad (AAUP, 2016). A federal court also found the University of Wisconsin's harassment code to be unconstitutionally broad, notably in its prohibitions against

> discriminatory comments, epithets or other expressive behavior directed at an individual . . . [that] intentionally . . . demean the race, sex, religion, color, creed, disability, sexual orientation, national origin, ancestry or age of the individual . . . and . . . create an intimidating, hostile or demeaning environment for education, university-related work, or other university-authorized activity.
>
> (AAUP, 2016)

These cases have turned on the problem of vagueness and illustrate the difficulty of distinguishing discriminatory speech from legitimate academic speech. They also, however, involve a novel assertion of administrators' power over speech.

The rules and procedures of universities in carrying out these laws do not have the usual features of actual law. They do not create visible precedent (as secrecy is the norm for many of these procedures, and no public record is created), nor do they provide guarantees of a due process similar to those in courts. Moreover, the responsible officials and committees carrying out these quasi-judicial functions are typically creatures of the administration, serving at its pleasure. Their findings are normally advisory and can be overruled by higher-level administrators. In this respect, they resemble administrative law generally, rather than proceedings in actual courts. Nevertheless, there are some constraints on administrative actions, and it is no coincidence that the issue of vagueness in policy statements plays a role in the relatively rare instances where courts intervene to protect academics from administrators. The policies are intentionally vague: this is what gives administrators discretionary power. These policies create or help define the contractual relation between an institution and its employee under employment law. Even the courts, which normally defer to a policy created to fulfill an administrative rule of the federal government and are reluctant to invoke constitutional considerations, recognize that the policies in question are too vague to support sanctions under employment law. The requirement that the regulations must meet some minimal standard of clarity does impose an important burden on administrators who act to sanction a faculty member in ways that curtail academic freedom.

Three Problem Areas

Title IX

According to the text of Title IX, "No person in the United States shall, on the basis of sex, be excluded from participation in, be denied the benefits of, or be subjected to discrimination under any education program or activity receiving Federal financial assistance" (US Department of Labor, 1972, Section 1681, Sex, (a)). This law has been quite radically extended, both by the relevant agencies, notably the Office of Civil Rights (OCR) of the Department of Education through letters of guidance, and by its implementation in university regulations, particularly in relation to ones involving the concept of "hostile environment," such as those that are understood as warranting restrictions on speech. Although some of the guidance relating to procedures governing student misconduct has recently been rescinded, the university regulations created in compliance with them have not, so this continues to be an important issue. According to the original guidance provided during the Obama administration, which did not go through the procedures necessary to make it an official regulation, there is a specific requirement for universities to educate students about what constitutes sex discrimination.

Title IX does not require a recipient of federal funds to adopt a policy specifically prohibiting sexual harassment or sexual violence. As noted in the "Revised Sexual Harassment Guidance" (2001), however, a recipient's general policy prohibiting sex discrimination will not be considered effective and would violate Title IX if, because of the lack of a specific policy, students are unaware of what kind of conduct constitutes sexual harassment, including sexual violence, or that such conduct is prohibited sex discrimination. The OCR therefore recommends that a recipient's nondiscrimination policy state that prohibited sex discrimination covers sexual harassment, including sexual violence, and that the policy includes examples of the types of conduct that it covers (Ali, 2011: 7).

This is an intrusion into academic freedom in one of the two meanings of this term: a university's autonomy from the state. It dictates what the students must be taught, even though the teaching, in this case, may not be in the classroom. Moreover, it is compelled speech, because it requires the university to say something. Yet it trades on an ambiguity between the task of informing students about the law and university regulations, and political indoctrination with respect to particular notions of proper gender relations.[4] The latter would be an intrusion on academic freedom; the former would not.

This issue takes a more extreme form when applied to faculty members. Because the use of anti-discrimination laws to justify various forms of preferential treatment in admissions has repeatedly been curtailed by the courts, universities have asserted an alternative argument: there is an educational value in "diversity" that warrants certain forms of discrimination in favor of particular underrepresented groups. The courts have partially accepted this argument in the case of university admissions, subject to some limitations. In addition to these measures, universities have sought to assure the commitment of its faculty members to the concept of diversity. The need to generate such commitment has taken both positive and punitive forms. In a widely publicized case, a Duke theology professor was disciplined for sending an internal email critical of a "racial equity" training program that the dean was promoting.

In an email to the faculty, the dean stated:

> It is inappropriate and unprofessional to use mass emails to make disparaging statements including arguments ad hominem-in order to humiliate or undermine individual colleagues or groups of colleagues with whom we disagree. The use of mass emails to express racism, sexism, and other forms of bigotry is offensive and unacceptable, especially in a Christian institution.
>
> (Stancill, 2017)

The dean and a professor sponsoring the training filed a complaint, which included a charge of sexual harassment on the basis of the theology professor's internal email. In response, the faculty member noted that there was nothing bigoted about his posts and objected that his intellectual freedom had been infringed. Nonetheless, he was disciplined. The sanctions included a ban from faculty meetings and a promise "that he would not receive future funds for research and travel" (Stancill, 2017). He subsequently resigned.

This case illustrates some of the problems of the interaction of employment law, contractual assertions of academic freedom, Title IX, and other anti-discrimination policies. The oddity of Title IX-based policies is that they are directed against such things as "racism, sexism, and other forms of bigotry," none of which is mentioned in Title IX or any other anti-discrimination law. Categories like racism and sexism are doctrinal and rooted in controversial theories rather than neutral rules, such as the one against discrimination in the actual statute. If we incorporate doctrinal statements into a policy, however, they are no longer merely doctrines, but instead are the official policies of the employer. In the Duke case, objecting to these policies, or even to the means of promoting them, was construed as a form of sexual harassment, or the creation of a hostile environment. The law offers no protection here: the employer has a right to demand agreement with the policy. If the faculty member's statement had been public (e.g., to a newspaper), this would have been grounds for discipline, and even for the firing of a tenured professor. Moreover, simply as an internal discussion, it would also be grounds for dismissal under normal employment law, because, as we have seen, there is no employment law provision for free speech within the normal activities of employment. A private university, such as Duke, is free, in principle, to demand doctrinal conformity.

112 Stephen Turner

The problem of doctrinal conformity in *public* institutions that also cannot, in principle, demand doctrinal conformity, arises in other ways, but it involves the same ambiguity between intellectual doctrines and policies. Ironically, given the long history of issues over oaths, Title IX and anti-discrimination law have generated oaths of their own. These take the form of "diversity statements," which faculty are required either to sign or to submit as part of the job application process (Oregon Association of Scholars, 2017; for guidelines, see UC, 2015). The statements are designed to compel the applicant to both affirm and prove their commitment to diversity. This form of oath taking has yet to be tested in court, although the requirement of oath taking to demonstrate commitment to diversity is widespread, and the statements are taken seriously. As sociologist Tanya Golash-Boza (2016), in an *Inside Higher Ed* article, advises job applicants:

> Many faculty members truly care about diversity and equity and will read your statement closely. I have been in the room when the diversity statement of every single finalist for a job search was scrutinized. The candidates who submitted strong statements wrote about their experiences teaching first-generation college students, their involvement with LGBTQ student groups, their experiences teaching in inner-city high schools and their awareness of how systemic inequalities affect students' ability to excel. Applicants mentioned their teaching and activism and highlighted their commitment to diversity and equity in higher education.

A typical statement (from a sociologist), which was recommended as a model on the official website of the University of California system, includes this example of evidence of one's commitment: "In my advising capacities, I encouraged my students to ponder the roles they might play in the alleviation of the vast inequities that continue to shape our world" (UCSD, n.d.). Are these oaths political tests of the kind rejected in the California loyalty case? It depends. If diversity is a political issue, these are political tests. To the extent that doctrinal statements of political beliefs, such as a conviction regarding the evils of inequality, are considered as a basis for employment, there are First Amendment issues, at least in a public institution. If it is a policy commitment, it is plausible for an employer to require adherence to the employer's policies. Separating the two presents the same kinds of difficulty as harassment guidelines.

Some of these oaths are simple affirmations that have to be signed off on by the applicant. It is an open question as to whether they are enforceable after employment—i.e., whether someone could be said to have violated the oath, have made it falsely, or have renounced it. Nonetheless, the requirement is designed to have an effect on hiring. The act of assessing a person's commitment to a policy—even if this were an appropriate requirement, consistent with academic freedom is a matter of largely arbitrary personal judgment, exercised by people who are unconstrained by rules or the possibility of appeal. Moreover, they may have an ideological commitment to the policy and to a personal view of its meaning, as the statement by Golash-Boza (2016) makes clear. When academics adapt their behavior to vague threats of this kind, they are giving up some of their freedom, and other academics are complicit in depriving them of it.

Research Misconduct Proceedings

Research misconduct operates in the same way as other administrative law domains, with the addition of a federal Office of Research Misconduct that issues federal funding bans for institutions involved in the individual cases that reach it. The primary bodies in this regard are internal to universities, which adopt their own research misconduct rules and procedures. The cases that have occurred in sociology include the highly visible University of Texas project, which indicated that children of same-sex marriages were harmed by this practice (Regnerus, 2012). It resulted in multiple misconduct and ethics charges. The citation of this research in a related court case led to a judicial examination of the editorial decision-making of the journal in which the study was published. Cases prosecuting research misconduct in the social sciences are quite rare and also extremely selective. Lenore Weitzman (1987) produced data showing differential economic harm for women as a result of divorce proceedings. These findings influenced legislatures and were warmly supported as an example of effective policy-oriented research. Yet such results, which fit a political agenda but did not mesh with the research's overall consensus, were dubious. As Christian Smith points out, it was never treated as a research misconduct case, and Weitzman's results were never subjected to juridical or quasi-juridical scrutiny, despite such red flags as missing data sets (Smith, 2014: 97–101). The risk to academic freedom by the combination of selective prosecution and unclear standards is that the threat of misconduct charges will deter research that undermines dominant political biases. If scholars adapt to vague standards and the likelihood of the threat of politically motivated complaints by self-silencing or by choosing to avoid controversial topics, they forfeit their academic freedom.

The IRB Puzzle

Institutional review boards (IRBs) were mandated as part of the same kinds of administrative law procedures as anti-discrimination and research misconduct rule making, but they work in ways that are especially problematic from the point of view of the First Amendment. They represent a form of prior restraint on speech, rather than a system of sanctions on speech. The issue of clear lines is thus particularly important here because enforcing sanctions on past actions requires some clarity in the rules in advance of the action. This is why courts have repeatedly ruled against universities' punishment of faculty for speech violations. IRBs, however, review research proposals on human subjects before that research is conducted. Moreover, they are, in the usual manner of administrative law requirements imposed on institutions, removed legally from the authorizing legislation and the possibility of judicial review.

The "Belmont Report" (HHS, 1979) provided the philosophical basis for the regulatory regime that was established. Medical research was the model. The report focused on such topics as informed consent and harms, as well as the confidentiality of records. Social scientists were not involved in the writing of the report, and the application of these standards to social science research was an accidental outcome. The bulk of research similar to that in the social sciences is psychological and educational research. As with medical research, anonymity and the protection of subjects, particularly through informed consent, have been a primary focus. The effect of applying these standards to academic social science fields has been to restrict social research in ways in which non-academics, such as journalists, were not hampered, even when the risk of harm was minimal. For example, IRBs have been prone to require elaborate statements regarding the purposes of projects, based on the requirement of informed consent.

Much of the discussion of issues over the application of these standards has involved ethnography and oral history, the areas closest to journalism and non-academic writing. The key topics have involved informed consent and anonymity requirements, which are hot-button issues for medical records, and thus strenuously enforced by IRBs. These issues have been partially resolved by a change in the rules, redefining "research" so that some kinds of human subjects research, such as oral history, journalism, biography, literary criticism, legal research, and historical scholarship, are no longer regarded as research per se.

The distinction that this redefinition was grounded in, however, produces an additional complication for social research. These activities were excluded because they were not "designed to develop or contribute to generalizable knowledge" (Abba, 2007: 575). Taken literally, many of the classics of social research (such as the Middletown books or the Yankee City series, as well as many classic ethnographies) included material that could be identified with specific incidents and persons and thus violate privacy requirements. The thin protection of not naming the cities in which the research was done speaks to the desire to generalize, but it did little to protect identities. Neither was informed consent, typically associated in medical research with consent forms, possible for public events or the casual conversations between participant and observer on which the researchers depended.

This change is not mandated for university IRBs, which can continue to treat federal regulations as the "floor" and thus do not exempt any researchers. An employee's relation to the IRB is mediated by employment law: the requirement to submit one's research proposals to an IRB is a matter of honoring the rules of the university. IRBs typically do not offer blanket exclusions. Ordinarily, exemptions must be specifically approved by the IRB. Many IRBs, which have become de facto representatives of a university's concerns about other subjects—including liability, bad publicity, and political exposure—have not adopted a permissive attitude to these projects, and some advocates of the IRB process bristle at the thought that the social sciences would not follow the rules imposed on medicine. Evidence on IRB workings is scant, because these boards operate secretly, and researchers tend to conform rather than risk sanctions. The AAUP, however, has collected a large number of horror stories about aggressive IRBs, some of which relate to social science projects (AAUP, 2006).

IRBs exercise considerable power. They can tell the applicants what kinds of research they may do and even rewrite protocols. Proponents of the IRB system treat these actions not as a matter of the application of clear rules, but as a means of balancing the interests of research against other interests. But do IRBs actually affect the kind of research that is done, and the topics studied, or are they merely a paperwork hurdle whose effects are largely random? Ceci et al. (1985) conducted a survey that showed IRB members were less likely to approve research that challenged left-wing biases. There is also much evidence of inconsistency. One ethnographic study of IRBs tells the story of a study of landlords in impoverished areas that was rejected at Brandeis for consent reasons but accepted at the University of Wisconsin (Stark, 2012: 54). Another case, reported in an AAUP journal, reflected the extensive sense in which the notion of "harm" could be applied outside of medical contexts to block research. A Caucasian PhD student studying ethnicity and career expectations was told that it might be traumatic for Black PhD students to be interviewed by him (Thomson et al., 2006: 96).

The overall effects of the IRB system on actual research choices are more difficult to detect. Within sociology, however, one can observe a few long-term changes that might well be attributed to the increased difficulty of performing human subjects research. Areas that require IRB approval have declined, while those that do not necessitate it have grown. Social psychology, as a field within sociology, has suffered a radical decline in section membership in the IRB era, and some forms of politically sensitive research, notably community power studies, have disappeared entirely. At the same time, areas such as cultural sociology, which can rely on public material and thus not have to face IRB scrutiny, and auto-ethnography, which does not directly involve subjects other than the author and, hence, does not require IRB approval, have flourished. IRBs present the clearest of all threats to academic freedom. They are explicitly designed to curtail research in the name of other goals and values. Yet it is controversial whether these restrictions represent the kind of abridgment of speech by the First Amendment doctrine forbidding prior restraint (Bledsoe et al., 2007; Charrow, 2007). It is apparent, however, that the absence of clear rules and the IRBs' use of their discretionary power to mandate changes in research protocols create an environment to which researchers must adapt, consciously or unconsciously.

Do the Two Forms of Academic Freedom Conflict?

In his history of the German idea of freedom, Leonard Kreiger (1957: 435) mentions the "traditional German notion of freedom as the essential harmony between popular liberty and monarchical authority." For most of the twentieth century, there was a similarly strong relationship between the two forms of academic freedom: freedom of the individual faculty member and freedom of the institution from state interference. Threats to a person's academic freedom often came from the state, such as from politicians incensed at something done at a state university, as in the California loyalty oath case. The freedom of a higher education institution was a means of protecting faculty from political interference, and, in turn, faculty members supported the freedom of their university as the basis of their own freedom. The current situation raises new issues that disrupt this commonality of interests. The conflict is especially well articulated in a recently decided Wisconsin Supreme Court case, which pitted a faculty member against Marquette University. Both concepts of freedom were articulated in detail in the rulings, which divided the court. The legal facts of the case, as recorded in the majority opinion, were the following:

> Marquette University suspended a tenured faculty member because of a blog post criticizing an encounter between an instructor and a student. Dr. John McAdams took exception to his suspension, and brought a claim against the University for breach of contract. He asserts that the contract guarantees to him the right to be free of disciplinary repercussions for engaging in activity protected by either the doctrine of academic freedom or the United States Constitution. The University denies Dr. McAdams' right to litigate his breach of contract claim in our courts. Instead, it says, we must defer to its procedure for suspending and dismissing tenured faculty members. It claims we may not question its decision so long as it did not abuse its discretion, infringe any constitutional rights, act in bad faith, or engage in fraud.
>
> (McAdams, 2018: 1)

The university was declaring its freedom from state supervision and the legal priority of its own procedures in relation to employment questions. McAdams was defending his constitutional rights and the guarantee of academic freedom explicitly written into his employment contract. The university believed—and asserted—that it could define, through its own procedures, what these guarantees meant and act accordingly.

The university won its initial case. The circuit court adhered to the notion that "public policy compels a constraint on the judiciary with respect to Marquette's academic decision-making and governance," out of a recognition that "professionalism and fitness in the context of a university professor are difficult if not impossible issues for a jury to assess" (McAdams, 2018: 55). The university nevertheless lost on McAdams's appeal to the Wisconsin Supreme Court. The majority opinion was that the university was not free to define the terms that appeared in its employment rules. The court also ruled that Marquette's quasi-judicial procedure, which was the basis for its actions, was merely an informal dispute-resolution process, and that "as a replacement for litigation in our courts, it is structurally flawed" (McAdams, 2018: 2). Thus, it rejected the circuit court's finding that McAdams had received due process. It noted as dubious the claim that juries could not assess fitness cases and rejected deference as an unsound practice. These responses recapitulate the standard issues with administrative law generally: lack of due process, lack of access to a jury trial, and quasi-judicial processes where their authority, particularly with respect to a question of the autonomy of the hearing officer, is suspect.

The definition of academic freedom came from the Marquette handbook itself, which was explicitly based on the AAUP definitions of academic freedom. As this is a frequent feature of faculty handbooks and thus forms part of the contract with faculty members, the aforementioned analysis is important. The higher court made the point that the 1940 AAUP statement is out of date and does not reflect current practice, which is that faculty members are largely unconstrained in their extramural comments. The current standard, rather, was one that was narrowly related to the performance of the faculty member's job: "The controlling principle is that a faculty member's expression of opinion as a citizen cannot constitute grounds for dismissal unless it clearly demonstrates the faculty member's unfitness for his or her position" (McAdams, 2018: 67).

As the AAUP pointed out (McAdams, 2018: 68), this was a stringent standard, one which was rarely invoked by universities. Marquette University, as the higher court indicated, did not show that the particular expression by McAdams proved his unfitness, and it invoked considerations that uncoupled the doctrine of academic freedom from any stable reference points. The form of this argument is important, for it goes to the heart of the notion of academic freedom as a right, rather than as just one consideration among many. The university argued that educational institutions assume academic freedom as just one value that must be balanced against "other values core to their mission." Some of those values, it said, include the obligation to "take care not to cause harm, directly or indirectly, to members of the university community"; to "respect the dignity of others and to acknowledge their right to express differing opinions"; to "safeguard the conditions for the community to exist"; to "ensur[e] colleagues feel free to explore undeveloped ideas"; and to carry out "the concept of cura personalis," which involves working and caring "for all aspects of the lives of the members of the institution" (McAdams, 2018: 69).

This line of argument would have the effect of eliminating academic freedom as a contractual right and subjecting its exercise to a wide range of other, largely subjective considerations. The minority opinion of the higher court, which may reflect the dominant legal reasoning on these issues, affirmed the superiority of an institution's academic freedom to the academic freedom of an individual. This argument was based on the concept of shared governance:

> Within academic freedom lies the concept of shared governance. It includes the right of faculty to participate in the governance of the institution on academic-related matters. Shared governance in colleges and universities has been forged over decades to address the specific issues that arise in the workplace of higher education.
>
> (McAdams, 2018: 139)

The relevant faculty right, in short, is to participate in shared governance.[5] Thus, as the dissent claimed:

> The majority [opinion] errs in conducting only half of the academic freedom analysis. It fails to recognize, much less analyze, the academic freedom of Marquette as a private, Catholic, Jesuit university. As a result, it dilutes a private educational institution's autonomy to make its own academic decisions in fulfillment of its unique mission.
>
> (McAdams, 2018: 140)

The dissent also rejected the idea that courts, rather than faculty operating in shared governance structures, should be able to define the meaning of academic freedom: "Apparently, the majority thinks it is in a better position to address concerns of academic freedom than a group of tenured faculty members who live the doctrine every day" (McAdams, 2018: 141). The dissent also added, significantly, that McAdams's "contract does not give him the full-throated First Amendment rights that would be given a private citizen vis-a-vis the government," despite its affirmation of his academic freedom (McAdams, 2018: 145). Therefore, the institution, in accordance with its autonomy, can regulate McAdams's extramural speech.

Conclusion

As all of these examples show, the present legal system produces an unequal conflict between academic freedom, which has only the most fragile and indirect legal basis, and employment law. The latter is backed by administrative law, which, in turn, is supported by the practice of judicial deference and the absence, in most cases, of statutory law providing for and defining academic freedom. A recent University of Texas lawsuit indicated how low on the legal hierarchy academic freedom is. A lawyer representing the state and the university affirmed the state's view that academic freedom was a "workplace policy," not a First Amendment right (Ellis, 2018). This is the language of standard employment law. If a university is allowed to define academic freedom as a workplace policy, then it has little legal significance. Policy is a prerogative of the employer. Employers have been reluctant to act on this prerogative, but they have been less hesitant in applying regulations backed by administrative law, which represent different policy values. In the cases we have discussed, academic freedom is considered to be one policy value among several and, therefore, subject to being balanced against other interests or public purposes.

The effect of this new regime of administrative law, which holds employers responsible for fulfilling a vast array of policy desiderata, is to create an equally vast array of new discretionary powers for academic administrators and committees, such as IRBs. The mere existence of these powers marks the end of academic freedom as it was traditionally understood: both as a right, instead of an interest against which other interests are balanced, and as a concept superior to employment policy, rather than subject to it. Without clear demarcations and the legal priority of a right—even if it is only an implied contractual right in employment law, with a defined meaning apart from the interpretation placed on it by universities—it is impossible to defend traditional academic freedom against the ever-encroaching body of administrative law and university procedures.

One may ask, however, whether there is much traditional academic freedom left to defend. The "marketplace of ideas" image referred to in the classic legal defenses of academic freedom depended on the real autonomy of faculty members to pursue inquiry as they saw fit and to occasionally express their opinions in public without penalty. The present regime of science is governed by a grant system that ties a scientist to the judgments of peers through a brutal system of competition for funds. The rest of academia is bound to a competitive system of quantitative reputation assessment, to which our submission is, as Gloria Origgi (2017: 218) has called it, a form of voluntary epistemic servitude that has the same effects. This coincides with, and perhaps produces, a cultural change in the professoriate. The constituency for traditional academic freedom within a university would be the people who were exercising freedom in accordance with the liberal theory of science. This constituency barely exists today. It is noteworthy that of the university cases discussed here, three of them (at Texas, Duke, and Marquette) involved objections to either an ideologically dominant position or to practices enforcing ideological conformity. The suppression of one faculty member was supported by much of the rest of the faculty. Conformity has an active constituency. Indeed, for topics involving diversity, it has an institutionalized presence in the university, many means to enforce it, and enthusiastic support among the faculty. Academic freedom has only the few legal means outlined earlier. We have come full circle, culturally as well as legally, from the California loyalty oath case.

My thanks to Joerg Tiede for the useful suggestions. I am responsible for errors.

Notes

1 One complication with this kind of "law" is that for most of its application to universities, there is no direct constitutional basis for them in the "enumerated powers" of the US Constitution, which do not include any authority to regulate research or education. The regulations instead are conditions of contractual relations between the federal government and universities or states, relations that result from grant programs.

2 This case involved a letter to the editor criticizing actions of the school board and affirmed Marvin Pickering's First Amendment right as a citizen to speak on public issues.

3 It is worth noting that a loyalty oath requirement was already under attack from the 1930s on by the Communists of the era, and the requirement was defended against their contestation of it by such figures as Michael Polanyi and Sidney Hook.

4 Seminars on "whiteness" directed at employees and students characteristically take the form of indoctrination, by directing them against resistance to the message and by declining to respond to counter-arguments, which are treated as pathologies (Watt, 2007).

5 As Henry Reichman points out in his commentary on this case, shared governance was something of a sham. This point is also made in the majority opinion. Marquette's president imposed an unusual and legally problematic demand that went beyond the advice of the faculty committee, namely, that McAdams apologize (Reichman, 2019: 101). This apology would have the effect of exposing McAdams to a civil lawsuit by the instructor who was criticized by him.

References

AAUP (American Association of University Professors). "1915 Declaration of Principles on Academic Freedom and Academic Tenure," In *Policy Documents and Reports*, 11th edn, 3–12. Baltimore: Johns Hopkins University Press, [1915]2015.

AAUP (American Association of University Professors). "1940 Statement of Principles on Academic Freedom and Tenure," *AAUP Reports and Publications*, 1940. www.aaup.org/reports-publications/

AAUP (American Association of University Professors). "Research on Human Subjects: Academic Freedom and the Institutional Review Board," *AAUP Reports and Publications*, 2006. www.aaup.org/reports-publications/

AAUP (American Association of University Professors). "The History, Uses, and Abuses of Title IX," *AAUP*, June, 2016. www.aaup.org/file/TitleIXreport.pdf.

Abba, Elmer D. "Promoting Free Speech in Clinical Quality Improvement Research," *Northwestern University Law Review* 101(2): 575–591, 2007.

Ali, Russlyn. *Dear Colleague* [re. Title IX and Sex Discrimination]. Washington DC: US Department of Education, Office for Civil Rights, 2011. https://www2.ed.gov/about/offices/list/ocr/letters/colleague-201104.pdf.

Bledsoe, Caroline H., Bruce Sherin, Adam G. Galinsky, Nathalia M Headley, Carol A. Heimer, Erik Keldgaard, James Lindgren, Jon D. Miller, Michael E. Roloff, and David H. Uttal. "Regulating Creativity: Research and Survival in the IRE Iron Cage," *Northwestern University Law Review* 101(2): 593–641, 2007.

Ceci, Stephen, Douglas Peters, and Jonathan Plotkin. "Human Subjects Review, Personal Values, and the Regulation of Social Science Research," *American Psychologist* 40(9): 994–1002, 1985.

Charrow, Robert. "Protection of Human Subjects: Is Expansive Regulation Counterproductive?" *Northwestern University Law Review* 101(2): 707–721, 2007.

The End of Clear Lines 121

Dickerson (Dickerson v. New Banner Inst. Inc.). 460 U.S. 103. *Justia*, 1983. https://supreme.justia.com.

Ellis, Lindsay. "What is Academic Freedom? Statement That Alarmed Professors at U. of Texas Sets Off Debate," *Chronicle of Higher Education*, 24 July, 2018. www.chronicle.com

Foraste (John Foraste, Plaintiff, v. Brown University and Laura Freid, Defendants). 290 F.Supp. 2d 234, *Justia*, 2003. https://supreme.justia.com

Garcetti (Garcetti v. Ceballos). 547 U.S. 410, *Justia*, 2006. https://supreme.justia.com

Gardner, David P. *The California Oath Controversy*. Berkeley: University of California Press, 1967.

Golash-Boza, Tanya. "The Effective Diversity Statement," *Inside Higher Education*, 10 June, 2016. www.insidehighered.com

Hamburger, Philip. *Is Administrative Law Unlawful?* Chicago: University of Chicago Press, 2014.

Hamburger, Philip *The Administrative Threat*. New York: Encounter Books, 2017.

HHS (Health and Human Services). *Belmont Report: Ethical Principles and Guidelines for the Protection of Human Subjects of Research*. Washington DC: US Department of Health and Human Services, Office for Human Research Protections, 1979. www.hhs.gov/ohrp/regulations-and-policy/

Kaplin, William A and Barbara A Lee. *The Law of Higher Education: A Comprehensive Guide to Legal Implications of Administrative Decision Making*, 5th edn, vol. 2. San Francisco: Jossey-Bass, 2013.

Keyishian (Keyishian v. Board of Regents of the State University of New York). 385 U.S. 589, *Justia*, 1967. https://supreme.justia.com

Kreiger, Leonard. *The German Idea of Freedom*. Boston: Beacon Press, 1957.

Lange, Greg. "University of Washington is Said on March 24, 1948, to Have More Than 150 Communists or Sympathizers," *HistoryLink.org*, 1999. www.historylink.org/File/1483/

McAdams (McAdams v. Marquette University). *Supreme Court of Wisconsin*, Case No. 2017AP1240, 2018. www.wicourts.gov.

McMahon, Paula. "Jury Rules Against Fired FAU Prof James Tracy in Free Speech Case," *Sun Sentinel* (Palm Beach, FL), December, 2017. www.sun-sentinel.com

Norman-Eady, Sandra. "Analysis and Holding," In "Summary of Garcetti et al. v. Ceballos and Impact of Decision on Connecticut Whistle blower Laws," OLR Research Report 2006-R-0399. Connecticut General Assembly, June 24, 2006. www.cga.ct. gov

North Haven (North Haven Board of Education v. Bell). 456 U.S. 521, Quoting United States v. Price, 383 U.S. 787, at 801 (1966), *Justia*, 1982. https://supreme.justia.com

Oregon Association of Scholars. "The Imposition of Diversity Statements on Faculty Hiring and Promotion at Oregon Universities," *Oregon Association of Scholars,* 2017. www.oregonscholars.org/wp-content/uploads/2017/01/DiversityStatements_Rev16Man 7.pdf.

Origgi, Gloria. *Reputation: What It is and Why It Matters*, translated by Stephen Holmes and Noga Arikha. Princeton: Princeton University Press, 2017.

Pickering (Pickering v. Board of Education). 391 U.S. 563, *Justia*, 1968. https://supreme.justia.com

Prelude to Controversy. *California Loyalty Oath Collection*. Berkeley: Bancroft Library, University of California-Berkeley, 1949. https://jbancroft.berkeley.edµ/collectionsjloyaltyoath/timeline_prelude.html

122 Stephen Turner

Ramadan, Lulu. "FAU Fires Professor Who Said Sandy Hook Shooting May Have Been Staged," *Palm Beach Post*, August 29, 2016. www.palmbeachpost.com/news-jlocal/fau-fires-professor-who-said-sandy-hook-shooting-may-have-been-staged/iqECze68gb WAxQ8DwKegRL/.

Regnerus, Mark. "How Different Are the Adult Children of Parents Who Have Same-Sex Relationships? Findings from the New Family Structures Study," *Social Science Research* 41(4): 752–770, 2012.

Reichman, Henry. *The Future of Academic Freedom*. Baltimore: Johns Hopkins University Press, 2019.

"Revised Sexual Harassment Guidance," *US Department of Education, Office of Civil Rights*, 19 January, 2001. https://www2.ed.gov/about/offices/list/ocr/docs/shguide.html

Schrecker, Ellen. "Political Tests for Professors: Academic Freedom during the McCarthy Years," *The University Loyalty Oath: A 5th Anniversary Perspective*, 1999. www.lib.berkeley.edu/uchistory/archives_exhibitsjloyaltyoath/symposium/schrecker.html.

Smith, Christian. *The Sacred Project of American Sociology*. Oxford: Oxford University Press, 2014.

Stancill, Jane. "Duke Divinity Professor Calls Diversity Training 'A Waste', Faces Discipline," *News & Observer*, 9 May, 2017. www.newsobserver.com

Stark, Laura. *Behind Closed Doors: IRBs and the Making of Ethical Research*. Chicago: University of Chicago Press, 2012.

Strauss, Peter L. *An Introduction to Administrative Justice in the United States*. Durham: Carolina Academic Press, 1989.

Svrluga, Susan. "Professor Who Says Sandy Hook Was a Hoax Sued the University that Fired Him: A Jury Ruled Against Him," *Washington Post*, 14 December, 2017. www.washingtonpost.com.

Thomson, Judith Jarvis, Catherine Elgin, David A. Hyman, Philip E. Rubin, and Jonathan Knight. "Research on Human Subjects: Academic Freedom and the Institutional Review Board," *Academe* 92(5): 95–100, 2006.

Tiede, Hans-Joerg. *University Reform: The Founding of the American Association of University Professors*. Baltimore: Johns Hopkins University Press, 2015.

UC (University of California). "Guidelines for Addressing Race and Gender Equity in Academic Programs in Compliance with Proposition 209," *University of California*, 2015. https://diversity.universityofcalifornia.edu/files/documents/prop-209-guidelines-ogc-full.pdf

UCSD (University of California-San Diego). "Examples of Diversity Statements," *University of California-San Diego*, n.d. https://facultydiversity. ucsd.edu/files/Ex-1to3-C2D-Statements.pdf

US Department of Labor. "Title IX, Education Amendments of 1972 (Title 20 U.S.C. Sections 1681–1688)," *US Department of Labor, Office of the Assistant Secretary for Administration & Management*, 1972. www.dol.gov/agencies/oasam/centers-offices/civil-rights-center/statutes/title-ix/

Watt, Sherry K. "Difficult Dialogues, Privilege and Social Justice: Uses of the Privileged Identity Exploration (PIE) Model in Student Affairs Practice," *College Student Affairs Journal* 26(2): 114–126, 2007.

Weitzman, Lenore. *The Divorce Revolution: The Unexpected Social and Economic Consequences for Women and Children in America*. New York: Free Press, 1987.

Part II

Fundamental Political Theory

Chapter 7

The Method of Antinomies
Oakeshott and Others

Stephen Turner

Several of Michael Oakeshott's writings, including *On Human Conduct* ([1975]1991), employ an argumentative device that is shared with several other twentieth-century thinkers, but which has not received much attention on its own terms. The device involves antinomies—the most famous of Oakeshott's being the antinomy between the state understood as a civil association and as an enterprise association. The antinomies between the politics of faith and the politics of skepticism, individualist and collectivist thinking, rationalist and pragmatic politics, and, in the essay "The Rule of Law" (1983), between the purely neutral rule of law and policy, work in the same way. These uses compare to some other prominent cases: Max Weber's antinomic distinction between the politics of conviction and the politics of responsibility; Carl Schmitt's claims about the ultimate incompatibility of liberalism and democracy; Hans J. Morgenthau's antinomy of love and power; in Edward Shils, who explicitly addresses antinomies in "The Antinomies of Liberalism" ([1978]1997) and in *The Torment of Secrecy* (1956), and more recently in Chantal Mouffe's *The Democratic Paradox* (2000).[1]

These thinkers exemplify a core project of de-mythification and de-ideologization which can be understood as a liberal counter-project to ideological liberalism and to ideology generally. A naïve reading of these thinkers treats them as relativists. But this is a misreading. The antinomic vision of politics is different from relativism in any simple sense of this term. It is specifically distinct from, and opposed to, the idea that there can be an ideological "solution" to the antinomies in question. This is not relativism: it is not relativistic about the ideologies in question. It denies that they can be correct doctrines. For these thinkers, ideological thinking is an error: a false escape from the irreducibly antinomic character of political life and political choice. From the point of view of antinomists, projects like "democratic theory" presume, in contrast, that the relevant antinomies can be reconciled in theory: that the antinomies are, in the end, false ones.

In this paper, I will examine the use and meaning of these antinomies and disentangle their use from misinterpretations, as well as show how their recognition represents a critique of and an alternative to standard modes

DOI: 10.4324/9781003360810-10

of political philosophy. In so doing, I will cover some familiar ground. My aim, however, will be different: to explicate the form of reasoning itself. Oakeshott says a good deal about the antinomic character of the specific antinomies he explores, and their conditions, though he uses a different terminology. But he does not discuss antinomies as a class, or, so to speak, from the outside. He does not say, for example, that freedom and equality are not antinomic in the sense of the antinomies he does explore, though this, and the antinomies of the term freedom, in the famous case of Isaiah Berlin's *Two Concepts of Liberty* (1958), formed a large part of the intellectual landscape in which he wrote. Nor does he distinguish the cases he focuses on from other binary oppositions—life and death, good and evil, *eros* and *thanatos*, yin and yang, and so forth. In what follows, I will attempt to distinguish the genuine antinomies from the mere oppositions and explain what makes these antinomies work, and what is implied by their existence. In doing so, I will draw from Oakeshott, especially from works such as *The Politics of Faith and Scepticism* (1996), where he is especially open and plain-spoken about their sources and nature. Oakeshott was famously disinclined to talk about method. As Kenneth Minogue says, "Oakeshott's inclination was to reject methodological formulae and to rely upon a philosophical self-consciousness about the precise relevance of the questions being asked and answered" (Minogue, 1993: viii). But he often did speak about the conditions for and the goals of understanding political ideas, if not in a way that readily answers the questions I have raised here, so there are resources in addition to the analyses themselves with which to answer them.

Principlism and Its Method

We can begin by describing a methodological contrast, which may itself have the character of an antinomy, between antinomism understood as a method or meta-theory of the political and what we might call principlism. This ugly term will be discarded, however, once the implications of the "antinomist" alternative become clear. The contrast can be seen in a simple recent case, Eric Beerbohm's *In Our Name: The Ethics of Democracy* (2012). The core of his argument is that citizens are responsible for actions taken in their name. As the argument was recently summarized, Beerbohm

> takes on the important question of citizen responsibility for policy decisions, and demonstrates that it should be the primary lens through which we should view the problem of self-government. He convincingly shows why many of our assumptions about representative government and institutional design are mistaken. He argues that democracies should make transparent the responsibility that each citizen bears for policies as a result of participating in elections. Current institutions often mask that

> responsibility and require redesign. They should be constructed to ensure transparency and so that citizen responsibility might be realized.
>
> (Brettschneider, 2015: np)

This is a simple example of the procedure. It tries to identify the underlying and grounding principle of democracy, "the primary lens," and derives a normative lesson from it, making this into a critical or standard-setting theory by which democracies can be judged, and also reformed, in accordance with the principle.

In this case, and in principlism generally, principles are held to be in some sense both derived from "current institutions" and superior to them. In this particular case, and indeed for "democratic theory" generally, antipathy to actual democratic institutions is at the heart of the argument. Here the argument is that the ordinary machinery of government, and indeed elections themselves, fail to make transparent the responsibilities each citizen bears and need to be given an institutional redesign in accordance with the principle. It is only a slight irony that this kind of democratic theory is itself anti-democratic: the procedures and institutions that are being challenged by the theory were themselves arrived at through democratic procedures and may rightly represent the enduring preferences of the people who are governed by them. Democratic decisions about the nature of the democracy under which people live are not, however, sufficient for "democratic theory." The theory tells us that the mode of democratic approval was itself not properly democratic, and therefore the actual untutored will of the people is to be ignored in favor of the design that follows the principle, which in turn is derived not from the will of the people but from some other source.

Interestingly, there is an antinomy produced by the unrealism of this principle. The creation and execution of policy require leaders—decision-making is normally concentrated. And it is difficult to see how a model with no leadership and no special concentration of responsibility in leaders would work, at least in many of the situations faced by democracies. This points to a question and provides a suggested answer. What, if anything, then, is the antinomy of "citizen responsibility"? Presumably, it would be something like leadership—or responsible leadership, the ideal promoted by Morgenthau and before him by Weber. The point of responsible leadership is that the leader takes responsibility—for persuading the citizens, if necessary by deception, to support him or her in acting in the national interest. And with this simple example, one can begin to see what the issue between the antinomist and the principlist is. In its pure form, "citizen responsibility" is not possible: decisions need to be made on behalf of others, by people who take responsibility for these decisions—this is the essence not only of leadership but also of government itself. One might want to minimize these kinds of decisions, and maximize "citizen responsibility for policy decisions" by such means as feeding information about the consequences of policies back to the citizens in a transparent fashion, but in

128 Stephen Turner

practice, some decision-making will always be made on behalf of citizens: it would be impractical for every citizen to know everything about policies. The ideal is an unrealizable ideal type. Dictatorship, in contrast, in which leaders take all the responsibility for decisions, is not an unrealizable type. But even dictators need legitimacy, and are in this sense at least accountable, and their followers "responsible."

The principlist deals with objections and obstacles, especially with incompatible ideals, in various ways. In the literature on Weber, which is also concerned with the problem of legitimacy and leadership and the antinomies it produces, the standard "democratic theory" strategy is to impute to Weber a "democratic theory" which makes democratic legitimacy a ground and principle (Breiner, 1996; Kalyvas, 2008) or alternatively to criticize him for having the wrong theory of this sort (Maley, 2011). Much of the effort of recent democratic theory has been focused on the troublesome idea of freedom: democracy is supposed to be the font of all good things, but of course, it is also a form of rule and engaged in coercion. So, these raw facts need to be reconciled with the ideal of rule by the people. One way is to redefine freedom, as, for example, Philip Pettit does (1997), in terms of non-domination, and then to define domination as that which the people regard as cases of domination. This salvages an idea of democracy by making freedom depend on what the people say, but indirectly: we are no longer talking about freedom in even the ordinary sense of the term. Another method is to reconcile justice and freedom by putting them in different categories: freedom can be seen as a good that must be distributed according to the principles of justice. Yet another way is to claim that there is a real, or at least possibly real, embodiment of the democratic idea in certain circumstances in which there is no state, and no machinery of democracy, in a revolutionary event in which all contradictions disappear: in which a kind of collective mental fusion occurs in which the people's will is simultaneously formed and expressed, without the impediments of procedures and authority, and therefore both freely and democratically at once.

The procedure of reconciling conflicts by subsuming them under a principle is particularly fertile in one respect: it provides the basis for academic writing which applies, refines, or generates alternatives to the principles proposed by others. Much of this reasoning depends on definitions and the refinement of definitions, redefinitions which are supposed, as Pettit's replacement of freedom in the sense of non-interference with "non-domination" does, to allow conflicts to be eliminated. It was an ironic consequence of neo-Kantianism that it aspired to identify the transcendental conditions of knowledge, its necessary and therefore unique presuppositions, but produced, rather than a unique list, a proliferation of competing and conflicting systems, all of which claimed to have identified the "necessary" conditions in question. Principlism in political philosophy has the same effect: after a long period in which Rawlsian principles and philosophical methods and their application held sway, only to become passé, the same goal of finding a single unifying principle rooted in a special philosophical method has lived on. The only lesson learned from the Rawlsian project was that system building grounded in a single principle is a good thing.

What we are dealing with in the case of antinomies are conflicts or incompatibilities in the domain of principles. The temptation to resolve the incompatibility at the level of principles is thus not surprising. From the point of view of logic, in any case, there is nothing inconsistent about choosing freedom over equality, or the reverse. So, why is there an issue about making them compatible in the first place? From a principlist point of view, it might be seen to be better to have a theory that can not only explain more than its rivals but also explain its rivals. So, there are clear motives for an argument that eliminates many apparently conflicting claims by redefining them and reducing them to a more fundamental principle.

What is the antinomist's motive? Without falling into principlism, she cannot simply be proving another principle by the same means. Nor can the antinomist provide principled reasons for the claim that a resolution in principle between the antinomic sides is impossible. But antinomic arguments nevertheless are about the relation between principles. The relation, however, is not philosophical: the antinomist assumes that the principles or ideas in question are, on the one hand, "ideal," and on the other that they cannot both be realized fully without conflict with the other: one cannot in the actual political world, for example, maximize freedom without producing as a byproduct some inequality. Nor can one reduce inequality, at least in the radical manner envisioned by equality understood as an ideal, without depriving people of some of their freedom.

These are banalities. Some of the ideals may be impossible to realize but can be realized partially. But the antinomist makes a more interesting point: that the achievement of the ideal requires, as a condition, in some sense, things associated with its apparent contrary. This is not a philosophical requirement, though in some cases it comes close to being one, but a practical requirement that holds in the particular world governed by a large set of particular or local contingencies, such as the world of modern European politics rather than in all possible worlds, as a genuine relation of entailment would. It involves factual conditions rather than logical ones. It is therefore a method, so to say, of political *theory* rooted in real political possibilities, rather than political philosophy rooted in ethical or other principles. But the factual conditions in question become apparent and relevant only through the lens of the conflict of ideals.

The obvious alternative conclusion—that there is a plurality of irreducibly competing and conflicting principles each of which has some attraction—cannot be addressed with the methods of redefinition and assimilating to a foundational principle. But there is a problem with this conclusion that the principlist will instantly recognize. Even acknowledging the fact of irreducible conflict turns into a discussion of the grounding principle of this acknowledgment. The principlist will immediately assimilate this acknowledgment to relativism and conclude that relativism is self-refuting, and consequently, this conclusion cannot be genuinely rational. And one can see that the antinomist can easily fall into this trap by providing non-relativist "grounds" for their position, for example, as Chantal Mouffe does, by in effect proposing a new doctrine of agonistic liberalism, in which the recognition of irreconcilable conflicts is given an implicit teleological justification, to stand alongside the teleological ends of principled, reductionist political philosophies. This creates its own antinomy— with the kind of politics represented by Jürgen Habermas, in which there is a teleological pull toward the elimination of disagreement. But Mouffe falls into the temptation of justifying agnostic liberalism as "progressive": Oakeshott famously denies that politics has a teleology, other than his comment to seeking coherence, to which we will return.

But what if principlism as a style of philosophizing is, as neo-Kantianism was, defective and inherently unable to achieve its goal of identifying the underlying true normative principles of politics? A plausible reason for thinking this to be the case would be that there are antinomies—that there are conflicting and incompatible ideas which have some sort of attraction or intellectual compulsion, but which cannot be reduced to a framework based on either of the ideas. This is the core thought of the antinomists. But it depends on a number of other ways of thinking about these issues which have never been fully articulated, and which may seem obvious, but which are perhaps worth making explicit, if only to clarify how antinomism both differs from principlism, and what principlism looks like if we accept the existence of irreducible antinomies.

What Are Antinomies?

One point about such principles should be already apparent: for each principle, there is not only an alternative but also something more: a kind of counter-principle that trades on the absences, qualifications, or deficiencies of the principle in question. Put a little differently, one situation of argumentation involving "alternatives" would be this: we agree on certain premises, perhaps many, and disagree on a few—opening up the possibility that these disagreements, once isolated, may be open to being resolved. Antinomism makes a different point: that there are attractions, independent of one another, of each pole of the antinomy. They are in tension. The tension is a result not of some sort of conceptual error, but of the real presence of attraction, either the attraction of an ideal or the attraction of practical necessities which cannot in the end be denied. Nevertheless, the two poles are bound to one another.

This binding is difficult to explain, in part because, as we will see, it is not a binding at the level of principle, but of contingent fact. But there are also other relations, which are important for historical interpretation, and therefore for understanding the principles and disentangling them from their counterfeits. One of these involves the ambiguity of political terms and their malleability, which gives an illusion of commonality and continuity as well as feeds the

The Method of Antinomies   131

hope that a further principle can resolve the ambiguities. Oakeshott makes the point that the term *salus populi* has been appropriated for a vast range of political purposes and has thus been given a variety of meanings. "Democracy" is not merely ambiguous but deeply ambiguous—the home of its own antinomic interpretations. Similarly for "a right":

> The word "right" when preceded by the indefinite article enjoys a scale of meanings which ranges from one extreme to another, the extremes of meaning being, I contend, the meanings respectively appropriate to our two styles of politics.
>
> (Oakeshott, 1996: 42)

These terms have a traceable genealogy, which can reveal how the antinomic interpretations arise and how they change.

But Oakeshott makes the further point that resolving these conflicts and ambiguities is not in principle impossible because the conflicts are contingent in the first place.

> Confucius, when he was asked what he would do first were he appointed governor, replied: "the one thing necessary is the rectification of names." He meant that "things" could never be "straightened out" while words remained equivocal. The observation was, of course, immediately appropriate to the politics of his situation, where government was not distracted between two opposed directions of activity.
>
> (Oakeshott, 1996: 132)

This was not an isolated comment. Oakeshott makes the more general point that certain kinds of societies may not experience these antinomies.

> In a community whose members, engaged in few activities and those of the simplest character, are not drawn in a variety of directions, the politics of faith will have some appropriateness. Indeed, a monolithic society may be expected to have a monolithic politics.
>
> (Oakeshott, 1996: 95)

These remarks raise a number of important questions. The contingency of these antinomic conflicts distinguishes them from disagreements, dichotomies, taxonomies, and mere alternatives. But what are the contingencies? Are they escapable, or deep? And the contingent character of the conflicts raises the question of whether the political approach to them should be to alter the contingencies themselves through revolutionary means.

Understanding the contingent character of the antinomies, in general and specifically those discussed by Oakeshott, may be helped by comparison to Weber's distinction between the ethics of intention or conviction and the ethics of responsibility. Weber's point about these "ethics," which of course are abstractions from commonplace ethical thinking conditioned by Christianity, is not that they are always and everywhere in conflict. In general, good things follow from well-intended actions: we would find it difficult to understand them as well-intended if the intender foresaw harms from them. But there are situations in which this is not the case, and for Weber, as for Oakeshott, it is in politics—or as Oakeshott puts it, in the activity of governance—that the antinomies reveal themselves.

The way the conflicts appear in politics, in the activity of governance, however, differs from the general case. In one sense, there is a categorical distinction between an ethic of consequences and one of intentions. Intentions in the Christian tradition from which Weber came were visible only to God, and sin was intended in a way contrary to His will. *Fiat justitia et pereat mundus*[2] is a slogan that makes sense in this tradition because the "world" which is allowed to perish is inferior to the other world promised by God. But the relation between this-worldly and other-worldly is not an antinomic choice: it is merely a choice—the choice Weber underlines by quoting Machiavelli on the Florentines who put their city above their soul in the war with the Pope ([1919]1946: 126). In the realm of the political itself, however, matters are different. Politics is a this-worldly affair. There, the extremes of the ethics of intention are barely intelligible. Weber's example is the bomb-throwing anarchist who has no hope for, or cares about, the realization of the this-worldly political goal of anarchism. This person can only be understood in other-worldly, which is to say non-political, terms. Similarly, for the extremes of the ethic of consequences: without intending to realize some ideal good, but seeking only power, the career of the power politician "leads nowhere and is senseless."

Within politics, it is a contingent fact that the two ethics conflict, and they conflict only over specific instances of political decision: a politician may never be faced with this conflict. To be sure, there is such a thing as an other-worldly politics: this is the politics of the Grand Inquisitor, as described by Carl Schmitt, who places the salvation of his subjects' souls above any earthly goal (Taubes, [1987]2013: 7). But there is nothing antinomic about this choice: the Grand Inquisitor is not an impossible figure, limited by a nemesis that arises from his own actions; neither is the politician with this-worldly goals. Nor is there any de facto requirement that each partake in the character of the other. In the case of Weber's distinction, it is different: when Weber quotes Luther in his comment that "here I stand I can do no other" ([1919]1946: 127), he is pointing to the limits of the politics of responsibility, its nemesis, and the need for an element of conviction that saves it from the senselessness of the power politician. And when he discusses the Christian in politics motivated by the law of love and the belief that only good comes out of good acts, he is pointing to the nemesis of either failure or morally compromising action, the moral compromise resulting from the fact that politics is an activity in which the morally dangerous and unpredictable means of violence is characteristic, because it is characteristic of states.

So, we have here a complex set of distinctions, including both antinomies and non-antinomic classifications. This-worldly and other-worldly, theory and practice, and political ideals and the governance—these are all categorical distinctions, rather than antinomies. Their use enables us to isolate and identify genuine antinomies. But antinomies are not, so to speak, in the Platonic eternal. They are contingent, and contingent in more than one way. One way is revealed by the phenomenon of nemesis, to which we will now turn. Another is the way pointed to by Oakeshott's references to Confucius and to primitive societies. Antinomies are antinomies for us—people with a particular background and history which is present in the attractions we have for particular ideals, which is itself a contingent fact. This contingency, which we may call a deep contingency, because it is not resolvable or alterable by short-term or political means, needs some explanation, for understanding this kind of contingency is central to understanding what binds the antinomic pairs together.

Binding and Nemesis

As we have noted, Oakeshott makes the observation that many of the key terms of political discourse are ambiguous and have developed conflicting meanings, or changed meanings, over time. The fact that the terms are the same binds these usages without our having to discover that they are bound. "Ambiguity," however, while it is a useful term for understanding the history of a concept, is not precise enough. There is ambiguity in the term bachelor, applied to unmarried men and also to graduates. There is no antinomic conflict here—merely multiple meanings. In the case of "democracy," however, the different meanings not only conflict but stand in a relation to one another that is not extricable by redefinition: the two meanings are bound to one another in a distinctive non-accidental way. So, what we need is an answer to the question "How are antinomic pairs bound to one another?" whether or not they are multiple meanings of the same term.

What makes them antinomic rather than merely typological? One answer is this: the practical exceptions one must make to the principle refer to the antinomic partner. Schmitt turns this into a methodological principle: that, as he quotes Kierkegaard, "the exception explains the general and itself. And if one wants to study the general correctly, one only needs to look around for a true exception" (2005: 15). This part of the idea is simple: the nature of the general claim is revealed by the exception. A simple example of this might be taken from Karl Polanyi's *The Great Transformation* ([1944]2001). The general principle he invokes is that capitalism dehumanized people by substituting the cash nexus for genuine social relations and that only socialism can restore them. The "exception" he acknowledges is this: some people will not accede to these genuine relations voluntarily and must be taken care of separately, as misfits. As Polanyi says, the "objector" should be offered a niche into which he can retire, the choice of a "second-best," that leaves him

134 Stephen Turner

a life to live. Thus, will be secured the right to non-conformity that is the hallmark of a free society. The general principle is revealed by this exception to the principle of socialist solidarity,[3] which is belied by the existence of "objectors" (Polanyi, [1944]2001: 255). Both the character of the antinomic principle and its antinomic pair are revealed by this strategy. The demand for conformism is concealed in the idea of solidarity; the need to punish or corral the non-conforming is revealed by the exigencies of the application of the idea.

Leo Strauss, commenting on Weber, dismissed his examples with the comment that the political conflicts could easily be resolved by considerations of prudence and the like. His thought was that issues of conflict in general could be resolved by a suitable Aristotelian hierarchy of ends in which these considerations could be balanced ([1953]1965: 68–9). But Strauss's appeal to prudential considerations has the effect of conceding Oakeshott's point: there are contingent situations in which an appeal to prudential considerations is necessary to resolve a conflict between principles. The question is whether these situations are central to actual political life, to the activity of governance, or are exceptions that can be ignored in favor of an otherwise applicable hierarchy of the good.[4]

For Oakeshott, in practice, conflicting ideals can be and are reconciled, though not definitively: this indeed is the essence of politics. But how do these antinomies work? Why are they not just alternative value choices? This requires some analysis. They are ideal types, neither of which is fully realizable because it is dependent in some manner on its antinomic pair.[5] The pairs are thus linked but in conflict. One can suppress one side of the pair, but not obliterate it. Even the state oriented fully to substantive rather than procedural justice, for example, cannot operate without procedures—Cadi justice requires the appointment of a Cadi, for example; the state which aspires to neutrality, similarly, must be legitimate, and seen to be effective in achieving some substantive goods for its participants. These are not hard analytic truths, but lessons that result from putting ideals into practice, as Oakeshott himself says.

Strauss, however, has a point: the argument depends on the identification of conflicts at the level of political ideals that may not be apparent in the ordinary course of politics. The use of extreme "conceivable but not realistic" examples to bring out these conflicts is worth examining. It appears repeatedly in Oakeshott's own writings. Take a simple example from Oakeshott:

> What we are seeking is an alleged mode of association in which the associates are expressly and exclusively related in terms of the recognition of rules of conduct of a certain kind, namely "laws." And what we have here is associates related expressly and exclusively in terms of seeking to satisfy substantive wants.

(1983: 124)

The "expressly and exclusively" phrase signals the unreality of these extreme cases. In practice, as Oakeshott himself says, the extreme case of a rule of law regime is not realizable. The alternative extreme is perhaps possible, though as we will see, the possibility depends on contingencies.

So, what is their function in the argument? As Walter Benjamin puts it:

> The general is the idea. The empirical, on the other hand, can be all the more profoundly understood the more clearly it is seen as an extreme. The concept has its roots in the extreme. Just as a mother is seen to begin to live in the fullness of her power only when the circle of her children, inspired by the feeling of her proximity, closes around her, so do ideas come to life only when extremes are assembled around them.
> (Benjamin, [1928]2003: 35).

Bloodless abstraction, the gray of theory, is a realm in which antinomies can be reconciled. Much of the time, as noted, they can be reconciled in practice. It is in the extremes of the empirical that they become recognizable.

Maxims of the sort quoted by Benjamin sound systematic, but they are not. This one is already in the form of a paradox, since the general has, by definition, no exceptions. To understand it, we need to see how it works in these arguments. Oakeshott, in *Politics of Faith*, uses the term "nemesis," which is closer to the point: which is that in practice a given tendency to realize an idea is undone or limited in distinctive ways; distinctive in that they arise from considerations associated with its antinomic pair. In discussing the nemesis of the politics of faith, or perfection, he lists a number of examples:

> the engagement to impose a single pattern of activity upon a community is a self-defeating engagement.
> (Oakeshott, 1996: 99)

The politics of skepticism, and its antinomic pair of the politics of faith or perfectibility, each have their own nemesis that points to the other in the pair:

> The disposition of skepticism to underestimate the occasion is another facet of this defeat. Faith recognizes every occasion as an emergency, and in the name of the "public interest" or the "public advantage" maintains its antinomian rule by calling upon the vast power at its command, which (because it is always insufficient) is always in process of being enlarged.
> (Oakeshott, 1996: 108)

The nemesis of the politics of perfectibility is that political power is always insufficient to achieve it—precisely the confession that Polanyi makes, justifying the "necessary" practices which he was well aware were characteristic of Stalinism when he admits that solidarism will never be complete.

136   Stephen Turner

But skepticism has its own nemesis.

> It is liable to confuse a genuine emergency with the counterfeit emergencies of faith, and to discount it. But in doing so it displays an insufficiency which puts it on the road to the other manner of self-defeat to which it is liable.
>
> (Oakeshott, 1996: 109)

This failure and the inadequacies it reveals are part of the "real" to which Oakeshott and antinomists more generally attend. But we can ask about other parts of the real as well: the nature of deep contingency, and the relation between ideals and the stuff from which they are, as Oakeshott puts it, "extricated."

Deep Contingency, Ideal Types, and the Data of History

Ideals need to be formulated for their antinomic character to be revealed. They are not necessarily apparent in the flux of ordinary political talk. The abstraction in question, because it is an imaginative enterprise, is not mechanical or scientific. The material with which it works is our way of talking about political things, and the way that they were talked of in the past. They

> reveal themselves in our manner of speaking, and they are cogent formulations only in so far as they make intelligible the current and historic distraction of our politics.
>
> (Oakeshott, 1996: 44)

Our talk about politics is not merely a mass of unconnected habits of speaking and acting, but a complex web underlain with purposes and with connected and conflicting purposes. We can find different coherences or ideal characters at the surface of this web.

As Oakeshott says, "The uninhibited character of each of these two styles of politics has, then, to be extricated." Formulating them provides a kind of coherence to ordinary talk, but "to elicit this is an imaginative rather than a logical exercise; not a purely logical exercise" (1996: 92). But the formulation is not merely a matter of providing a definition identifying a family of notions that correspond roughly to what is in effect a kind of ideal type, and indicating what the pull or attraction of these ideals (or rather the underlying purposes and aspirations which they articulate) is. It also requires revealing their character by identifying their nemesis or the exceptions that appear as they are put into practice. As Oakeshott explains,

> Whenever the politics of modern Europe have moved decisively in the direction of either of these extremes, the shadow of the nemesis has

appeared: our task is to reconstruct from these shadowy intimations the hidden character, or at least the hidden characteristics which they signify.

(1996: 2)

So, finding the coherence of an ideal, or constructing it imaginatively out of the raw material of political speech, is more than a matter of logic in a variety of ways. It relates to the pushback of the real world in the form of nemesis, exception, and unintended consequences. But it also, because the antinomic relations depend on contingencies, relates to the contingencies of the real world as well.

This relationship is difficult to explain, for epistemic reasons that will become obvious. The principlist regards such contingencies as mere conditions to be altered in pursuit of the ideal and the elimination of the antinomy: as bumps in the road, or eggs needing to be scrambled to make a revolutionary omelet. But the failure to realize the ideals points to the difficulty of knowing what the relevant contingencies are. The topic is a theme of Oakeshott in "On Being Conservative" (1962) where a contrast is identified between those who think that large-scale change can be planned with predictable outcomes and those who believe the world is complex in ways that belie our ability to predict the consequences of our actions, especially those involving large scale change.

Some of the contingent facts that bear on antinomies, and which form their conditions, are what we might call "shallow": altering them is possible, and there are predictable risks, costs, and benefits from doing so. Deep contingencies, however, are those which we cannot readily alter or predict the outcome of altering and typically are unable to conceptualize clearly in the first place. They exist in the longue durée. It is this kind of contingency that Oakeshott has in mind when he says that

> Political activity in the conditions of modern Europe is movement within a certain field of historic possibilities. During this half-millennium these possibilities have expanded in some directions and contracted in others: what may be contemplated now is in some respects a smaller and in others a larger range of activity than it was five hundred years ago. But these contractions and expansions are relatively insignificant. The range of internal movement is fundamentally unchanged.

(Oakeshott, 1996: 117)

This is not to say that rapid change is not possible: he also adds that

> modern history may be said to have been inaugurated by a peculiarly large and rapid expansion of political possibilities, and its course, from this point of view, has been the more and more thorough exploitation of a range of movement then opened up.

(Oakeshott, 1996: 117)

138   Stephen Turner

This was not the aim of the people who produced this change: their aims were not even political. Oakeshott locates a major component of the changes that allowed for the expansion of state power as the rise of individualism which eventuates in the Reformation (Oakeshott, 1993: 22).

This is very murky territory. The deep contingencies that may become salient in the future, as conditions for previously unrealized or unconceived antinomies, may already be present in the deep history of a culture or even more deeply rooted. Morgenthau, under the influence late in the life of psychoanalysis, argued that the antinomy of love and power was fundamental. But because the salience of antinomies comes and goes, we need to avoid the temptation to ascribe these antinomies to human nature, without denying the possibility that they are indeed that deeply rooted.

Antinomism Versus Principlism: Is This a Methodological Antinomy?

In passing, I earlier commented that the relation between principlism and antinomism might itself be an antinomy. There is something to be said for this: the two approaches are in some important respects kindred. Both are abstractions from political experience and ordinary political speech; both aim at clarifying it or giving it greater coherence. Principle-seeking is, in any case, part of the political life the antinomist is concerned to study.

> To abridge conduct into general principles is . . . a supremely important level of political thinking. And even at first sight it is obvious that some of these generalizations refer to the constitutions of government and others to the office or conduct of government.
>
> (Oakeshott, 1993: 14)

But the motives we might have for this kind of reconstruction will vary. One is "to understand what forms of behavior they represent or are intended to represent, and to recognize the part that they play" (Oakeshott, 1993: 14). Oakeshott himself acknowledges that this is a hazardous affair. But more hazardous is the attempt to ground these principles in something more fundamental—to make them more than articulations of our practices, and into fundamental truths, beyond the contingencies that give rise to antinomies.

An asymmetry between principlism and antinomism prevents them from being true antinomies. What the existence of contingent antinomies shows is that there are circumstances, contingencies, under which principles cannot resolve antinomies. Antinomism acknowledges that there are situations in which principlism, in the form of the Confucian rectification of names, which might be the same as the articulation of a new concept of citizenship to match what has become the practice of citizenship, as Marshall did, might be appropriate and successful. But principlism cannot acknowledge that its own truths are contingent, or that its exceptions undermine its principles: they would be placed in a category below truth itself.

Notes

1 The pairing of Weber and Oakeshott might at first glance seem odd, but there is an important and somewhat startling textual basis for this connection. Oakeshott reviewed Morgenthau's *Scientific Man versus Power Politics* (1946) shortly before writing "Rationalism in Politics" ([1947–48]/1962). The review, which comments that "This is a book good enough to wish it were better, and profound enough to wish it were more lucid" ([1947]/1993: 97), reads like of a draft of Oakeshott's classic paper, which provides exactly this lucidity. Morgenthau's text does not mention Weber but is the most overtly Weberian of his writings (see Turner and Factor, 1984). It was based on lectures at the New School which were part of a special émigré genre, in which Americanizing German scholars presented their views by eliminating German sources and substituting Anglo-American ones. This had a distorting effect but was also the source of novel connections, for example, Morgenthau's appropriation of Lincoln as the exemplary great leader.
2 Let justice be done though the world perish.
3 Oakeshott discusses this impulse to enforced conformism at length under the heading of solidarism (1993: 89–99).
4 Strauss exempts the conflict between ethics of intention and ethics of consequences from his reduction to the prudential, but on ground familiar from Schmitt: Strauss interprets the conflict in its theological sense, as one between other-worldly and this-worldly, or between the human and the divine, or theology and philosophy. These are non-antinomic, categorical distinctions.
5 The term "pairs" is important, but should not be misinterpreted. Nothing excludes an antinomic trilemma or indeed any number of antinomic elements. To be antinomic, however, the elements must be antinomic to each of the other elements, that is to say, form a pairwise antinomic relation with each of the other elements.

References

Beerbohm, E. *In Our Name: The Ethics of Democracy*. Princeton: Princeton University Press, 2012.

Benjamin, W. *The Origin of German Tragic Drama*, translated by John Osborne. London: Verso, [1928]2003.

Berlin, I. *Two Concepts of Liberty*. Oxford: Clarendon Press, 1958.

Breiner, P. *Max Weber and Democratic Politics*. Ithaca: Cornell University Press, 1996.

Brettschneider, C. "Philosophy Tag," Eric Beerbohm, *In Our Name: The Ethics of Democracy*, 10 February, 2015. http://dailynous.com/2015/02/10/philosophy-tag-14/

Kalyvas, A. *Democracy & The Politics of the Extraordinary: Max Weber, Carl Schmitt, and Hannah Arendt*. Cambridge: Cambridge University Press, 2008.

Maley, T. *Democracy & the Political in Max Weber's Thought*. Toronto: University of Toronto Press, 2011.

Minogue, K. "Introduction," In *Morality and Politics in Modern Europe: The Harvard Lectures*, Edited by Shirley Robin Letwin. New Haven/London: Yale University Press, 1993, vii-xii.

Morgenthau, H. *Scientific Man versus Power Politics*. Chicago: The University of Chicago Press, 1946.

Mouffe, C. *The Democratic Paradox*. London/New York: Verso, 2000.

Oakeshott, M. "Scientific Politics: A Review of Hans Morgenthau: Scientific Man versus Power Politics," In *Religion, Politics and the Moral Life*, Edited by Timothy Fuller. New Haven/London: Yale University Press, [1947]1993, 97–110.

140 Stephen Turner

Oakeshott, M. *Scientific Politics: Morality and Politics in Modern Europe: The Harvard Lectures*, Edited by Shirley Robin Letwin. New Haven/London: Yale University Press, 1993.

Oakeshott, M. "Scientific Politics. On Being Conservative," In *Rationalism in Politics and Other Essays*. London: Methuen, 1962, 168–196.

Oakeshott, M. *Scientific Politics: On Human Conduct*. Oxford: Clarendon Press, [1975]1991.

Oakeshott, M. "Scientific Politics. Rationalism in Politics," In *Rationalism in Politics and Other Essays*. London: Methuen, [1947/48]1962, 1–36.

Oakeshott, M. *Scientific Politics: The Politics of Faith and the Politics of Scepticism*. New Haven/London: Yale University Press, 1996.

Oakeshott, M. "Scientific Politics: The Rule of Law," In *On History and Other Essays*. Oxford: Blackwell, 1983, 119–164.

Pettit, P. *Republicanism: A Theory of Freedom and Government*. Oxford: Oxford University Press, 1997.

Polanyi, K. *The Great Transformation: The Political and Economic Origins of Our Time*. Boston: Beacon Press, [1944]2001.

Schmitt, C. *Political Theology: Four Chapters on the Concept of Sovereignty*, translated by George Schwab. Chicago: University of Chicago Press, 2005.

Shils, E. "The Antinomies of Liberalism," In *The Virtues of Civility: Selected Essays on Liberalism, Tradition, and Society*, Edited by S. Grosby. Indianapolis: Liberty Fund, [1978]1997, 123–187.

Shils, E. *The Torment of Secrecy: The Background and Consequences of American Security Policies*. Glencoe: The Free Press, 1956.

Strauss, L. *Natural Right and History*. Chicago: The University of Chicago Press, [1953]1965.

Taubes, J. "Carl Schmitt: Apocalyptic Prophet of the Counterrevolution," In *To Carl Schmitt: Letters and Reflections*, translated by Keith Tribe. New York: Columbia University Press, [1987]2013, 1–18.

Turner, S and R. Factor. *Max Weber and the Dispute over Reason and Value*. London: Routledge, 1984.

Weber, M. "Politics as a Vocation," In *From Max Weber: Essays in Sociology*, translated by H. H. Gerth and C. Wright Mills. New York: Oxford University Press, [1919]1946, 77–128.

Chapter 8

Decisionism and Politics
Weber as Constitutional Theorist

Stephen Turner and Regis Factor

Weber's constitutional and legal thinking developed and replaced the utilitarian views of Ihering and was followed by the critique of liberalism of Carl Schmitt. This chapter explains how Weber went beyond utilitarian with a relativistic view of values and showed how a politics focused on the achievement of shared intermediate values could proceed under a parliamentary order that preserved human freedom. This is a crucial and largely unnoticed intellectual innovation that avoids the idea that democracy is and must be based on a shared worldview or sense of destiny. Schmitt's alternative was to affirm the reality and importance of arbitrary sovereign authority that transcended normal politics.

The National Assembly held in the Frankfurt *Paulskirche* in 1848, which opened with high hopes for the unification of Germany on parliamentary constitutional principles, was left to die a year later, in the telling phrase of Donoso Cortes, "like a street woman in the gutter" (quoted in Valentin, 1940: 263). In the period of reaction that followed, during which the *Paulskirche* convention came to be described as the "parliament of professors," one of its members, Georg Gottfried Gervinus, was accused, in a trial for high treason, of attempting to prove the historical inevitability of the supersession of monarchical forms by republican forms. This was Gervinus's second experience as a professorial martyr. In 1837, he had been one of the professors at the University of Gottingen, the "Gottingen Seven," who protested the revocation of the Hanoverian constitution. For this, he had been banished and given three days to leave the kingdom. The lesson he, and many other liberal thinkers, learned from these experiences was that the German middle classes were incapable of performing the historical role assigned to them; they lacked the political will to establish a republican order.

Both unification and parliamentarization occurred despite the political failures of liberalism. The creation of a parliamentary structure was part of the complex half-treaty, half-constitution that made unification possible, and the National Liberals became the leading party in the new parliament. The "unpoliticality" of the middle classes, the source of support for the party, led to its slow destruction. The great division in strategy that crippled the party was a

DOI: 10.4324/9781003360810-11

142   Stephen Turner and Regis Factor

result of the dilemma created by Bismarck's attacks on the parliament that had come into being with unification, and by usurpations of its powers. The liberals were faced with the alternatives of resisting and risking diminishing what popular support they still retained, or accepting the sham parliamentarism that Bismarck allowed. Liberal politicians chose the latter, and the party gradually degenerated into an interest party without principles.

The realm of liberal thought developed differently. The combination of feeble popular support and the predominance of intellectuals made for a situation parallel to the circumstances of the members of the Frankfurt School in this century, who were forced to turn their intellectual energies from the failures of capitalism to the failure of the proletariat. Liberal thinkers made idiosyncratic accommodations in theory to the politics of power from which liberal politicians were excluded in practice. Weber grew up in this intellectual ambiance of professorial liberalism. Many of its leading figures had connections to the Weber household; Gervinus himself had been the tutor of Weber's mother.

When Weber wrote on the German constitution in 1917, the political fundamentals were unchanged. Parliament was weak, and the bourgeoisie lacked political will. He proposed to strengthen parliament but saw that the support of the bourgeoisie could not be counted on.

> One can be quite assured that the beneficiaries of the old order and of uncontrolled bureaucracy will exploit every outbreak of syndicalist putschism, no matter how insignificant, in order to scare our philistine bourgeoisie which, unfortunately, still has pretty weak nerves.
>
> (Weber, [1968]1978: 1461)

This was the ever-renewed lesson of 1848.[1] Yet fate was again to intervene on the side of reform, and Weber's constitutional proposals of the wartime period (Weber, [1968]1978: 1381–469) were to have a significant influence on the Weimar constitution, in large part because they were virtually the only proposals for fuller parliamentarization in existence when President Wilson forced the dismantling of the monarchy. On the strength of his proposals, Weber became a member of a working group that drafted the proposal that, after considerable modification, became the Weimar constitution. Weber presented no constitutional theory as such. To reconstruct the premises of his constitutional thinking, we are obliged to proceed by making something of the scattered critical remarks and observations he made on the themes of the legal and historical constitutional thinkers he read, discussed, and had relations with. It happens that there is a wealth of remarks of this sort and that Weber had a close personal relationship with a figure who plays an important role in the development of German legal thinking, Gustav Radbruch (Radbruch, 1951: 84; Marianne Weber, 1975: 452, 454). Radbruch based a full-fledged relativistic philosophy· of law on premises about the rationality of value-choice that Weber shared. Weber's explicit statements do locate him in relation to his peers

Decisionism and Politics 143

and immediate predecessors; he was a link in the progressive transformation of fundamental premises about constitutional order. The aim of this chapter is to show what the progression was and how Weber contributed to it.

Ihering's The Law as a Means to an End

Weber was well aware of the great names of contemporary constitutional thinking and legal philosophy. When he entered university studies in Heidelberg, he read Ranke and Savigny, representatives of "conservative" approaches to German legal and constitutional development. In Immanuel Bekker's course on Roman law, a subject in which Weber was ultimately to be habilitated, and which was then among the most prestigious of the academic disciplines, he was introduced to the work of Rudolph von Ihering, the polemical opponent of Savigny (Marianne Weber, 1975: 65; cf. Mommsen, 1984: 4). Later, as a student in Berlin, he attended the lectures of Rudolf Gneist on German constitutional law and on Prussian administrative law (Mommsen, 1984: 11). The ideas of several of the legal thinkers prominent in his student days are found, transformed, at the center of Weber's sociology; Rudolph Sohm was the source of "charisma," Gneist of the idea of the centrality and indispensability of bureaucracy. His emphasis on the centrality to the Western civilization of the "rationality" of Roman law reflected the dispute between Romanists and Germanists, including Friedrich Karl von Savigny and his successors, whose historiographic views Weber rejected as so much mysticism.

In Radbruch's textbook on the philosophy of law, he identifies Ihering as the thinker in whose mind "all motifs of thought" of earlier philosophy of law "were gathered and joined" to produce "the renascence of legal philosophy" that had taken place during the time Weber was trained in the law ([1932]1950: 66). The general analytic thesis of Ihering's major work, *Der Zweck im Recht (The Element of Purpose in Law)*, was that laws are analyzable in terms not just of abstract concepts, the method of the then dominant "conceptualist" school, but also of ends: "It is not," he said, "the sense of right that has produced law, but it is law that has produced the sense of right. Law knows only one source, and that is the practical one of purpose" (translated in Stone, 1950: 301). The premise that laws were compromises that served practical purposes grounded a practical, historical method of analyzing the ends of given laws in terms of the interests they are designed to accommodate.[2] As it happens, Ihering provides us with a direct link to liberal political philosophy, for he was the most prominent German admirer of Utilitarianism, and especially of Bentham, whose own discussion of laws provided part of the vocabulary for the historical, evolutionary approach Ihering developed.

"Acting, and acting with a purpose," Ihering said, are synonymous ([1877–83]1968: 9). Purpose, as Ihering used it, is the "ideational form" of an interest ([1877–83]1968: 7); interest is the "real force which moves the human will" ([1877–83]1968: 39). However, "the will is not under the law of causality, but under the law of purpose" ([1877–83]1968: 18), which is to say that, while action is moved by interest, it is not the mechanical product of external causality ([1877–83]1968: 17). The dialectical target of these definitions was Kant, whose ethics separated ideation and will, and of whom Ihering tartly remarked that "You might as well hope to move a loaded wagon from its place by means of a lecture on the theory of motion as the human will by means of the categorical imperative" ([1877–83]1968: 39). The attraction of Kant's theory was that it was part of a solution to a traditional problem for German liberals, the question of the relation between individual purposes and the purposes of "higher" entities, such as the state. Gneist had supposed the existence of a mysterious harmony between the two types of purposes. Ihering gave a different solution to this problem, designed to be an improvement both on the German liberal tradition and on the Utilitarians: "The answer is, the world exists by taking egoism into its service, by paying it the reward which it desires. The world interests egoism in its purposes, and is then assured of its co-operation" (Ihering, [1877–83]1968: 25).

The reasoning built on Bentham. The world has two levers; the first lever is given by nature in the form of pleasure and pain (Ihering, [1877–83]1968: 26–7), and a second arises by *"connecting one's own purpose with the other man's interest"* ([1877–83]1968: 28; italics in original) and securing "agreement of wills" between parties. Ihering was rather vague on the character of this "subjective" or psychological "lever" and said only that it is an "indirect compulsion" ([1877–83]1968: 34) and that the agreement of wills in such paradigmatic cases as commercial agreements may depend on salesmanship. The basic properties of the commercial transaction are preserved in the state. The state, as Ihering defined it, is an association that is distinguished as a type of association by its claim of an exclusive right to exercise certain forms of coercion. Ihering went beyond mere definition to inquire into the justification of the state's claim to this exclusive right. The justification he arrived at was necessity; coercion was found to be indispensable to the achievement of the purposes for which these associations were formed.

Ihering made his reputation in Germany for an argument against Utilitarianism. Identifying egoism with individual purposes, Ihering argued, led to a fundamental conceptual difficulty. Mill conceded the propriety of the interest of society in various regulations designed to keep an individual from acting against the interest of others but denied the propriety of laws that have the purpose of forcing an individual to act for his own good against his will. In doing this, as Ihering pointed out, he conceded the validity of a standard of the interest of society. But Mill's attempts to draw a line between justified and unjustified intrusions into individual freedom were, Ihering showed, hopelessly ad hoc. Mill had said, for example, that law could forbid a person from selling himself into slavery on the grounds that freedom cannot be used for its own destruction. But every contract, Ihering observed, "contains a partial renunciation of freedom" (quoted in Stone, 1950: 302). Mill's difficulties were not, as it happened, purely theoretical. In 1905, Dicey opened the published form of his *Lectures on the Relation between Law and Public Opinion during the Nineteenth Century* (1962: xx) by quoting the same passage in Mill, with the purpose of showing how far toward a recognition of collective interests public opinion had gone in the preceding 50 years. The conceptual consequence of admitting the validity of collective interests is that "individual" interests become only one set of ends among many interests, which may have equal or superior force.

The Evolution of Law

The source of all interests is to be found in "egoism." But egoistic interests or purposes create *social* interests by virtue of the fact that the realization of most egoistic interests is possible only through other individuals (Stone, 1950: 305) and, in particular, through "associations" with distinct purposes. These "associational" interests have a degree of autonomy; for just as a contract involves the renunciation of freedom, the subordination of the interests of the individual in an "association," legal or informal, that defines a purpose is a necessity for the achievement of many purposes. Social interests of this sort not only persist historically over longer periods than the particular individual egoistic interests that compose them but are also subject to evolution and alteration. New circumstances and conflicts create new coincidences of interest and new opportunities for artificially creating coincidences of interests. In commerce, the salesman secures an "agreement in wills" by his "ideational representations" of new purposes, which in turn produce new circumstances under which new purposes may be created. Similarly, for law: "One purpose of law is produced out of the other with the same necessity with which, according to the Darwinian theory, one animal species is developed from the other" (translated in Stone, 1950: 303). This, Ihering saw, was "a new inexorability, but not," he thought, "one before which men may remain passive; rather one which requires constant struggle and conscious seeking of ends on the part of men" (translated in Stone, 1950: 303).

Understanding the ends that men formerly sought to achieve through law provided Ihering with a method of *Ideologiekritik*. Past doctrines and laws could be understood as ideational representations of the purposes of past associations, based on former coincidences of interest. The ideas and practices of the past thus came to represent not "merely the arbitrary and the obsolete," as they had for Bentham, but also "the imperfect realization of the principle of utility" (Stone, 1950: 303). Ihering also attempted a better formulation of this principle, which took cognizance of those egoistic interests of the individual that arise from the fact that one must realize one's egoistic interests through others, a project he did not live to complete. The attempt itself presumes that "egoistic interests" are in some sense natural or fixed, and that the collective or social purposes that are served, in different social and historical circumstances, by different laws, arc themselves more or less fixed. The similarity between this premise and the doctrine of the mutability of law in Aquinas must have been pointed out to him after the first edition of *Der Zweck im Recht* appeared, for in the second he not only admitted it but also chided intervening generations for having overlooked it (Stone, 1950: 301n.).

Force and the State

Law is a *modus vivendi* that is recognized as binding and hence as a standard for judging individual conduct. There is one fixed interest in which it is rooted: peace. Intelligent egoism and moderation counsel peace, so it is rational to obey, and states arrange matters so that one is punished for disobedience. But such utilitarian reasons for obedience do not of course always obtain, which suggests that there are occasions when this *modus vivendi* ought not to be honored. Ihering acknowledged this: "Law can conflict with life," he said, and went on to add that in these conflicts "we choose life" (Ihering, [1877–83]1968: 189), because "law is not the highest thing in the world, not an end in itself; but merely a means to an end, the final end being the existence of society" ([1877–83]1968: 188). The character of these special occasions is a point of some importance for Ihering's historical argument. In the normal case, individual and collective interests do coincide. Ihering stated this as a "law" to the effect that common interests are always preponderant over individual interests, by which he meant that because of the necessity of achieving our ends through others, there are real, more or less fixed interests in a peaceful social order that are always greater than the real individual interests against any such order.

But the form that this order may take is not *strictly* determined by these interests, in part because new combinations or coincidences of interests may be conceived and articulated, and new forms of association invented. In the unusual occasion, the situation of revolution, where "unorganized force" faces the organized force of the state, or the situation of dictatorship, where the law must be suspended to preserve society,[3] politics is replaced by force. So, where we must

> choose either law or life, the decision cannot be doubtful: force sacrifices law and rescues life. These are the *saving deeds* of the power of the government. At the moment when they are committed they spread fear and terror, and are branded by the advocates of law as a criminal outrage against law's sanctity; but they often need only a few years or decades, until the dust which they have raised has settled, to gain vindication by their effects.
>
> (Ihering, [1877–83]1968: 189, italics in original)

Any successful use of organized force is better than anarchy, the impotence of state force ([1877–83]1968: 234–5). But the exceptional moments are when law is made and new orders are established. These moments are also a source of the political maturity of nations, for the experience of upheaval teaches the necessity of the state and law (Ihering, [1877–83]1968: 416–17).

The *de facto* predominance of organized power over unorganized power usually gives the state the upper hand against revolution. But the *possibility* of conflict means that vigilance in preventing "any organization that threatens it on the part of the forces of the people" ([1877–83]1968: 237) is an essential task of the state. This "negative task" of the state means that the state's right to coerce must be an absolute monopoly, such that other associations can coerce only with the implied but revocable consent of the state. The positive task of the state is the achievement of greater efficiency in the organization of force: "The State organization of forces may be designated as the proper *technique of the political art*," and the state has the practical obligation to achieve "the highest possible perfection of the organization of its own forces" ([1877–83]1968: 237; italics in original). The "State of modern times which has understood as no other has how best to make up for the insignificance of its forces by an exemplary organization" is Prussia (Ihering, [1877–83]1968: 237).

Purposes as Decisions

Much of Ihering's analytic practice was retained by Weber. Like Ihering, he assumed both that the interests of a particular historical period are more or less fixed, and that the interests articulated as the purposes of associations would in fact be largely without force if they did not coincide with pre-existent interests. Weber also retained Ihering's method of *Ideologiekritik;* when he encountered a legal doctrine, he asked what interests or compromise between interests it articulates (e.g., Weber, [1968]1978: 874–5). The seeds of Weber's destruction of Ihering's assumptions about the relative fixity of interests, and the basis for Weber's radicalization of the concept of interest, are planted in Ihering's own texts. In *Der Zweck im Recht* Ihering made, in passing, the comment that some "rewards" are "ideal" (Ihering, [1877–83]1968: 147). In a widely read speech on the historical importance of the defense of "rights" where the cost of this defense goes beyond any benefit to immediate material interests, he used the term "ideal interests" as a means of describing the motivation for these struggles (Ihering, [1872]1915: 127). In Ihering's uses, the term is never drastically separated from the interests of a more tangible sort that the ideal articulates. But the usage itself laid the foundation for the transformation of the concept which is used to transform Ihering's project.

Ihering expected that human purposes could be systematically related in an impersonal hierarchy, with an order determined by the historical evolution of one collective purpose out of another—an inexorable process itself largely determined by the existence of more or less fixed "egoistic" interests. Weber and Radbruch insisted on the irrationality of the relations between these choices. Anarchism, to choose a familiar example, becomes for Radbruch a form of individualism. He understood "individualism" as a category of value-choice antinomic to the categories in which the values of the nation and culture fell ([1932]1950: 94, 99). In place of the necessity of ordering purposes in an impersonal, "objective" hierarchy—in which, for example, the choice of individual values over collective values can be understood as a kind of self-contradiction—they insisted on the necessity of ordering value-choices in a personal hierarchy, i.e., to recognize the potential conflicts between choices and to make "responsible decisions," conscious decisions between fully understood alternatives (Weber, 1949: 18; Radbruch, [1932]1950: 136). They insisted on the irrationality of the relations between the array of choices present at any historical moment. Radbruch called this doctrine, whose premises Weber shared,[4] "decisionism" or "relativism." When Radbruch called it "relativism," he was careful to insist that it was not, as he puts it in one book,

> cognate to Pilate of the Gospel, in whom practical as well as theoretical reason becomes mute: "What is truth?" It is cognate rather to Lessings' Nathan, to whom the silence of theoretical reason is the strongest appeal to practical reason: "May each of you vie with the other then in bringing out the power of the gem in his own ring."
>
> (Radbruch, [1932]1950: 58)

The philosophical basis of the doctrine was formulated repeatedly in their writings: "Statements concerning the Ought may be established or proved only by other statements concerning the Ought. For this very reason, the ultimate statements concerning the Ought are incapable of proof. axiomatic. They may not be discerned but only professed" (Radbruch, [1932]1950: 55).

Law is an arena in which persons with potentially different ultimate values may share common subordinate or intermediate values. Radbruch quoted a French jurist to this effect.

> Peace and security—these are the first benefits the Law is to afford us. Even if we should be in profound, irreducible disagreement on the higher ends of the law, we could nevertheless arrive at an understanding so as to make it achieve these intermediate ends in which we are all interested.
>
> (quoted in Radbruch, [1932]1950: 108n)

The understanding or "agreement of wills" with respect to these common intermediate ends itself contains "decisions" between rationally irreconcilable options (cf. Radbruch, [1932]1950: 109). Radbruch argued that in law, the choices were further structured by the fact of the mutual dependence on the three basic values—individuality, collectivity, and community that constituted the sphere of law. The achievement of each required, he argued, the achievement, to some extent, of the others. Radbruch was a socialist and held to what he called a "social view" of the law. His analysis of private property exemplifies his point: "even the individualistic theories of ownership were never

Decisionism and Politics 149

purely individualistic. They were based on the assumption of a pre-stabilized harmony between individualistic selfishness and the common weal" (Radbruch, [1932]1950: 166). Consequently, "even in the legal view of today, private ownership appears as an area of activity for private initiative, entrusted to the individual by the community, entrusted in the expectation of its social use, always revocable if that expectation is not fulfilled" (Radbruch, [1932]1950: 167). This formulation, he thought, turned the question of nationalization into a factual question of its effects. Weber neither considered that the evidence supported such a policy nor believed in absolute rights, such as property rights. Nor did "rights" figure in his historical analyses; the notion that the evolution of law proceeded through the struggle for rights, one of Ihering's central historical conceptions (Ihering, [1872]1915), is absent in Weber.

Constitutional arrangements are means or intermediate ends. As Weber put it, "forms of State are for me techniques like any other machinery" (translated in Mayer, 1956: 76).[5] Ihering believed that the problem of the efficient use of force, the positive task of the state, was inherent. "Politics as a Vocation," written at a time when constitutional issues were very much in the air, begins with an assertion of the diversity of constitutional forms:

> What is a "state"? Sociologically, the state cannot be defined in terms of its ends. There is scarcely any task that some political association has not taken in hand, and there is no task that one could say has always been exclusive and peculiar to those associations which have been the predecessors of the modern state. Ultimately [he agrees with Ihering] one can define the modem state sociologically only in terms of the specific *means* peculiar to it, as to every political association, namely, the use of physical force.
>
> (Weber, 1948: 77–8; italics in original)

When Ihering discussed the evolution in law he assumed that, in the evolution of purposes, the purposes of peace and security provided by Attila continued to be provided by regimes with higher purposes. Weber repeated this, giving it a decidedly Hobbesian twist:

> In the final analysis, in spite of all "social welfare policies," the whole course of the state's inner political functions, of justice and administration, is repeatedly and unavoidably regulated by the objective pragmatism of "reasons of state." The state's absolute end is to safeguard (or to change) the external and internal distribution of power; ultimately, this end must seem meaningless to any universalist religion of salvation. This fact has held and still holds, even more so, for foreign policy. It is absolutely essential for every political association to appeal to the naked violence of coercive means in the face of outsiders as well as in the face of internal enemies.
>
> (1948: 334)

Beneath the benevolent veneer of the modern Welfare State are the realities of power. But Weber did not conclude, as Ihering did, that peace was a basic purpose of law. Instead, he rejected the distinction between peace and struggle:

> "Peace" is nothing more than a change in the form of the conflict or in the antagonists or in the objects of the conflict, or finally in the chances of selection. Obviously, absolutely nothing of a general character can be said as to whether such shifts can withstand examination according to an ethical or other value-judgement.
>
> (1949: 27)

Where Ihering believed that success stemmed from the use of force for the right, by which he meant the predominant collective interests, Weber said,

> The very success of force, or of the threat of force, depends ultimately upon power relations and not on ethical "right," even were one to believe it possible to discover objective criteria for such "right" . . . "reasons of state" thus follow their own external and internal laws.
>
> (1948: 334)

If we read Weber's remarks as a selective repudiation of Ihering, we are faced with some questions. Ihering's philosophy of the state, for all its inadequacies, was a more or less coherent whole. How do Weber's revisions of Ihering fit together and how do they fit with those doctrines, such as interest, *raison d'état*, and law as compromise, that Weber does not reject? In particular, how do they bear on the special concerns of his constitutional writings? Here the comparison with Ihering is striking, for Weber rejected the idea of a fixed *ultima ratio* for the state that Ihering had made the basis for his own theory of state form.

The Constitutional Decision

The rhetorical community Weber addressed in his "political" writings on the constitution is not the community of those who share or could be made to share his particular values or interests, but a community of persons whose party and material interests Weber took as given. In his conduct on the constitutional committee, Weber's tendency to accept interests as unalterable pre-conditions, and to focus on the devices of the constitutional structure that serve to relate given institutionally articulated interests, was especially marked. He was attentive to the domestic interests given by the pre-existing federal system—the part-constitution, part-treaty of the first Reich—as well as to the class and religious interests articulated by the parties. His readiness to face up to and accept these interests had the defects of its virtue of realism—he thought solely in terms of the compromises made possible by these interests, and tended—as he did in his accounts of English and Russian constitutional history—to ignore

Decisionism and Politics   151

those political ideas, public sentiments, and traditions that could not be easily reduced to his formula of "material and ideal interests."[6] Yet, on his own premises, one can discuss the question of forms of state as a "technical" problem *only* by reference to ends. Weber's audience was constituted by some shared circumstances. To the extent that it shared values, they were not shared values in the sense of shared *ultimate* values, for it was an audience composed of members of parties with *opposed* interests and *opposed* ultimate values. Whether the audience could be said to share some set of subordinate values— peace, order, and the like, for example—is another question. One might pursue the question of constitutional form by seeking common interests or by proposing a compromise between interests that could become a common purpose. Weber proceeded as though in this realm of means a choice of intermediate ends remained, and the point of his primary essay, "Parliament and Government in a Reconstructed Germany," was to define this choice.

The circumstance that limited the possibilities of choice was the inevitability of greater parliamentarization and democratization. As he correctly perceived, those who had served in, and sacrificed for, the war would not be willing to return to a political community in which their enfranchisement was partial and of doubtful effect. Weber attempted to impress this inevitability on his readers and ridiculed those who longed for a "German" "integrative" state form.

The problem that occasioned the essay was leadership. In the context of 1917, in the midst of a constitutional crisis brought on by the failures of the war, this was a *pragmatic* problem, which Weber used to turn away his readers from immediate concerns over leadership to focus on the constitutional system. He gave examples drawn from a wide range of parties and origins, of leaders and persons with leadership potential whose talents had been badly used by the system. He also gave examples of leadership failure that could not be blamed on parliamentarism but represented the failures of leadership which he blamed on the monarchy and on traditional bureaucratic elites (Weber, [1968]1978: 1425–6). Elaborate examples were not necessary to make the point that stronger and better leaders were needed. The problems were evident to everyone in the face of Ludendorff's intervention into the political affairs of the Office of Chancellor, actions whose consequences were still being played out at the time Weber's articles were appearing in the *Frankfurter Zeitung*.

The air was already thick with recriminations over this episode, over the failure of peace initiatives, and over the handling of naval mutinies, recriminations that were to become only more dramatic and inclusive in the postwar period. Weber assimilated these present problems into an older problem, revealed by the careers of Bismarck and his unimpressive successors. The older problem was a familiar liberal theme—the Junkers had presented themselves as the leadership class indispensable for national greatness—liberals from the time of unification and before had disputed this claim, comparing the Junkers unfavorably to the English aristocracy (cf. Gneist, 1886, vol. II: 392). Weber continued this polemical tradition. In 1917, he wrote that only one thing is indisputable: every type of social order, without exception, must, if one wishes to *evaluate* it, be examined with reference to the opportunities which it affords to *certain types of persons* to rise to positions of superiority through the operation of the various objective and subjective selective factors.

(1949: 27; italics in original)

In "Wahlrecht und Demokratie," also published in 1917, Weber assailed the Junkers as a pseudo-aristocratic caste whose "conventions and forms" were "supported by the structure of bureaucracy" (1948: 392) and whose characteristic social institutions, such as the duel corps, "serve as a convenient way of taming men" (1948: 393).

Weber's solution to the problem of creating a pool of leaders was vague in its details but simple in design. The career of Bismarck revealed a weakness within the older constitutional system, the problem of succession. The rise of a worthy successor, i.e., a leader with the capacity to amass popular support for his measures despite the reluctance of the parliamentary parties, could have developed neither in the bureaucracy nor in. the parliament. In Germany, there was a legal obstacle that prevented parliamentary figures from holding significant posts in the administration. Thus, the person with power instincts was forced to choose between bureaucratic office and its discipline and political "responsibility" in a powerless body. In fact, Weber argued, the born leaders in Germany chose neither. Bismarck was himself largely to blame for this; he had emasculated parliament politically and rendered it hopelessly unattractive as a career for a person with the political talents that make for leadership. The manifest inadequacies of parliamentary leadership were thus the consequence, not the cause, of parliamentary impotence. "The level of parliament depends on whether it does not merely discuss great issues but decisively influences them; in other words, its quality depends on whether what happens there matters" (Weber, [1968]1978: 1392).

The tactical problem of the text is to persuade his readers of the merit of a particular constitutional arrangement, in which parliament had expanded powers, but where one of its major purposes—to be a nursery for leaders—was served indirectly. The model for this is countries like England, which have proper parliaments, with ministerial responsibility and the possibility of votes of no confidence, where parliaments select the leaders, and where the leaders are accountable to parliament and must run their departments according to guidelines set by parliament (Weber, [1968]1978: 1408). In these systems, Weber says, one finds a particular kind of struggle.

Every conflict in parliament involves not only a struggle over substantive issues but also a struggle for personal power. Wherever parliament is so strong that, as a rule, the monarch entrusts the government to the spokesman of a clear-cut majority, the power struggle of the parties will be a

Decisionism and Politics 153

contest for this highest executive position. The fight is then carried by men who have great political power instincts and highly developed qualities of political leadership, and hence the chance to take over the top positions; for the survival of the party outside parliament, and the countless ideal, and partly very material, interests bound up with it require that capable leaders get to the top.

(Weber, [1968]1978: 1409)

But *only* where there is real power to be had through these struggles "can men with political temperament and talent be motivated to subject themselves to this kind of selection through competition" (Weber, [1968]1978: 1409).

Beneath the formal arrangements of parliamentary decision-making, Weber saw other processes. In England, Weber said,

the broad mass of deputies functions only as a following for the leader or the few leaders who form the government, and it blindly follows them *as long as* they are successful. *This is the way it should be.* Political action is always determined by the "'principle of small numbers,'" that means, the superior political maneuverability of small leading groups. In mass states, this Caesarist element is ineradicable.

(Weber, [1968]1978: 1414, italics in original)

It was the Caesaristic clement itself that he took to be the only basis upon which high politics might be conducted. "Since the great political decisions, even and especially in a democracy, arc unavoidably made by few men, mass democracy has bought its success since Pericles' times with major concessions to the Caesarist principle of selecting leaders" (Weber, [1968]1978: 1452).

The Selection of Intermediate Ends and Means

When he remarked that Bismarck had reduced parliament to "nothing but the unwillingly tolerated rubber stamp of a ruling bureaucracy" (Weber, [1968]1978: 1392), Weber appealed to an old liberal fear. Ihering had expressed this anxiety, in the older language of the opposition between state and society, when he spoke of the danger that arises from "applying the common means in opposition to the society and in favor of its administrators" ([1968]1978: 223). One might expect that the likelihood of this happening would increase as a natural consequence of the process of the concentration of force that he regarded as the positive task of the state. Ihering had no solution to this danger. Weber expressed the point in much more colorful language. The "animated machine" of bureaucratic organization, together with the inanimate machines of industry, is, he says, "busy fabricating the shell of bondage which men will perhaps be forced to inhabit someday, as powerless as the fellahs of ancient Egypt" ([1968]1978: 1402). Weber claimed that this is not an inevitability, but the result of a value choice. The circumstances of modern society are such that "if a technically superior administration *were to be the ultimate and sole value* in the ordering of the affairs of state, it would certainly come to pass" ([1968]1978: 1402; italics in original). Weber's concern was to show that another value choice is possible and preferable.

Weber sought the rejection of bureaucratization as an intermediate value, on the ground that this intermediate value was inconsistent with the value of national greatness. For Germany, to accept bureaucratic rule, he said, would be to accept the political fate of being

> condemned to remain a small and conservative country, perhaps with a fairly good public administration in purely technical respects, but at any rate a provincial people without the opportunity of counting in the arena of world politics—and also without any *moral* right to it.
>
> ([1968]1978: 1462, italics in original)

Weber, of course, did not think of "Swissification" as a serious alternative, and he was aware that this was not what his audience wished. The real question was not of wish but of will. The challenge posed by the "choice" was to the quality of the will of his audience- in the face of the cruel realities of politics (hence his quotation of a passage in *The History of Florence*, where Machiavelli "has one of his heroes praise those citizens who deemed the greatness of their native city higher than the salvation of their souls" (1948: 126) and in view of the necessity of a reach that exceeds the easily grasped (hence Radbruch's praise of Don Quixote: Radbruch, [1932]1950: 53; cf. Weber, 1949: 46).

When the war ended and the form of government changed, the parliamentary leadership proved to be as ineffective in power as the wartime chancellors had been, and Weber grew disenchanted with the prospect of a true parliamentary system. In the complex politics of the development of the Weimar constitution, he fought for a "Strong President," elected by popular vote for a long term[7]—the closest practical equivalent that could be found to what he considered the specifically Caesarist constitutional technique, the plebiscite, i.e., "not an ordinary vote or election, but a profession of faith in the calling of him who demands these acclamations" ([1968]1978: 1451). The impulse behind this attempt to strengthen the office of the president is not new, as Weber's 1917 discussion of Caesarism makes clear ([1968]1978: 1381–1469).

In Weber's original proposal, the formal rules strengthening parliament are the *de jure* means to a *de facto* constitutional order that has particular properties, of which the existence of a nursery for leaders is one. These properties, together with the underlying realities of modem politics—the indispensability of bureaucracy, the ineluctability of the principle of Caesarism, the necessity of making concessions to Caesarism for there to be great politics in democracies, and the inevitable rule of the few—create what might be called the "consequential" constitution, the constitution as it really works.

When Weber discussed the level of underlying practical realities, the significance of parliament is defined by its relation to Caesarism. In the course of discussing the problem of succession in a Caesarist polity, Weber observed that "the rise, neutralization and elimination of a Caesarist leader occur most easily without the danger of a domestic catastrophe when the effective co-domination of powerful representative bodies preserves the political continuity and the constitutional guarantees of civil order" ([1968]1978: 1457). Here we glimpse a particular constitutional ideal: a regime in which the leader has the fullest means of validating his popular support but limited means to remain in power after failures and in which there is the *de facto* constraint on his power to destroy political continuity of a parliament made up of ambitious persons with an interest in maintaining a system in which they have a stake. This is the order that Weber held out as the best available means to the common intermediate end of national greatness. It is not, of course, a guarantee. Whether this end is itself to be merely professed or truly meant is a matter of will—of national will, which can be destroyed by excessive class conflict, and of the will of the individuals who make up both the masses who acclaim and the leaders, who must act with the sober strength of those truly called to politics and tested in its ways.

The parliamentary leaders who negotiated the final constitution whittled away the powers to be granted the president, against Conservative opposition, until the sole unlimited power of the president was to declare a state of exception (a state of siege), suspending the fundamental rights established elsewhere in the constitution (article 48) (Brunet, 1922: 165). The article required that parliament be informed immediately of such declarations and that they be revoked at its demand. The requirement could be temporarily evaded by the use of article 24, which empowered the president to dismiss parliament, by requiring a new election within 60 days. Weber apparently took no special interest in article 48 (Mommsen, 1984: 378), later made notorious by its role in the quasi-legal Nazi seizure of power. He could not have been oblivious to it, however, in view of the stress writers like Ihering placed on the indispensability to the state of legally arbitrary power for self-protection, and in view of his own insistence on the doctrine of *raison d'état*, and of the central place of the practice of declaring states of exception in German government from the time of unification. In the period after the war, when the empire had gone out of existence and the Weimar constitution had not been adopted, the Spartacist rebellions were suppressed on the basis of the practice and precedent of the old constitution (Koch, 1984: 133–4, 254). The same powers were freely invoked by Ebert's Socialist government, with Radbruch as Attorney General (Koch, 1984: 254). This government's suspensions of basic legal principles, such as the principle of *nulla poena sine lege*, and its one-sided application of the Law for the Protection of the Republic, established precedents that were used in turn by the Nazis (Koch, 1984: 284). The persistence of these political practices puts the reliance on the doctrine of *raison d'état* in this legal tradition in a particular light. Neither were the powers abstractions nor were they curtailed by restrictive conventions. This qualifies any interpretation of Weber's Caesarism. His endorsement of the principles behind the practices was itself given without qualification and reflected his belief that the fundamental realities of politics to which the practices were a response would not change under any constitutional arrangement.[8] He must have expected leaders to use these powers, and for a responsible parliament to assent routinely to their use—the ambitious being mindful that, as leaders, they would themselves want to have these powers at their disposal.

The Realm of Necessity

"What is the spiritual basis of parliamentarism today?" When Carl Schmitt asked this question in 1923, he went to the core of the problem that Weber's transformation of the constitutional problem had created. Weber and, before him, such thinkers as Gneist had been liberals by sentiment even as they gave increasingly illiberal formulations to their fundamental political ideas. Read without these liberal sentiments, Gneist's slogan "freedom is order, freedom is power" (quoted in Krieger, 1957: 358) is totalitarian mysticism, and Weber's constitutional vision of charismatic competition between aspiring Caesars is a celebration of irrationalism. Schmitt, who came to this tradition of constitutional reasoning without sharing these liberal sentiments, was able to discern the contradictions behind it.

By the time Schmitt raised this question, it was evident that the Weberian constitutional formula, in which plebiscitarian parliamentary democracy was justified as a socio-technical device for producing leaders, was no longer plausible, and that the foundational question had to be asked anew. Schmitt made the point that in the times of Burke or Mill, parliamentarism was linked with a belief in public discussion, but that in the time of Weber, Preuss, and Naumann, the conditions of mass democracy had reduced the discussion to propaganda appealing to interests and passions (1979: 11). Schmitt traced the difficulty to the inherent conflict between liberalism and democracy, a conflict he saw embodied in the Weimar constitution itself. The democratic idea, Schmitt said, was "the assertion of the identity of law and the will of the people" (quoted in Schwab 1970: 62). The legal forms of this identity include the practices of popular initiatives, referendums, and acclamation, the first of which was directly provided for in the Weimar constitution. Liberalism, in contrast, rests on the idea of public debate and the enactment of laws as the result of free parliamentary discussions, also provided for by the constitution. In fact, he observed, the condition of the public debate did not obtain in Weimar politics; parliamentary discussion itself was not taken seriously; decisions were made behind closed doors by party or coalition committees (Schwab, 1970: 68–9).

Schmitt's alternative returned him to the fundamental problems of modem legal and political thought, but the tools he used were for the most part the tools of the tradition of nineteenth-century legal "positivism." This tradition was itself defined only retrospectively, and the term, in its German applications, is best used with caution. Weber used the term to make historical observations on the development of law, as when he commented that "legal positivism has . . . advanced irresistibly" ([1968]1978: 874), but here, he meant little more than the disappearance, in legal thinking, of the idea of natural law and its manifestations. The Hobbesian formula that *auctoritas, non veritas*, makes law, which Schmitt placed at the center of his own legal theory, was the alternative to natural law theory accepted by nineteenth-century positivism, and for that matter by such twentieth-century relativists as Radbruch ([1932]1950: 115–17). Schmitt used it to re-emphasize the issue of authority in polemical opposition to the normativism of the twentieth-century "positivist" Kelsen, who, he considered, had mistaken part of the law—the part that dealt with a deduction from basic legal norms—for the whole.

Normativism, Schmitt argued, has a hidden presupposition; it presupposes that the normal situation obtains, and therefore cannot account for the abnormal situation. The legally paradigmatic case of "abnormality" is the situation in which a state of exception is declared in response to "necessity," and this case reveals a level more basic than Kelsen's *Grundnorm;* the power to decide on questions of necessity, to decide on the declaration of a state of exception, is a power that transcends the presupposition of a normalcy and thus places its holder in a position that is more fundamental than positions whose powers presupposed normalcy, such as the position of a judge. It is from this observation that Schmitt constructs his distinctive theoretical contribution, which we can best understand by returning to Ihering. For Ihering, the fundamental character of the law was determined by relatively fixed egoistic interests—such as peace. Peace is secured by the order-creating actions of the dictatorial law giver and is the primal basis of law: the binding of norm and force (Ihering, [1877–83]1968: 186–8). This was also Schmitt's conception and the conception he attributed to Hobbes when he described him as a "decisionist." The sovereign is the *summa auctoritas* and the *summa potestas* in one, as Schmitt put it, and the sovereign decision is an absolute beginning, which grounds the norm as well as the order (1934: 27–8).[9] To show that force is indispensable to the *establishment* of order is only part of the story, of course; the achievement of normalcy, as Ihering recognized, is never final. Occasions when it is threatened by force may arise, and the primal basis of law in the binding of force and norm again becomes visible. At this primal level, there is a large clement of moral arbitrariness. Ihering stressed, for example, that in entering into alliances, it is not right, but accident, that determines which alliances will enable the preservation of order ([1877–83]1968: 220).

Weber accepted these conclusions, but he varied Ihering's premises in a way that minimized the possibility of rational reconciliation of conflicts of interest

158 Stephen Turner and Regis Factor

through law. As we have seen, Ihering considered that ideal interests which have been historically effective have never been far removed from tangible material interests, interests of the sort that compromise may readily preserve. The ideal interests Weber identified in history, such as the other-worldly interests of Protestantism and the various ideals of which charismatic leaders have been the bearers, are not the sort that can be reconciled through compromise. They are, as Weber said, like warring gods. The plebiscitarian democratic form that he promoted as a constitutional structure served to *make* values compete by subjecting their charismatic champions to the test of public acclamation. In this ideal, we see the last vestige of the liberal faith in public discussion no longer as a faith in its rationality, but as a faith in the power of leadership appeals to command voluntary devotion.

Ihering could benignly contemplate the state of struggle that he believed history to be because he believed that progressively better compromises would arise through struggle. Weber did not share this optimism, but he believed that the struggle between charismatic politicians could be harnessed by a plebiscitarian democratic constitution to serve the end of national greatness. He knew that "the fact that both [the Centre and the Social Democratic] parties dissociated themselves from the parliamentary system made parliamentary government impossible" (Weber, 1948: 112). He expected that the plebiscitarian presidency, in contrast to parliament, would be less weakened by the conduct of these parties. The Weimar presidency, however, was much weaker in relation to parliament than the presidency Weber desired.

During the Weimar era, Schmitt observed, some of the parties were "totalizing." They followed their adherents from cradle to grave, attempting to instill in them the correct *Weltanschauung*,[10] and were in a fundamental sense unwilling to engage in political debate in the sense envisioned by liberal parliamentarism. Their anti-parliamentarism went beyond "dissociation," as practiced by the parties of the old Reich. By defining its "enemies" directly, that is not by pressing for laws through public debate, but by making these identifications the basis of their politics and often of direct action, these new parties, such as the Nazis and the Communists, undermined what Schmitt regarded as the most significant political monopoly of the state, its capacity to draw the distinction between friend and enemy (Schwab, 1970: 78). Schmitt saw that constitutional order could not withstand the pressures of the plural and unrestrained demands of these parties.

Schmitt discussed the problem of the legal tools for the defense of the state, notably the dictatorial means of article 48, and studied the underlying theory of dictatorship. He concluded that, in the Weimar system, it was the responsibility of the president to act in defense of the constitution. The constitution, he held, is "inviolable" in essence; its provisions must be interpreted in light of the necessities of the defense of the constitutional order as a whole (Bendersky, 1983: 97). This suggested that the president was not only obliged to use the legal means provided by the constitution for its defense but also obliged by his oath to go beyond the letter of the constitution, if necessary, to preserve its essence.

Where the legal order is itself threatened, and the threat cannot be resolved by "normal" means, it is not "values" but what Weber calls the "objective pragmatism of 'reasons of state'" (1948: 334) that governs politics. The sphere of politics reduces to the elemental problem of decision: the problem of identifying the enemy and choosing allies. Weber made no attempt to theorize the situation of necessity or to relate it to his theory of value choice. He simply acknowledged it. Schmitt's account of necessity served to circumscribe the place of value choice by drawing the contrast between ordinary politics and occasions when action is a response to an autonomous and distinct "necessity." This step transformed the structure of political reasoning Weber developed. Necessity, which had been to Weber an unintegrated category, became for Schmitt a large and autonomous realm of the irreducibly "situational" and unique: *necessitas non habet legem*. The enlarging of this realm, as Schmitt's critics saw, was a further step in the de-rationalization of politics.

Schmitt did not limit his constitutional thinking to the realm of necessity. He proposed eliminating parts of the constitution in order to arrive at a document accepted by all significant parts of the population, a strategy closer to Ihering's or Weber's. The range of common ground, however, had never been very large; the contradictions in the original document itself testify to that. In the end, this common ground diminished and the president, Hindenburg, who was reluctant to rule by article 48, appointed Hitler as Chancellor in the hope that effective parliamentary rule could be restored. Hitler had different hopes. His aim was to change the "essence" of the constitution, and his manner of doing so embodied an image that had become successively more central in the de-rationalizing progression from Ihering through Weber to Schmitt—of the primal bond between the order-creating law giver and the obedient multitude.

Notes

1 For a discussion of the events of 1848, which shows the character of the proletarian and peasant threat and suggests how it would have been seen by the bourgoisie, see Valentin (1940: 220–46).

2 The principle gave rise to a school of *Interessenjurisprudenz*, based on the doctrine that the judges' application of the law should respect the implicit compromise between interests contained in a given law.

3 Ihering treated dictatorship in "conditions of necessity" ([1877–83]1968: 188) as abnormal, but not as historically unusual, even for a more or less stable legal order. In case of necessity, a dictator was named in Rome, the guarantees of civil freedom were set aside, law receded, and unlimited military power stepped into its place. Corresponding measures at the present day are the right of the government to declare a state of siege and to issue provisional laws without the cooperation of the estates of the realm; such measures acting as safety valves, to enable a government to remove the distress by course of law ([1877–83]1968: 188; cf. Schmitt, 1928).

4 In the early pages of his 1917 essay, 'The Meaning of "Ethical Neutrality"', Weber comments, in a footnote, that 'as to the "irreconcilability" of certain ultimate evaluations in a certain sphere of problems, cf. G. Radbruch's *Einführung in die Rechtswissenschaft* I diverge from him on certain points but these are of no significance for the problem discussed here' (MSS, p. 11). Radbruch's views on these issues in this text were consistent with other of his works quoted in this chapter. Cf. also Chroust, 1944.

5 Weber amplifies this thought elsewhere, when he says that it is possible to defend quite meaningfully the view that the power of the state should be increased in order to strengthen its power to eliminate obstacles, while maintaining that the state itself has no *intrinsic* value, that it is a purely technical instrument for the realization of other values from which alone: it derives its value, and that it can retain this value only as long as it does not seek to transcend this merely auxiliary status (Weber, 1949: 47; italics in original).

6 Cf. Pipes 1955, esp. pp. 398–9.

7 Weber's later constitutional writings, which were addressed to the day-today development of constitutional discussion, are analyzed in Mommsen (1984: 332–81).

8 Although these vast emergency powers have analogs elsewhere in western European constitutions, the sheer extent of their use in Germany may be said itself to alter the character of the office of president, especially in relation to parliament. Carl Schmitt appreciated, as Weber perhaps did not, the *constitutional* significance of these practices.

9 Ethical decisionism, the position of Weber and Radbruch, is distinct from, though not inconsistent with, this legal theory. Radbruch, indeed, suggests that what Schmitt would call decisionism could be derived from relativism ([1932]1950: 116–17). Nevertheless, the passages usually cited in support of the claim that Schmitt was a nihilist, relativist, or decisionist in the ethical sense are open to a different interpretation: that, in the historical circumstance of a plurality of values, authoritative decision remains the *fons et origo* of legal order, and that even when the fundamental principles are agreed, as in the church, this fundamental necessity obtains, and takes the form of the problem of authoritative interpretation of basic principles (cf. Schwab 1970: 46). Both these problems arise, Schmitt says, from the same source, the wickedness of man. "In a good world among good people . . . only peace, security, and harmony would prevail. Priests and theologians are here just as superfluous as politicians and statesmen" (quoted in Bendersky 1983: 87–8).

10 A contemporary example of this would be the radical movements in Israel which pursue settlement policies contrary to those that the government approves.

References

Bendersky, J. W. *Carl Schmitt: Theorist for the Reich*. Princeton: Princeton University Press, 1983.

Brunet, R. *The New German Constitution*, translated by J. Gollomb. New York: Knopf, 1922.

Dicey, A. V. *Lectures on the Relation between Law and Public Opinion during the Nineteenth Century*. London: Macmillan, 1962.

Gneist, Rudolf von. *The English Constitution in Its Transformations through a Thousand Years*, translated by R. Jenery Shee. Boston: Little Brown & Company, 1886. https://commons.wikimedia.org/w/index.php?title=File:Rudolf_Gneist,_The_English_Parliament_in_its_Transformations_through_a_Thousand_Years_(1886).pdf&page=7

Ihering, R. von. *Law as a Means to an End*, translated by I. Hasik. South Hackensack: Rothman Reprints, [1877–83]1968.

Ihering, R. von. *The Struggle for Law*, translated by J. Lalor. Chicago: Callaghan, [1872]1915.

Koch, H. W. *A Constitutional History of Germany in the Nineteenth and Twentieth Centuries*. London: Longman, 1984.

Krieger, L. *The German Idea of Freedom: History of a Political Tradition*. Boston: Beacon Press, 1957.

Mayer, J. P. *Max Weber and German Politics: A Study in Political Sociology*. London: Faber, 1956.

Mommsen, W. J. *Max Weber and German Politics*. Chicago: The University of Chicago Press, 1984.

Radbruch, Gustav. *Der innere Weg: Aufriß meines Lebens*. Stuttgart: Koehler, 1951.

Radbruch, Gustav. "Legal Philosophy," In *The Legal Philosophies of Lask, Radbruch, and Dabin*, translated by Kurt Wilk. Cambridge: Harvard University Press, 43–224, [1932]1950.

Schmit, Carl. *Die die drei Arten des Rechtswissenschsftlichen Denkens*. Hamburg: Hanseatische Verlagsanstalt, 1934.

Schmitt, Carl. *Die Diktatur*. Munich: Duncker & Humboldt, 1928.

Schmitt, Carl. *Die geistesgeschichtliche Lage des heutigen Parlamentarismus*. Berlin: Duncker & Humboldt, 1979.

Schwab, George. *The Challenge of the Exception: An Introduction to the Political Ideas of Carl Schmitt between 1921 and 1936*. Berlin: Duncker & Humboldt, 1970.

Stone, Julius. *Social Dimensions of Law and Jurisprudence*. London: Stevens, 1950.

Valentin, Veit. *1848: Chapters of German History*, translated by E. Scheffauer. London: Allen & Unwin, 1940.

Weber, Marianne. *Max Weber: A Biography*, translated by H. Zohn. New York: Wiley, 1975.

Weber, Max. *Economy and Society: An Outline of Interpretive Sociology*, edited by G. Roth and C. Wittich Berkeley. Los Angeles: University of California Press, [1968]1978.

Weber, Max. *From Max Weber: Essays in Sociology*, edited by H. H. Gerth and C. W. Mills. New York: Oxford University Press, 1948.

Weber, Max. *Methodology of the Social Sciences*, translated and edited by Edward A. Shils and Henry Finch. New York: Free Press, 1949.

Chapter 9

The Rule of Law Deflated

Weber and Kelsen

Stephen Turner

Max Weber and Hans Kelsen may seem unexpected sources for a discussion of the normative concept of the rule of law. Neither addresses the issue directly, despite being contemporaries of people like Albert Venn Dicey who made it a central concern ([1885]1959, [1914]1962). Despite the fact that Weber avoided the term "*Rechtsstaat*" and referred instead to rational-legal *Herrschaft*, and that Kelsen said that the term *Rechtsstaat* was ideological, both Weber and Kelsen haunt this literature. The distinctive language they used in discussing the law reappears with regularity in the literature, usually without mentioning them by name[1]. So do their distinctive concerns.[2] Both, moreover, were engaged in projects that bear directly on the concept of the *Rechtsstaat*, the German language variant of the concept of the rule of law.[3] So why did they decline to embrace what has become a standard topic in discussions not only of the nature of legal order but of social and political orders as well?

The Kelsen-Weber response, as I will reconstruct it here, is this: to divide legal orders into "rule of law" and non-rule of law legal orders is not to make a legal distinction; it is a matter of imposing a non-legal distinction, a distinction that is, from the point of view of purely legal considerations, arbitrary. The distinction as formulated by "rule of law" theorists is typically rooted in ideological considerations masquerading as legal distinctions. Defenders of the rule of law conception claim otherwise: they think they are making legal distinctions between legal orders, distinctions that can be based on philosophical considerations rather than ideological preferences for particular types of political orders. Ronald Dworkin, for example, argues that what are treated as ideological and non-legal concepts are in fact required by adjudication and that a proper understanding of the nature of adjudication and of legal interpretation will show that these concepts and considerations play an ineliminable role (Dworkin, 1988). For these thinkers, as for Kelsen, for the concept of the rule of law to be reduced to a mere political preference is a failure. They thus agree on the terms of the dispute: the concept has to be derived from legal considerations solely. They disagree on what is entailed by legal considerations. This, however, is not the only approach to the topic. A long tradition has been concerned to argue that there is a need (presumably a moral or political need)

DOI: 10.4324/9781003360810-12

The Rule of Law Deflated   163

to distinguish legal orders from oppressive orders and that there are characteristics of legal systems that allow one to make these distinctions. The large number of lists of criteria for evaluating the degree to which a country is a rule of law regime reflects this basic idea: the criteria are themselves based on features of the legal systems of the countries, but it is not clear that the preference for these features is or can be grounded in legal considerations alone. To the extent that they reflect political or moral preferences for particular kinds of legal systems, the distinction is no longer a legal one.

Deflationary Arguments

The argument Weber and Kelsen present has several elements, but the core is this: they are deflationary arguments. In each case, they articulate an account of the relevant facts and logical implications in a particular domain which is designed to be substituted for a "metaphysical" version of the same conception—such as "sovereignty"—which shows that there is nothing more to sovereignty than that which is included in the substituted conception. Kelsen's argument is indirect. It shows that the general considerations that determine what counts as a legal regime also are sufficient to account for the legal aspects of the supposedly distinct phenomenon of a "rule of law" legal regime. The supposed distinction on which the "exclusive" notion of the rule of law depends, in short, is a distinction without a difference. This assertion appears in connection with the identity thesis:

> There cannot therefore be any State not bound by its own order, free in relation to it, insofar the idea of a State bound by its order, free from hypostatization, has a meaning, because the State is this order itself, can- not be anything but order, and the idea of State liberated from "its" order is a contradiction in terms. Since this order can be only the legal order, no State is conceivable other than the *Rechtsstaat*, and the *Rechtsstaat* is a pleonasm.
> (Kelsen, [1922]1928: 187; translated in La Torre, 2010: 30)

The last sentence has a striking, and intended, implication for the discussion of the rule of law. It amounts to a rejection of "exclusive" concepts of the rule of law as adding nothing. What is of interest, however, is why it is the case that legal orders are necessarily rule of law orders.

Kelsen's argument, and what I will show to be Weber's variant of this argument, are not merely "inclusive" conceptions of the rule of law. Nor do they depend on a meta-philosophy of law such as legal positivism. They are deflationary analyses of the concept that show that the concept adds nothing of explanatory value and is merely ideological. Both Kelsen and Weber used deflationary arguments in the context of law, but they were of different kinds.

Weber's deflationary definitions were "empirical" in the sense that they asserted that there was no empirical difference between the implications of the

164 Stephen Turner

definitions he gave and the definitions given by other, essentialist or metaphysical theories of the same thing. Weber's famous definition of the state as the monopoly of legitimate violence in a geographical territory is a classic example of deflation: nothing of the metaphysical view of the state is left, but the definition enables one to describe the empirical facts about statehood with no empirical remainder. Kelsen did something similar with sovereignty, but in Kelsen's usages, the examples are legal rather than empirical differences and involved the claim that there were no legal implications of supposed differences, for example, between sovereign units of a federal system and units with specified authorizations under a legal order. The rest of the theory of sovereignty was, for him, mystical leftovers from the metaphysical theory of monarchy.

For them, such notions as the *Rechtsstaat* were ideologically encrusted, historical half-truths, only partially emancipated from their origins in religiously tinged natural law thinking, with misleading affective associations that had developed in the longue durée of political and philosophical contestation, which sufficed neither as sociological nor legal ideas. Their goal was to strip them of their ideological content to get down to their factual core. They went about doing this in different, but parallel, ways.

Kelsen and Weber: Core Concepts

For Weber, the answer to the question of why he did not employ the concept of the *Rechtsstaat* is straightforward: he discusses it under a different heading. As part of his typology of forms of legitimate rule, he included "rational-legal authority," which is a formulation of the main features of the *Rechtsstaat* with the valuative overtones removed. His account of rational-legal authority placed "calculability," which appears as "predictability" in standard lists of characteristics of the rule of law, in a central position, and his historical writings treat the separation of office and person as one of the defining features that distinguish Occidental political and legal orders from those found elsewhere (Weber, [1968]1978, 957–958): this is the distinction between the rule of law and the rule of men as it can be grounded in the history of law and administration.

A sociological "ideal type" is an abstraction designed to provide an interpretive entry point for analysis, in this case of a distinctive form of legitimating belief. He contrasts it to two other conceptually purified forms, charismatic and traditional domination. Kelsen has a parallel list, adding religious, customary, and statutory law (Kelsen, [1945]2005: 110–116). Weber treats these as ideal types, rarely or never found in reality in their pure forms, and regards actual present legal orders as mixtures; Kelsen, similarly, describes modern constitutions as mixtures of customary and statutory law, and he also uses the language of ideal type.[4] Rational-legal authority, according to Weber, rests on the acceptance of the validity of the following (three) mutually dependent ideas:

1. That any given legal norm may be established by agreement or by imposition, on grounds of expediency or value rationality or both, with a claim to obedience at least on the part of the members of the organization. This is, however, usually extended to include all persons within the sphere of power in question—which in the case of territorial bodies is the territorial area—who stand in certain social relationships or carry out forms of social action which in the order governing the organization have been declared to be relevant.
2. That every body of law consists essentially of a consistent system of abstract rules that have normally been intentionally established. Furthermore, the administration of law is held to consist in the application of these rules to particular cases; the administrative process is the rational pursuit of the interests that are specified in the order governing the organization within the limits laid down by legal precepts and following principles which are capable of generalized formulation, and are approved in the order governing the group, or at least not disapproved in it.
3. That the typical person in authority, the "superior," is thus himself (still) subject to an impersonal order by orienting his actions to it (this order) in his own dispositions and commands. (This is true not only of persons exercising legal authority who are in the usual sense "officials," but, for instance, the elected president of a state) (Weber, [1968]1978: 217).

Kelsen puts the same issues in a very slightly different way, reflecting his different purposes, and the difference between a sociological de-ideologization and one based on normative minimalism.

The first item concerns "sovereignty" and extends Weber's famous definition of a state: "A Compulsory political association will be called a state insofar as its administrative staff successfully upholds the claim to the monopoly of the legitimate use of force" ([1968]1978: 54). This is a "sociologized" restatement of the concept of sovereignty and one that radically demystifies it. "Legitimacy" for Weber is no more than the belief by at least some of the affected population, namely, the members of the ruling organization themselves, in the right of the rulers to rule. Elsewhere Weber speaks of legitimacy in terms of the combination of this belief and the probability that the rules in question will be obeyed ([1968]1978: 37, 53–54; [1913]1981: 175–9).

For Kelsen, the core idea is that the law consists in the production of norms in accordance with norms, that legality is a matter of action in accordance with legal norms, norms which in turn are produced in accordance with other norms. State action is the action of individuals or bodies that are authorized by norms to produce norms according to norms. The acts of the state are no more than these norm-governed or authorized acts. Kelsen's distinctive contribution to the philosophy of law is his relentless insistence on the idea that law is norms created in accordance with norms, and the key implication of this idea, the hierarchical structure of the normative order itself, the *Stauffenbautheorie*, which was already part of his Vienna background:

166 Stephen Turner

> Law regulates its own creation inasmuch as one legal norm determines the way in which another norm is created, and also, to some extent, the contents of that norm. Since a legal norm is valid because it is created in a way determined by another legal norm, the latter is the rea- son of valid- ity of the former. The relation between the norm regulating the creation of another norm and this other norm may be presented as a relationship of super- and subordination, which is a spatial figure of speech. The norm determining the creation of another norm is the superior, the norm created according to this regulation, the inferior norm. The legal order, especially the legal order the personification of which is the State, is therefore not a system of norms coordinated to each other, standing, so to speak, side by side on the same level, but a hierarchy of different levels of norms. The unity of these norms is constituted by the fact that the creation of one norm—the lower one—is determined by another—the higher—the crea- tion of which is determined by a still higher norm, and that this *regressus* is terminated by a highest, the basic norm which, being the supreme rea- son of validity of the whole legal order, constitutes its unity.
>
> (Kelsen, [1945]2005: 124)

The two definitions are closely related. For Weber, the characteristic of rational-legal authority is the existence of a body of laws that constitutes a consistent, abstract, impersonal order. Officials are governed by or "oriented" to this order, and this includes not only the officials and political authorities who exercise the authority of administration but also elected officials, such as Presidents and legislators. Kelsen makes the same points: that the law is a consistent normative order, that it is a system of norms, rather than one of personal authority. Weber does not say precisely that law is norms produced in accordance with norms, but the third item in his list implies something very close to it. Officials, including elected ones, are oriented in their actions to an impersonal order, a "consistent system of abstract rules which have normally been intentionally established" ([1968]1978: 217), to which they are subject. This system of rules is the law: the legitimating principle which characterizes the orientation to the law that gives these rules a specifically "legal" meaning is the belief in the validity and authority of the impersonal order itself, and not merely a belief in its contents.

Whether a "belief" in this impersonal order as such is different from a belief in Kelsen's *Grundnorm* is a question that can be asked in two ways: sociologically, there seems to be no difference; legally, from the point of view of Kelsen's own account of the problem of international recognition of legal authority, there seems to be no difference either, because Kelsen's account of the recognition of legal authority under international law requires only effective authority, a version of Weber's first item, and the existence of the *Grundnorm* can be inferred back via regression from any functioning legal authority.[5] The difference comes down to the difference in disciplinary purposes: the sociologist explains without justifying; the jurisprudential thinker seeks the ultimate ground of justification. For Weber, the principle of rational-legal legitimacy must be accepted as a value: it is not possible to ground it on anything deeper. Similarly, for Kelsen, with this difference: for Kelsen, the ground of the law cannot be outside of the law but must be itself a legal norm. So, the legitimating principle must be a law itself, a law presupposed by the law as a normative system of positive laws, without which the law would not be normative.

The "Nothing More" Question

Kelsen's point in the *Pure Theory of Law*, and in other texts, is that not only is the *Grundnorm* or Basic Law the normative ground of a dynamic legal system, but it is also the sole and sufficient normative ground. Kelsen pursued this argument by systematically re-analyzing traditional legal notions in order to show that the implications for legal and political thought that had been read into them by previous theorists did not follow from what was logically required to account for the law.

Kelsen's claim was that the complete legal meaning of the concepts could be adequately analyzed in terms of the idea that norms are produced by norms. The project in this sense resembles, though in a different sphere and by means of different kinds of arguments, Weber's own procedure of systematically stripping traditional terminology for teleological thinking about human action and society of any teleological content.

So where does the rule of law fit into their picture? As has been already noted, many of the properties of legal orders that the label "rule of law" has been applied to appear in their accounts already. Both of them emphasize the subordination of officials to the law. This consideration alone accounts for much of the traditional notion of the rule of law: a state in which the laws are largely obeyed, in which official power is circumscribed by the law, and that authorizes the use of the coercive power of the state only within limits. Writers like Lon Fuller add to the rule of law such notions as the idea that the laws should not be contradictory (Fuller, 1964), a consideration explicitly addressed in both Weber's definition and *inter alia* by Kelsen. The idea of legal rationality and the idea of non-contradiction seem inseparable. Both also add the consideration of effectiveness: whether the legal order actually commands obedience. If we limit ourselves to these three very simple considerations, we have the following: the rule of law is the effective operation of a state under an impersonal rationally organized order that is accepted as valid by a significant number of people, especially officials, and that has a reasonably high level of compliance, especially by officials. Deviations from the rule of law are illegal acts, and the abrogation of the rule of law would consist in the commission of acts not authorized by the law or forbidden by it, especially by officials, in significant numbers.

Extending the Deflationary Argument

We can take these anodyne definitions of legal orders or in the case of Weber the specifically modern legal order as the basic answer to the question "what is the rule of law"? The question to be asked is this: what of the elements of a "rule of law" regime that are at the core of most conceptions of the rule of law are accounted for by the Weber-Kelsen account of law? What is covered, and what is left over? Here the differences between Weber and Kelsen with respect to their different purposes, constructing an ideal type to understand empirical reality in the case of Weber and understanding a normative order in the case of Kelsen, lead them in somewhat different directions. Both are relevant to the notion of the rule of law, which is ambiguous between two aspects: typically lists of properties defining the rule of law focus on both facts, such as the extent of corruption, and properties of the legal system itself. Weber's approach deals with the factual side; Kelsen's with the properties of the legal system. But some of the criticisms of Kelsen are more appropriately directed to the empirical side, and Weber points to a dark side of the rule of law, a side which Kelsen himself acknowledges.

The notion of an effective impersonal order in which officials act and generate norms according to norms accounts for much, if not most, of what is normally referred to as the rule of law. In the developing world, much of what is meant by a lack of the rule of law is a matter of ineffectiveness in enforcing the law, and especially ineffectiveness in enforcing the laws relating to official conduct, which for Kelsen would include the improper generation of norms, for example, by judges or bureaucrats acting in unauthorized ways. Weber discusses these issues under the heading of predictability, which is an empirical feature of legal systems. The normative and empirical aspects are of course entangled. There are some typical legal institutions, such as an appellate court system, that serve the purpose of enforcing judicial consistency, for example, and the existence and legal properties of these institutions are often included in lists of criteria evaluating the rule of law.

Discretion and the Rule of Law

How do their accounts of an effective norm-governed regime relate to the traditional claims for the rule of law? The issues can be broken into parts, but the parts are intertwined in complex ways. The four issues that seem most important are these: the issue of legal oppression; the problem of the role of discretion, administrative and judicial; the problem of judicial independence; and the problem of the role of legal interpretation, especially in connection with Dworkin's claim that adjudication requires or implies a commitment to a large set of interrelated political values and moral *desiderata*. Discretion is at the heart of this issue and most of the other issues as well.

An influential tradition in the rule of law literature outside of law is associated with Hayek and is concerned with administrative and judicial discretion

(Hayek, [1960]1978, 212–15, 225) and the idea that the central feature of the rule of law is the limitation of discretion, especially administrative discretion: this is the modern meaning of the idea of the rule of law, not men. This tradition has its roots in the experience of the *Obrigkeitstaat* or magistrate state, where there was a wide range of discretionary power and consequently arbitrariness of legal process and state action. Weber in particular contrasts this more traditional form with the modern bureaucracy, a machine made of men whose hallmark is predictability, and with modern rational-legal authority, which also achieves the maximum degree of predictability ([1968]1978: 1394–95). The maximum conformity with the ideal type of rational-legal authority would eliminate arbitrary authority: it would not be arbitrary because it would be impersonal and part of an order; the fact that it maximizes predictability means that it is not arbitrary. So, this kind of regime, if it is oppressive, must be oppressive in another way. We will return to the notion of oppressive law after dealing with oppressive discretion.

As Hayek himself was forced to acknowledge, however, some discretion is ineliminable. Even the courts regularly acknowledge this and defer to administrators.[6] Thus, there can be no sharp line between a rule of law regime and one involving discretion: it is a quantitative rather than a qualitative distinction. But although judges have discretionary power, this power is limited. And this poses a number of interesting conundrums for any rule of law account. If we grant that some discretion is ineliminable, how are we to understand discretion and its limitation? For now, it will suffice to say that it erases this way of making a legal distinction between the *Obrigkeitstaat* and the *Rechtsstaat*: both involve discretion. The difference, as Weber puts it, is that while each is a form of legitimate rule, that is to say, a legal order, they rest on different legitimating beliefs, the latter a form of what Weber calls traditional authority and Kelsen calls customary law.

In the case of jurisprudence proper, the issue of the limits of discretion is bound up, in the Anglo-American literature, especially since Dworkin's *Law's Empire* (1988), with the problem of legal interpretation. Kelsen, notoriously, rejected theories of legal interpretation. But Kelsen avoided many of the problems associated with the language of interpretation and what Dworkin attacked as the false dichotomy between inventing and finding law by his argument that the judge, in passing a sentence, was enacting a norm, an individual norm in most cases, and that this is what the judge is authorized to do. The judge is thus a law giver just as the legislator or the executive giving a directive is.

This reflects a fundamental difference in the understanding of what judges do, especially when they justify their decisions. What is the purpose of justifying a decision if it is not to supply a justification of it that is at the same time an interpretation of the law? Begin with two core facts: that judges have discretion, and that it is limited discretion, with the limits enforced legally by courts of appeal. Part of the point of justifying a decision reflects the limits on discretion. To provide an adequate reason is at the same time to immunize the decision from the claim that discretion had been abused. What is an abuse of discretion? A large part of it is spelled out in the judicial oath. Here is an American example:

> Each justice or judge of the United States shall take the following oath or affirmation before performing the duties of his office: "I . . . do solemnly swear (or affirm) that I will administer justice without respect to persons, and do equal right to the poor and to the rich, and that I will faithfully and impartially discharge and perform all the duties incumbent upon me as . . . under the Constitution and laws of the United States. So help me God."[7]

The content of the oath makes clear what an abuse of discretion would consist of: a failure to be unbiased first, and to perform the duties specified in the law second. The latter would be a failure to apply the law; the former a failure to use the discretion implied in the oath itself in an unbiased manner. It would follow that the justifications given by the judge of their decisions are attempts to fulfill these commitments: these are the controlling commitments, and failures with respect to them would be and are the subject of discipline and even removal. Appeals courts respect the reality of discretion and do not simply give their own opinions of an appealed case. They apply both commitments and adhere to them as judges, with the expectation that they will potentially be judged in the same way. These constraints also assure the claimant of a degree of predictability, with respect to both the initial decision and the appellate decisions. This account is entirely consistent with Kelsen's picture of adjudication as norm giving. Theories of legal interpretation of the sort Kelsen disparaged are more readily construed as guides to the construction of justifications. But the underlying purpose of the justification is contained, explicitly, in the two elements of the oath. And as Kelsen would have noted, these are norms with sanctions attached to them, and in this sense real law, unlike any norms of "interpretation" such as those found in Dworkin (2011). Dworkin is correct, however, in one limited respect: appeals to democratic principles are one potential way of justifying a claim that the decision was unbiased and thus within the realm of acceptable discretion. But it should be added that there are many other ways to justify this claim, including, for example, a law and economics analysis.

There is a variant of the "discretion" tradition in the discussion of the rule of law, which is more straightforwardly "legal" rather than political. It is exemplified in Dicey's concern with the increasing role of administrative law and administrative courts for the supervision of administration (Dicey, [1885]1959: 213–237). This comes very close to Hayek's concerns. But it raises the question of whether this concern is accounted for by predictability. What is the difference between predictability and effectively restricted discretion? An independent judiciary is often included in lists of elements of the rule of law. But the function of an independent judiciary is to serve as a means of controlling the actions of state officials—it is they who the judiciary is independent of.

The Rule of Law Deflated   171

Independence also protects the judiciary from the influence of private persons. So, the role of "independence" in relation to the rule of law is to assure consistency and predictability in the application of the law. This independence is not an end in itself, or a new criterion, but a means to the end of predictability, among perhaps other ends, such as protection against bureaucrats' misuse of their discretion.

The legal issue here, as Dicey understood it, had to do with the independence of the common courts and the less-than-independent character of administrative courts. This seems like a clear conflict with Kelsen, who argued that the notion of the independence of the judiciary in the English tradition resulted from a particular historical experience, but was an illusion: English judges are appointed by the state and are part of it, and therefore not independent. Kelsen acknowledges the historical role of the judiciary in restraining royal power in England but suggests that these events created an illusion of independence: in fact, the selection of judges and their control by the administration was a matter governed by law just as other executive functions were. In each case, the decision-makers were producing norms in accordance with norms, including norms that authorize them to take particular kinds of actions. It is, and should be, a technical issue as to the distribution of executive powers of this kind, but it should not be pretended that the courts are outside of politics. The notion of "powers" and thus the idea of the independent power of the judiciary is a mystification: there are no "powers" here other than the ones produced under norms: the same body of norms that authorizes legislatures and executives to produce norms (Kelsen, [1945]2005: 255).

One can turn the idea of separation of powers into a political ideology—and indeed, the use of the extra-legal metaphysical language of "powers" facilitates its absorption into a political theory or ideology. But the phrasing has no legal meaning beyond the sense of legal authorization. But there is another issue here that undermines the idea of judicial independence as an absolute value standing on its own, rather than understanding it as an instrumental value. Too much judicial discretion has the potential for undermining predictability, not to mention democratic values. Kelsen's own constitution writing reflected his recognition of this.[8] One can say the same for the rights associated with the legal process, the demand for due process itself, and for other elements of the legal order that have been associated with the rule of law. These are not stand-alone legal values but instrumental legal values, a point made by Raz (1979). And such values as transparency may also be understood as instrumental.

Instrumental values, more generally, have two sides: they may serve the primary value, or they may undermine it. Thus, transparency, another criterion found in lists of elements of the rule of law, under some circumstances, will make it more likely that the law will be followed, and also that it will be accepted as legitimate and thus that the legal regime will be effective. But whether this is true in a given situation is a contingent, empirical fact. Weber points to the universal phenomenon of bureaucratic secrecy ([1968]1978:

172   Stephen Turner

992–93), and it must be said that secrecy may also, in some circumstances, promote legitimacy and effectiveness: instrumentality cuts both ways, here and elsewhere.

The Oppressive Regime

Law itself is instrumental, from the point of view of politics. And this exposes a division in Weber's own thinking about the law. From 1914 on, he takes the view that the law is a coherent system, an intellectual object, to be understood as such on the model of mathematics. In this form, it is not instrumental or directed by values. His earlier writing is perhaps closer to his friend Gustav Radbruch, who had a "values" account of law of a kind Kelsen was intensely critical of. These perspectives are not entirely inconsistent: legal order, understood in terms of the valuative language Weber (and Radbruch) employed was not an "ultimate" value, or at least not a meaningful one, but rather an intermediate value, a value that needed to be accepted by people with different ultimate values as instrumental for the achievement of these ultimate values, by providing the order that made the achievement of ultimate values possible (Turner and Factor, 1987). This way of thinking meant that Weber could see the legal order from, so to speak, the outside. Kelsen, in his writings on democracy, did so as well, a point to which we will return, for it is important to answer a common criticism of both Kelsen and Weber: Kelsen for failing to call distasteful regimes non-legal and Weber for failing to distinguish genuine "rational" legitimacy from de facto legitimacy (Friedrich, 1958; see also B. White, 1996).

One can imagine, though empirical cases are lacking, a highly aggressive and intrusive legal regime that conformed to the predictability aspect of the rule of law that nevertheless afforded little protection for the individual against the state: a well-oiled police state with a long list of enforced unfreedoms. Weber's hostility to the inexorable rise of a bureaucratic order based on rational-legal authority and his sense that the last vestiges of human freedom had to be protected from it indicate that he agreed with this concern. However, it is also true that a large part of what is terrifying about the police state has to do not with the laws themselves, but with the discretion granted to those who enforce it and to their unpredictability: the situation Kafka describes, in which the charges, violations, and processes are a mystery rather than predictable. Yet these officials might very well have their unpredictable actions authorized by law.[9] The problem posed by the critics of Kelsen and the proponents of an exclusive account of the rule of law is this. Is there a response to either of these concerns within the Kelsen-Weber view of law? Or does the deflationary approach to the rule of law amount to the acceptance of this kind of regime as an example of the rule of law?

If we grant that the issue of discretionary power is a quantitative rather than a qualitative difference, the problem of "oppression" can be clarified. One form of "oppression" is the sheer existence of arbitrary power—an argument made in political philosophy by Philip Pettit (1997, 2012), who calls this "domination." He has in mind primarily the private use of arbitrary power, for example, the power to deny a person needed services for no reason or to order a person to do something for no reason. This formulation is designed to permit an activist, but still limited, state, which is permitted to interfere for good reasons. His account points to a problem with the concepts of arbitrariness and oppression themselves.

There is a peculiar problem with the relationship between "objective" and "subjective" aspects of oppression. If one thinks that there are objective standards of oppression that apply even when the people involved do not regard the relevant acts as oppression, one is obliged to provide a source for these standards. Philosophical intuitions do not help: they would not be the intuitions of the people to whom the standards are being applied. If they merely reflect local political ideologies, they are not objective standards. If there is a generic notion of oppression that is not relative to a community, it must derive from some other sort of theory—such as a Marxian theory of history—not from the idea of the rule of law. Pettit avoids these problems by arguing that what counts as arbitrary is a matter neither of natural law nor positive law but rather of common knowledge within a community, and therefore "objective" in a factual sense but at the same time relative to the community. If the community regards committing a person to drug treatment as non-arbitrary, it is; if this is not part of the community ethos, it is arbitrary. This redefinition gives a source for the relevant notions or arbitrariness and has for him the virtue of justifying state intervention that restricts a person's freedom, and solves the problem of what is or is not oppressive. It solves it, however, in a way that reveals the problem with the concept. If a given legal regime allowing discretion conforms to community standards, it is not oppressive, however oppressive it might seem to outsiders. Indeed, any legal order using discretion would be non-oppressive if it conformed to community standards of non-arbitrariness, on Pettit's account.

There is of course a question of whether there is such common knowledge. Pettit has difficulties with the possibility of minorities with different community standards, and there is also the problem of individuals asserting freedoms that the community rejects. Why should we be bound to the judgments of the community? These are questions that are ordinarily resolved politically: indeed, the point of political procedures is precisely to produce decisions in the face of disagreement. Moreover, the idea that the law should conform to public opinion is a particular political ideal rather than a legal principle. As Dicey pointed out, it was only in the late eighteenth century that the idea that law should comport with public opinion took hold. From the perspective of the deflationary argument, this means that the concept of the rule of law is logically independent of the normative political idea that legal structures should match community notions of arbitrariness.

The problem of oppression and freedom from oppression has a logical structure that parallels the logical structure of the problem of discretion, and with

174　Stephen Turner

similar consequences: it does not serve to distinguish between different rule of law regimes. Even the most oppressive regime, to the extent that it is law governed, does not forbid everything, and therefore permits something: thus all legal regimes allow freedom of some sort. There is no qualitative distinction between an oppressive and a free order, only a quantitative one. What counts as permitted or forbidden under the law is a political matter. For Kelsen, this was an argument in favor of democracy: majority rule implied that the majority could not oppress itself. For Weber, the protection of the last vestiges of genuine human freedom, which he thought were threatened by bureaucratization, was also political: the constitutional regime he designed preserved the possibility of political leadership and the political control of bureaucracy. In this respect, they both rejected the traditional view of German liberalism that the best protection of freedom was the law and the courts, rather than the people.

Conclusion

Why would it matter that one could construct a deflationary argument for the rule of law, an alternative which strips it of its ideological elements? One superficial reason is obvious and would have been obvious to Weber and Kelsen. The ideas of the rule of law and the *Rechtsstaat* both present themselves as something other than political programs, ideologies, or personal value choices. The terms purport to refer to something broader—a way of life, a spirit animating the legal life of a society, and a means of protecting other important values, of basic equity and fairness, rights, and so forth. The contrast to tyranny and the rule of men and the frequent claim that the rule of law is under threat testify to the emotive power of these notions. Yet the promise is illusory.

The rule of law, because of its historical associations, is a concept that promises a great deal. But if we ask what the rule of law actually consists of, within a sociological reality, we get a less alluring answer. There is nothing in the subordination of officials to an abstract order that guarantees the achievement of values of freedom or protection from state power. States which operate under the strict observance of an abstract order are machines that can be turned for many purposes. The preservation of the values that we ordinarily group under the notion of the rule of law must come from someplace other than the notion of law itself. Kelsen was relentless in separating the legally meaningless ideological provisions of treaties and constitutions from those which had actual legal force.[10] He regarded the flowery but empty promises of such constitutions as a kind of fraud. The rule of law is a concept with similar properties. It is usually treated as an unalloyed good, seen through the haze of associations with English freedom, the rise of democratic constitutionalism, liberal rights, and the achievement of a decent society in which everyone is accorded equal respect of the law. But the legal meaning of the rule of law is simply that the law is obeyed and effective. Weber and Kelsen allow us to cut through the haze to see that the law is a coercive order, that the rule of law is consistent with a

The Rule of Law Deflated   175

wide range of values, and intrinsically connected to a few of the political ideas and values with which it is normally associated. The associations are decorative and historical. With Kelsen and Weber, we have something startling: an impeccably liberal *Ideologiekritik* of a liberal shibboleth.

Notes

1 Paul Craig (1997), for example, discusses "Formal and Substantive Conceptions of the Rule of Law"; the distinction is central to Weber's sociology of law.
2 In "Rule of Law versus *Rechtstaat*" (2000), Michel Rosenfeld considers the problem of the irrationality of the common law one of Weber's themes; cf. Melissaris (2004).
3 The relations and differences between the two concepts have been widely discussed, but a traditional view was that the *Rechtsstaat* represented the German conception of the English legal system, especially as depicted by Rudolf von Gneist ([1882]1886), 1886; see also Blaau (1990); Costa and Zolo eds. (2007); Craig (1997); Dietze (1985, 1973); Fallon (1997); Gozzi (2007); and Rosenfeld (2000).
4 The term comes from Georg Jellinek, whose lectures Kelsen attended in Heidelberg, who used it to represent a valuative ideal. Weber uses the term non-valuatively, as a value-neutral means of interpretation and aid to conceptually clear description. This is also how Kelsen uses the term ([1945]2005: 284, 288, 441–44).
5 This problematic is discussed at length in Turner (2010: 74–7).
6 Hayek himself makes this concession ([1960]1978: 213).
7 U.S. Code, Title 28, Part I, Chapter 21, § 453, www.law.cornell.edu/uscode/text.
8 The Austrian Constitution (*Bundes-Verfassungsgesetz* [*B-VG*]) was based on a draft by Hans Kelsen and first enacted on October 1, 1920 (cf. Kelsen, 1942).
9 Though it must be said that empirical regimes of this sort seem to involve issues with discretion, often punished by other people with discretionary power, thus collapsing into a system of terror. Thus, even a high Soviet official under Stalin would not be sure of what discretionary powers, or even duties, he had.
10 This is especially visible in his discussion of the treaties creating the League of Nations (Kelsen, 1939).

References

Blaau, Loammi. "The Rechsstaat Idea Compared with the Rule of Law as a Paradigm for Protecting Rights," *New Contrast* 107: 76–96, 1990.
Costa, Pietro and Danilo Zolo. *The Rule of Law: History, Theory, and Criticism.* Dordrecht: Springer, 2007.
Craig, Paul. "Formal and Substantive Conceptions of the Rule of Law," *Public Law* 467–487, 1997.
Dicey, Albert Venn. *Introduction to the Study of the Law of the Constitution,* 3rd edn. London/New York: Macmillan, [1885]1959.
Dicey, Albert Venn. *Law & Public Opinion in England: During the Nineteenth Century,* 2nd edn. London: Macmillan and Company, [1914]1962.
Dietze, Gottfried. *Liberalism Proper and Proper Liberalism.* Baltimore: Johns Hopkins University Press, 1985.
Dietze, Gottfried. *Two Concepts of the Rule of Law.* Indianapolis: Liberty Fund, 131–133, 1973.

176   Stephen Turner

Dworkin, Ronald. *Justice for Hedgehogs*. Cambridge: Harvard University Press, 2011.

Dworkin, Ronald. *Law's Empire*. Cambridge: Harvard University Press, 1988.

Fallon, R. A. " 'The Rule of Law' as a Concept in Constitutional Discourse," *Columbia Law Review* 97(1): 1–56, 1997.

Friedrich, Carl J. "Authority, Reason, and Discretion," In *Authority*. Cambridge: Harvard University Press, 28–48, 1958.

Fuller, Lon. *The Morality of Law*. New Haven: Yale University Press, 1964.

Gneist, Rudolph von. *History of the English Constitution*. New York: G.P. Putnam & Sons, [1882]1886.

Gneist, Rudolph von. *The English Parliament in Its Transformations through a Thousand Years*, translated by Richard Jenery Shee. Boston: Little Brown, 1886.

Gozzi, Gustavo. "Rechtsstaat and Individual Rights in German Constitutional History," In *The Rule of Law: History, Theory, and Criticism*, Edited by P Costa and D. Zolo. Dordrecht: Springer, 237–259, 2007.

Hayek, F. A. *Constitution of Liberty*. Chicago: The University of Chicago Press, [1960]1978.

Kelsen, Hans. *Der soziologische und der juristische Staatsbegriff. Kritische Untersuchung des Verhältnisses von Staat und Recht*, 2nd edn. Tübingen: J.C.B. Mohr, [1922]1928.

Kelsen, Hans. *General Theory of Law and State*. Oxfordshire: Routledge, [1945]2005.

Kelsen, Hans. "Judicial Review of Legislation: A Comparative Study of the Austrian and the American Constitution," *The Journal of Politics* 4(2): 183–2000, 1942.

Kelsen, Hans. *Legal Technique in International Law: A Textual Critique of the League Covenant*. Geneva: Geneva Research Centre, 1939.

La Torre, Massimo. *Law as Institution*. Dordrecht: Springer, 2010. https://link.springer.com/content/pdf/bfm%3A978-1-4020-6607-8%2F1.pdf (accessed 2 March 2022)

Melissaris, Emmanuel. "Is Common Law Irrational? The Weberian 'England Problem' Revisited," *Northern Ireland Legal Quarterly* 55(4): 378–395, 2004.

Pettit, Philip. *On the People's Terms: A Republican Theory and Model of Democracy*. Cambridge: Cambridge University Press, 2012.

Pettit, Philip. *Republicanism: A Theory of Freedom and Government*. Oxford: Oxford University Press, 1997.

Raz, Joseph. *The Authority of Law: Essays on Law and Morality*. Oxford: Clarendon Press, 1979.

Rosenfeld, Michel. "Rule of Law versus *Rechsstaat*," In *Menschenrechte und Bürgerrechte in einer vielgestaltigen Welt*, Edited by P. Häberle and J. P. Müller. Basel-Genf-München: Helbig & Lichtenhahn, 49–71, 2000.

Turner, Stephen. *Explaining the Normative*. Cambridge: Polity Press, 2010.

Turner, Stephen and Regis Factor. "Decisionism and Politics: Weber as Constitutional Theorist," In *Max Weber, Rationality and Modernity*, Edited by Scott Lash and Sam Whimster. London: Allen and Unwin, 334–354, 1987.

Weber, Max. *Economy and Society: An Outline of Interpretive Sociology*, Edited by G. Roth and C. Wittich. Berkeley-Los Angeles: University of California Press, [1968]1978.

Weber, Max. "Some Categories of Interpretive Sociology," In *The Sociological Quarterly 22,* translated by Edith Graber, 145–150, [1913]1981.

White, Brigita. "Is There a Place for Morality in Law?" *QUT Law Review* [S.l.] 12: 229–242, 1996. https://lr.law.qut.edu.au/article/view/421 (accessed 2 March 2022)

Acknowledgments

We are pleased to acknowledge the previous publication of the following papers in this volume, and especially for the permissions granted for publication in this volume:

Turner, Stephen. "Democracy, Liberalism, and Discretion: The Political Puzzle of the Administrative State," In *Reclaiming Liberalism*, Edited by David F. Hardwick and Leslie Marsh. London: Palgrave, 2020, 41–62.

Turner, Stephen. "Improving on Democracy Stein Ringen, What Is Democracy For? On Freedom and Moral Government," *European Journal of Social Theory* 14(4): 561–570, 2011.

Turner, Stephen. "Religious Pluralism, Toleration, and Liberal Democracy: Past, Present, and Future," In *Religion and the Political Order: Politics in Classical and Contemporary Christianity, Islam, and Judaism*, Edited by Jacob Neusner. Atlanta: Scholars Press, 1996, 275–299. With thanks to the University of South Florida.

Turner, Stephen. "The Ideology of Anti-Populism and the Administrative State," In *The Condition of Democracy*, 3 vols, Edited by Jürgen Mackert, Bryan Turner, and Hannah Wolfe. Abingdon: Routledge, 2021, 131–148.

Turner, Stephen. "The End of Clear Lines: Academic Freedom and Administrative Law," In *Challenges to Academic Freedom*, Edited by Joseph Hermanowicz. Baltimore: Johns Hopkins Press, 2021, 49–79. With thanks to the Johns Hopkins University Press for permission.

Turner, Stephen. "The Method of Antinomies: Oakeshott and Others," *Cosmos + Taxis. Studies in Emergent Order* 6: 54–63, 2018.

Turner, Stephen. "The Rule of Law Deflated: Weber and Kelsen," *Lo Stato* 6: 97–115, 2016. With thanks to Mucchi Editore for permission.

Turner, Stephen and George Mazur. "What are Democratic Values? A Neo-Kelsenian Approach," In Πολιτεία [*Politèia*]. *Liber Amicorum Agostino Carrino*, Edited by Carmine De Angelis and Antonino Scalone. Milano: Mimesis, 2020, 525–540. With special thanks to Mimesis Edizioni.

Turner, Stephen and Regis Factor. "Decisionism and Politics: Weber as Constitutional Theorist," In *Max Weber, Rationality and Modernity*, Edited by Scott Lash and Sam Whimster. London: Allen and Unwin, 1987, 334–354.

Index

AAUP (American Association of University Professors) 103–105, 109, 115, 117
abortion 90, 93–94, 97
absolutism 69, 80
abstractions xi, xix
academic freedom 15, 100–105, 109–110, 115; conflicts 116–118; diversity and 112–113; liberal theory of 106; Title IX and 108–111; as workplace policy 118–119; *see also* rule
academic tenure 103, 105–106, 111, 116, 118
accountability 13, 26, 33, 60–64, 71–72, 82; democratic 68–69, 75; electoral 76–78; political 31, 40; standing and 29
Adams, Samuel 12, 40–41, 72
administration 28, 34–35, 70, 74–79; and democracy 72; European models of 30–31; law and 13, 15–16, 164–166, 170–171; and metamorphoses xxiv; public 30, 32; public review 29, 36–37; *see also* professional administration; triadic balance
administrative agencies 28–29, 36–38, 40
administrative discretion xxiii, 10, 75
administrative law 27–29, 37, 48, 101, 107–109, 113–114, 117–119; Prussian 143; *see also* administration
administrative power 78–79, 100, 103, 107, 109, 119; *see also* Institutional Review Boards (IRBs)
administrative practice 12–13
Administrative Procedure Act (1946) 30, 107; public comment system 36–37
administrative regulation 48–49, 101, 119

administrative science 30–31
administrative state 30–33, 39, 64, 72, 78–80; democracy and 26, 28, 40–41; discretionary power 28, 32–35, 38–40; *see also* courts; democracy; discretion
affirmative action 39
agency 37–38, 101, 107–108, 110; discretionary power of 37, 40; government 5, 12; regulatory 29; *see also* regulation, regulatory regimes
agency theory *see* political theory
agent relationships xxii–xxiv, xxvi, 6, 8–9, 19–20; problems 11–13, 22; *see also* democracy
agreement xiv, xxii–xxiii
anarchy 132, 146
antinomic 136–137; argument 129, 132; interpretations 131; pair 133–135, 139n5; politics 125
antinomies xx–xxii, 4, 9, 16, 22, 125–126, 135, 137; contingent 131, 133; and priciplism 129–130, 138; values 6–7, 19; Weber 125, 128
"Antinomies of Liberalism, The" (Shils) 125
anti-discrimination law 110–113
anti-Populism 67, 69, 72, 82; and discourse 67; ideology 13
arbitrary officialdom 27, 32, 34
argument 167; deflationary 163, 168, 173–174
association 146–147; state as 145, 149
Austrian Constitution (*Bundes-Verfassungsgesetz [B-VG]*) 175n8
authority 33, 38–40, 48, 57–58, 64, 90, 96; experts and 63; legislative 59; of the people 61; rational-legal 164–166, 169, 172; *see also* epistemic authority

Index   179

authority of the state *see* state, the
autonomy 28–29, 43–45, 117–119,
145; from the state 100–101, 110;
professional 102

Babeuf, François-Noël xi; Babeufism 7,
56, 59
Beerbohm, Eric: *In Our Name: The
Ethics of Democracy* 126
belief 164–166, 169
Bentham, Jeremy 19, 143–145
Berlin, Isaiah 49; *Two Concepts of
Liberty* 126
Bismarck, Otto von 142, 151–153
Bourdieu, Pierre 43
Buchanan, James 2
bureaucracy 2, 74, 80, 82, 142–143,
152–154; plebiscitary 48; power 47;
responsible 11; secrecy 172; *see also*
European bureaucracy; Friedrich, Carl;
Weber, Max; Wilson, Woodrow
bureaucratic discretion *see* discretion
bureaucratic rule *see* rule
bureaucrats 69, 74, 79–80, 82
Burgess, John 30, 80
Butterworth, Joe 104

Caesarism *see* Weber, Max
Caldwell, Christopher *The Age of
Entitlement* 3
California Loyalty Oath 104–107, 116,
119, 120n3
California Regents 104–106
capitalism 72–73, 133, 142
centralization 75, 80
certainty xx, xxii
charisma 143, 156, 158
charismatic leaders 69, 71
checks and balances 80–81
Chevron case 29, 37
choice 26, 30–31, 38; democratic 27
citizen 32–33, 35, 38; democratic 3–5,
7–8, 13
citizen responsibility 15, 126–128, 139
citizen speech 103, 106
civic action 90, 92–94
civil peace xviii–xxix
civil rights 57; Office of Civil Rights
(OCR) 110; rights 91, 94, 97
civil violence 87, 89, 95, 97
class 45, 50–52, 68, 73–74, 78;
bureaucratic 80; conflict 54; expert 72;
middle 45, 50–52, 70, 141; working 45

classical liberalism 43, 48
coercion 128, 144; *see also* legal
coercion
coherence 130, 136–138
collective commitment 62–64
collective interests 145–146; *see also*
interests
collective values *see* values
common law *see* law
communities of experts *see* experts
community 150–151; law and 148–149
complexity 60, 62–64
compromise 91, 93, 95, 143, 147, 151,
158, 159n2
conflicts, reconciling 128, 130, 134–135
conformity 108, 119; doctrinal 111–112
Confucius 131, 133
consensus 43, 47, 52, 90, 95–96, 98n1;
consensus democracy 48–49; religion
and 93–96
constitution xxii–xxiv, 27–29, 36–37,
39–40, 156; form 149, 151; structure
150, 152, 158; US xvii, xxvi; Weimar
142, 154–6; *see also* German; Weber,
Max
constitutional consent 59–60
constitutionalism 39, 55
constitutional order 8, 10, 14, 17, 143, 155
constitutional system 151–152
constitutional theory 142–143, 155–156,
159
contingency 133, 136–137
contract 100, 102–103, 106–109,
116–119
contract law 101, 111, 120n1
Cortes, Donoso 39–40, 141
courts 28, 33, 40; and administrative
state 27–29, 35–39
criminalization 88, 92, 98n1
customary law xx, 102, 169

Dahl, Robert xvii, 7, 9, 12, 54–55; *A
Preface to Democratic Theory* 54
decisionism 148, 160n9; *see also*
Schmitt, Carl
decisions *see* political decisions
deference 37; judicial 107–108, 117–118
delegation 28, 36
deliberation 62–63
della Porta, Donatella 62–63; *Can
Democracy be Saved?* 62
democracy ix–xi, xv, 2–4, 13–14,
26–27, 44–49, 131, 133; conditions

180 Index

for 54–55; genuine 9–10, 12; homogeneity 78; modern 63; parliamentary 156; scalar concept 6, 8; values and 13–14, 16–19; *see also* accountability; administrative state; anti-Populism; consensus; freedom of speech; ideology; Kelsen, Hans; legal positivism; liberal democracy; majority, rule; Populism; rights; Ringen, Stein; rule of law; Scandinavia; social democracy; state, the; Weber, Max; Wilson, Woodrow

democracy indices 46–47
democratic control 71, 81
democratic mentality 14–15
democratic procedures xvii, xx, xxiv, xxvi, 39, 55–59, 61–64; legal x–xi
democratic theory xiii, vii, 1, 4–9, 56–57, 63, 68, 127–128; validity 7; *see also* political
democratic values 58–59, 61–64
Dicey, Albert Venn 27, 35, 162, 170–171, 173; *Lectures on the Relation between Law and Public Opinion during the Nineteenth Century* 145
dictatorship 128, 146, 158, 159n3
discretion 15, 18–21, 36–38; administrative 168–170; and democracy 40; oppressive 173; power of 169, 171–172
discretionary power xxii–xxv, 9–10, 12–13, 18, 20, 108–109, 115; *see also* accountability; administration; administrative power; Institutional Review Boards (IRBs); state power; Wilson, Woodrow
discretionary state *see Obrigkeitstaat*
discrimination 38; sex 107, 110; sexual harassment 109–111; Title IX 107–108, 110–112
discussion xix, xxvi, 26–28, 30, 89, 92; government by xxiv–xxv, 27; liberal 39, 40; public discussion 90–94; *see also* anti-Populism; political
diversity 108, 110–111, 119; statements 112; of thought 106; *see also* academic freedom; religious pluralism (diversity)
domination 44, 50, 56, 58, 68, 164, 173
due process 102, 105–106, 108–109, 117

Dworkin, Ronald 17, 162, 168–170; *Law's Empire* 169

economic power 46, 49–50, 52
edicts of toleration 87, 89–90; *see also* liberalism, toleration and
efficiency 30–31, 33, 36, 38, 77, 79–81; government 59
egalitarianism 49; economic 26, 55
egoism 144–147, 157
electoral control 71, 75–78, 80, 82
electoral politics 2, 11, 13, 20–22
electoral process 31–32, 41, 71, 76
elites 3; and populism 68–69, 71, 73, 76, 78; *see also* rule
Elster, Jon 64
employment law 102–103, 111, 114, 118–119; First Amendment and 106, 109
ends xxi, 145, 151; intermediate xiv, xix, xx, 17, 148–149, 153, 155; law and 143, 146, 148; means-ends reasoning xviii; ultimate xviii
epistemic authority 63
equality xxi–xxii, 43–44, 55–56, 59; of opportunity 50; political 55; *see also* freedom
equal opportunity 101, 108
ethics: Strauss 139n4; Weber 131–132
ethnic conflict 6, 13
European bureaucracy 30–31
expertise 8, 20, 32, 60, 63, 66–67, 71, 75–77; source of authority 68, 78–79, 82; *see also* Populism; triadic balance
experts xii–xiii, xxv, 2–4, 6, 21, 67, 69, 71, 81; community 40
EU (European Union) 4, 61

fact xiv, xvi–xviii, xix, 3, 6, 8; administrative xi; political xxi; procedural x; *see also* ends; fact-value distinction; legal facts
fact-value distinction ix, xiii, xv–xvii, xxviin1, 60, 63
faith, politics of 125, 131, 135–136
false consciousness 44, 55
federal agencies *see* agency
federal regulation *see* regulation
First Amendment (US) 46, 88, 103, 105–106, 112–113, 115, 118; *see also* employment law

Index 181

force 146–147, 149–150, 153, 157; *see also* Ihering, Rudolf von; interests; state, the
freedom xix–xxi, 44–47, 50, 56–57, 59, 61, 128–129, 144–145, 159n3, 172–174; conflict with 43, 52; equality and xxi–xxii; metamorphosis and x; negative 49; as non-intervention 58; positive 49–50; Voltaire and xx; *see also* academic freedom; democracy; Gneist, Rudolph; intermediate values
freedom of speech xi, 2, 27, 48, 67, 102; and democracy 10, 13, 21; *see also* First Amendment (US)
French wars of religion 87–88, 95
Friedrich, Carl xxv, 3, 11, 21; and bureaucracy xxiv
fundamental political theory ix, xi, xxiv; *see also* political theory

Gervinus, Georg Gottfried 141–142
Gewirth, Alan 43
Gneist, Rudolph 77, 143–144, 151; and freedom 156
Gold Standard 73, 76, 83n4
governance 45, 47, 67, 69, 70, 77, 79; faculty 101–102, 116; shared 118, 120n5
government x, xii, xxii, xxvi, 48–52, 77–79, 80–82; by discussion xiv, xxiii, 61, 89; and good life 45; trust in 46; *see also* discussion; Friedrich, Carl; Kelsen, Hans; Populism
government agencies *see* agency
government by the people 66–68, 70, 74
government power 68, 74–75, 146
group identities 3, 12, 14
Grundnorm see Kelsen, Hans
Gundlach, Ralph 104

Habermas, Jürgen 43–44, 130
happiness x, xix
Hart, H.L.A. xviii
Hayek, Friedrich 12, 168–170
health care 44, 46, 48
Hochschild, Jennifer 12
hostile environment 110–111
human freedom *see* freedom
human rights 56, 91

Iceland 46–47, 51
ideal interests *see* interests

ideals 8–9, 15, 128–129, 133–134, 136–137
ideal type 4, 128, 134, 136, 165, 168, 175n4
ideology xiii, xv, xxiii, 13–15, 70; anti-Populism as 69, 72; political 171; or representation 12
Ihering, Rudolf von 141, 144–145, 159, 159n3; *Der Zweck im Recht (The Element of Purpose in Law)* 17, 143, 146–147; *Ideologiekritik* 145; and law 143, 145–147, 149, 157; Weber 143, 147, 149–150, 153, 155, 158; *see also* force; interests; purpose; Utilitarianism; Weber, Max; will 141–145, 148
improvisations xxiv–xxvi
individual 144, 149, 155; interests 145–146; values 147–148; *see also* Radbruch, Gustav
individualism 138, 147
Institutional Review Boards (IRBs) 12, 100, 107, 113, 115, 119; *see also* administrative power
interests 146, 156; as force 144–145; ideal 147, 151, 153, 158; material 147, 150–151, 158; social 145; *see also* collective interests; egoism; individual
intermediate ends *see* ends; fact; values
intermediate values *see* values
interpretation: conflicts of ix, xvii, xxii, 28–29, 36–37; interpretation 162, 168–170

Jefferson, Thomas xxii, 12
Jellinek, Georg: "the normative power of the real" xv
judicial review 27, 37–39, 80
justice xii–xiii, xx, 4, 7–9, 16, 43–45, 128, 134; expedience and xxii; metamorphosis and x, xx, xxiii; social 26; theories of 5

Kammen, Michael "A Machine that Would Go of Itself" xxvi
Kelsen, Hans 14, 17–18, 21, 22n3, 60–62, 162–165; democracy 56–59, 172, 174; *The Essence and Value of Democracy* 57; facts xiii, xv–xvi; fact-value distinction xvii–xviii, xxviin1; government x, xxii; *Grundnorm* 166–167; law xvi, xix–xx;

182 Index

metamorphosis x, xxii, xxiv, 7, 12;
norms 63–64, 165–168, 170–171;
Pure Theory of Law 167; relativism
59; representation xxiii; rule of law
9, 19, 162–163, 167–168, 171, 174;
Stauffenbautheorie 165; Weber 4–6, 8,
11, 16; *see also* arguments, deflationary;
customary law; Friedrich, Carl; Jellinek,
Georg; law, primitive; representation

law xvii–xviii, xxviiin1, 6, 8–11,
15, 18–22, 27–30, 32–34, 38–40,
73–74, 103, 169–170, 172–174;
bureaucracy xxv–xxvi; case 104,
106; common 135; as compromise
143, 147, 150; constitutional 107;
democracy and xi–xi, xix–xx,
xxiv–xxv, 1, 4, 9, 11; genuine xii;
primitive xx; statutory 108, 118,
164–165; values and xv–xix,
xxii, xxviiin2; *see also* academic
freedom; administrative law;
anti-discrimination; contract
law; customary law; employment
law; legal facts; legal positivism;
metamorphosis; natural law; rule of
law; Schmitt, Carl; triadic balance;
Weber, Max
Lawlor, Patrick 11
leadership 127–128, 151–154, 158
legal authority *see* authority
legal coercion xxiv, 57–58, 61, 64
legal distinctions xvii, 162–163
legal facts xiii, xv–xvi, xxiv
legal interpretation *see* interpretation
legal order x, xii, xv–xvi, xxiv–xxvi,
57–59, 162–164, 166–169, 171–173
legal positivism xii, 17, 21, 163
legal regime 163, 171–174
legislation 101, 107–108, 114; *see also*
Populism; power
legislative authority *see* authority
legislative power *see* power
legitimacy 68–70, 80, 128, 165, 167,
172; religious legitimacy 96–98
letters of guidance 101, 110; *see also*
Institutional Review Boards (IRBs)
Levitan, David 32
liberal democracy xiv, xvii–xviii, 37, 46,
57, 82, 98, 105, 125; narrow theory
of 26; and religion 93–97; *see also*
democracy; discretion; liberalism;
populism

liberalism xi, xx–xxi, 27, 29–30, 39–41,
87, 90, 91, 130, 142, 156; critique of
141; toleration and 88, 91, 94; *see also*
democracy; Schmitt, Carl
liberal political theory 3, 7–8, 12, 14,
20–21; *see also* theory
liberty: as license 45, 49
licensure; exclusion from 28
limited government 12, 14
Little League 96, 98
Loewenstein, Karl 11
loyalty oath *see* California Loyalty Oath

MacKinnon, Catharine 9–10, 13
majoritarian legal procedure x, xxiv
majority(ies) x, xxiv, 55, 82; rule 26, 47,
58; vote 62–63, 92
Mansfield, Harvey 66
Margalit, Avishai 44
marketplace of ideas 105–106, 119
McAdams v. Marquette University
116–118, 120n5
metamorphosis x, xvi, xix–xxv, 5, 7–8,
14–16, 22; of law xv, xxiv; of values
14, 19, 21; *see also* administration;
democracy; freedom; government;
justice; Kelsen, Hans; law
method 126, 128–129
middle class *see* class
Mill, John Stuart 144–145, 156
Minogue, Kenneth 126
minorities xxiv, 14, 20–21, 82
modern state, the 87–88
morality 17–18, 44, 91–92
Morgenthau, Hans J. 125, 127, 138,
139n1
Mouffe, Chantal 125, 130; *The
Democratic Paradox* 125
myth 66–68, 81–82

National People's Party 73–75, 82
National Socialism xxi
natural law xvii, xx, 5, 18, 57, 164, 173
natural rights 5, 18, 54, 57
nemesis 132–133, 135–137
neo-Kantianism 56, 128, 130
neutrality 15, 17–18, 20, 55, 60;
neutralization 82; *see also* political
neutrality
New Deal 39, 54
non-intervention *see* freedom
"normative power of the real, the" *see*
Jellinek, Georg

norms 4–5, 14–15; democratic xvii, 64; legal 34, 39, 165–167, 169; *see also* Kelsen, Hans

Northern Ireland (Ulster) 94–95, 98

Oakeshott, Michael 131, 133–134, 139n1; ideals 136–137; "On Being Conservative" 137; *On Human Conduct* 125; politics 130–132, 136–138; *The Politics of Faith and Scepticism* 126; rule of law 135; "The Rule of Law" (Oakeshott) 125; *see also* antinomies; Confucius; method; nemesis

Obrigkeitstaat 169; discretionary state 36, 40–41

O'Donnell, Guillermo 46

Office of Civil Rights (OCR) *see* civil rights

Olivecrona, Karl xv

open societies xxv, xxvi

parliamentarism 147, 151, 156, 158

parliamentary democracy 88–89, 91

Parsons, Talcott xvii, xviii, 3

parties, political 56, 60, 62, 64

paternalism 45, 48, 69

peace 146, 148–151, 157, 160n9

people, the x–xiii, xv, xvii, xxiii–xxiv, xxvi–xxvii, 11, 17, 20–21, 57, 59, 62–63, 66, 72–74, 79, 81–82; opinion of the street 79–80; and pluralism 71; rule by 67–68, 72; values and xvi–xix; *see also* electoral control; government; Populism; relativism; triadic balance; will of the people

persuasion, rational 89–98

Pettit, Philip xvii, xxi, 43, 49, 58, 128, 173

Phillips, Herbert 105

pluralism 70–71, 75; religious 98

Polanyi, Michael 133–135

polarization xxvi, 14

political decisions 82, 91–92

political discussion 90–92, 94, 97; *see also* discussion

political equality *see* equality

political fiction xiii, 18; useful xi

political interference 102, 116

political myth *see* myth; triadic balance

political neutrality 26, 33, 79, 88, 104

political participation 55, 61

political parties 68–71, 77, 81–82

political theory ix, xii, xx, xxii–xxiv, xxvi; agency theory x; *see also* democratic theory

politics 87–88, 94–96, 129–134, 136; liberal 90–91, 95; parliamentary 89; reform 45; and religion 95–96

politics of faith *see* faith, politics of

politics of power *see* power

politics of responsibility *see* citizen

politics of skepticism 125–126, 135

Populism 66, 68, 70–73, 80, 82n2; and democracy 67, 69; hostility to 70; legislation and 29, 32, 37; *see also* anti-Populism; citizen; elites; faith, politics of; Oakeshott, Michael; people, the

poverty 46, 49, 52

power xxvi, 2, 4, 11–13, 43, 51, 125, 147, 155–158, 160n4, 160n5, 160n8, 165, 171–173; arbitrary 26, 32, 34; economic 44, 46, 49, 52; executive 28–29, 39; judicial 28, 37; legislative 28, 34–36; politics of 142; populism and 75–76; *see also* administrative power; agency; bureaucracy, power; discretionary power; government; separation of powers; state, the

practices xv, xxi, xxvi, 135, 138; *see also* administrative practice

principal-agent problem/theory xxii–xxv

principlism 126–130; antinomism *vs.* 138

privacy 90–91, 93

private realm 90–92, 96, 98

procedures xiv, xiv, xix, 29–30, 39; legal 26–27; *see also* Administrative Procedure Act (1946); democratic procedures; voting

professional administration 31, 33

professional autonomy *see* autonomy

progressivism 66–67, 82

Protestantism 93, 97

PTA (Parent Teachers Association), the 96–98

public, the 29, 32–33, 37, 39; bureaucracy and 31–32

public administration *see* administration

public discussion *see* discussion

public opinion 26–27, 32–33, 40–41

public/private distinction 90, 96, 98n2

public realm 90–91, 94, 96

public sphere 5, 19, 63

purpose 144–145, 147–149, 151, 152; Ihering 143, 144, 147

184 Index

quasi-judicial process 102, 107, 109, 117

Radbruch, Gustav xv, xx, 9, 142–149,
154–155, 157
Rakoff, Judge Jed xxii
rational-legal authority *see* authority;
Weber, Max
Rawls, John xvii, 5, 7; *Theory of Justice*
(John Rawls) 44
realism xii, 150
reasoned persuasion *see* persuasion
Rechtsstaat 27, 169, 174, 175n3;
liberalism 8; *see also* Kelsen, Hans;
Weber, Max
regulation 2, 15, 16, 74, 80;
administrative 101, 119; agencies
64; federal 100, 108, 114; regulatory
regimes 28, 61; university 100,
107–108, 110; *see also* administrative
regulation
relativism 5, 16, 59, 61, 125, 129, 148
religion 92–93, 95–97; limits of 96;
neutrality 88–89; United States (US)
and 88, 93, 95, 97, 98n1; *see also*
abortion; consensus; French wars of
religion; liberal democracy; politics
religious pluralism (diversity) 94, 96, 98
representation xiv, xx, xxiii, xxv, 13,
19, 67, 69–70, 78; ideology and 12;
theory of 66
representative government 79
research: misconduct 101, 107, 113;
protocols 115; *see also* Institutional
Review Boards (IRBs)
responsibility *see* citizen
rights xii, xxiii–xxiv, 2, 15, 26, 36, 134,
147, 149; democratic 131; self-defense
91; *see also* civil rights; human rights;
natural rights
Ringen, Stein 7, 45–52, 56
Rorty, Richard 22n1
rule 66–67, 71–72, 88, 89, 92, 108,
110; academic freedom and 107–108,
112–113; by the people 67–68, 73;
bureaucratic 79–80, 82; democratic
82; elite 70; universities and 100,
103–104, 108–109, 114, 117; *see also*
Institutional Review Boards (IRBs)
rule of law xi, xii, xix, 30, 34–35, 55,
125, 128, 169, 172–174; democracy
and 1, 9, 12, 17–19; *see also* Dicey,
Albert Venn; Kelsen, Hans; law;
Weber, Max

rule making 107–108, 113
rules 2, 15–16, 28, 40, 75, 165–166;
bureaucratic 7

salvation xiv, xix
sanctions xi, xvii, xx, 101–102, 109, 111,
113, 115
Savigny, Friedrich Carl von 143
Scandinavia 50–52; democracy
46–47
Schmitt, Carl xviii, xxi, xxiii, xxviin2,
12, 27–28, 80, 125, 132–133,
157–159, 160n9; constitutional theory
47; decisionism 17, 39, 40; liberalism
critique of 141; parliamentarism 156;
positivism 157; *see also* dictatorship
scholars, individual freedom of 101–102,
105, 113
science 14, 16, 89, 92
segregation 94–95, 98n2
self-government 77–79, 81
Sen, Amartya 43
separation of powers 37, 68–69, 80–81,
171
sex discrimination *see* discrimination
skepticism *see* politics of skepticism
Small, Albion 30
social democracy 43–44, 47, 50, 52,
54–55
social justice *see* justice
social order 58, 60
Sohm, Rudolph 143
sovereignty 163–165
Sowell, Thomas 3
standing, legal 29, 37–38, 60
state, the 34, 44–46, 58, 125, 134, 138,
151–154, 158–159, 163–166; action
47, 91, 169; administrative law 27–31;
authority of 39, 87, 98; benevolent
44, 48; bureaucracy 80; coercive 44;
democratic 55, 59, 63; legitimacy
40; police 172–173; *see also*
administrative state; civil association;
Ihering, Rudolf von; *Obrigkeitstaat*;
Populism; power; Ringen, Stein;
triadic balance; trust; value-conflict;
welfare state
state force 88, 146–147, 150
state power 15, 30, 39–40, 54–55, 60,
75, 82, 149, 167, 174
state practices *see* practices
state neutrality *see* political neutrality
Strauss, Leo 134, 139n4

subordination 79, 167, 174
Supreme Court (US) 91
Sweden 46, 52
Sykes, Charles *A Nation of Victims* 3

Tawney, R. T. xi
tenure *see* academic tenure
Thach, C. E. 27, 34–36
theory 26, 31–33; legal 30; liberal
  political theory 28
Title IX 10, 38; *see also* academic
  freedom; discrimination
tolerance xxi, 14, 97–98, 88, 94, 97–98,
  98n1; *see also* edicts of toleration;
  religion
Torment of Secrecy, The (Shils) 125
traditional authority *see* authority
triadic balance ix, 67–69
trust xxiii, xxv, xxvi, 6, 13–15, 19–20,
  33, 46–48, 75–76, 78–79, 81; *see
  also* government

ultimate values xiv, xxviii–xxix
United Nations: Charter 55; UNICEF 46
United States 46–52; *see also* religion;
  trust
university autonomy 100, 111, 118; *see
  also* autonomy
University of California loyalty oath *see*
  California Loyalty Oath
university regulation *see* regulation

valuations xiii, xvi–xvii
value-choice 142, 148
value-conflict xiv, xvii, xix, xx,
  xxii, 6, 8, 9, 14, 16, 19, 22,
  60–61; *see also* Kelsen, Hans;
  Weber, Max
values 5, 12–13, 15–17, 21–22, 59–60,
  158, 160n9, 165, 174; democratic
  58–59, 61–64, 171; individual *vs.*
  collective 148; instrumental 171–172;
  intermediate xiv, xviii, xix, xxvi, 14,
  17, 59, 141, 148; shared 151; ultimate
  148, 151; value neutrality 60; Weber
  and 141, 151, 159, 160n4, 160n5; *see
  also* democracy; ideals; law; legal;
  ultimate values; value-conflict
del Vayo, Julio Alvarez *March of
  Socialism* xii

voters 31, 36; *see also* majority
voting xiii, xiv, xx, 75–76, 78

Weber, Max ix, xii, xxviin1, 8, 11,
  16–19, 22n2, 68, 71, 82, 139n1,
  163; bureaucracy xxiii, xxv,
  153–154, 169, 171–172, 174;
  Caesarism 153–156; constitution
  and 142–143, 149–150, 152,
  156, 160n8; definition of the state
  165–167; democracy 128; fact-value
  xiii–xviii; *Herrschaft* 162; "ideal
  interests" xxi; *Ideologiekritik* 175;
  Junkers 151–152; law 150, 157, 172;
  parliament 151–156; "Parliament
  and Government in a Reconstructed
  Germany" 151; politics 132;
  "Politics as a Vocation" 149;
  pragmatism 149, 159; *Rechtsstaat*
  162, 164; "Rights of Man" 19; rule
  of law 162–164, 167–168; state
  149; Strauss 134; ultimate values
  xiv, xviii; value neutrality 60;
  "Wahlrecht und Demokratie" 152;
  Weimar constitution 142, 154–156;
  see also antinomies; arguments,
  deflationary; charisma; decisionism;
  ethics; Friedrich, Carl; Gneist,
  Rudolph; ideal type; ideology,
  Ideologiekritik; Ihering, Rudolf
  von; Kelsen, Hans; leadership;
  legitimacy; *Obrigkeitstaat*; peace;
  power; purpose; Radbruch, Gustav;
  Schmitt, Carl; values
welfare state xi–xii, 49–51, 54, 56
White, Leonard 32, 39–41
will x, xi, 143–145, 148, 154–156;
  political 141–142
will of the people 56, 61, 67, 127
Wilson, Woodrow 13, 28, 30–34, 36,
  38, 75–78, 80–82, 142; "Democracy
  and Efficiency" 30; "The Study of
  Administration" 30
women 10, 12–13
workplace policy *see* academic freedom
worldview 95–96, 141–142

Yeoman Farmer 76

Žižek, Slavoj 70–71

Ingram Content Group UK Ltd.
Milton Keynes UK
UKHW022029060623
422995UK00009B/89